ENDORSEMENTS

Over the years I have kept a watchful eye out for emerging prophets who are not only gifted, but have content found in the Word of God to correspond to the revelatory dimension. I also look for the fruit of the Spirit so that there will be a sustainable wineskin to carry the new wine. With joy, it is my honor to commend to you the life and ministry of Naim Collins and now his writings as well! God is raising up a generation of diverse new prophetic voices who have the character to carry the gift.

DR. JAMES W. GOLL
Founder of God Encounters Ministries
Author, Recording Artist and Communications Trainer

You can't write about prophetic dimensions unless you've walked in them. Naim Collins has walked in prophetic dimensions most of his life, finding his gift at an early age and cultivating it. In the process of navigating these dimensions of the prophetic, he has discovered keys to unlock and declare the secrets of God, which He reveals to His servants, the prophets. You don't have to be a prophet to move in the prophetic dimension. You just need activation, training—and faith. In *Realms of the Prophetic*, Naim hands you the keys to open doors in the prophetic you haven't entered before. Anyone who wants to move in the prophetic at higher dimensions should read this book.

JENNIFER LECLAIRE
Author, *The Making of a Prophet*
Founder, Awakening House of Prayer

Realms of the Prophetic is a golden key that unlocks the prophetic in a person's life! This is more than a book, it's an encyclopedia masterpiece.

Anyone looking to "dive deep" into what the prophetic is and how it flows into this natural world, this book is for you. This book is genius!

Dr. Jeremy Lopez
CEO, IdentityNetwork.net

My life and ministry have been shaped by mature-heart prophets who know how to hear the Father's voice and see His face. Naim Collins is a true prophet who is raising up a prophetic people who are shaping our world today. A must-read for anyone desiring an upgrade in the prophetic.

Leif Hetland, Founder & President
Global Mission Awareness
www.globalmissionawareness.com
www.calledtoreignbook.com

As I did, I'm sure you will enjoy reading Dr. Naim Collins' book, *Realms of the Prophetic*. As a prophet of many decades, I found it to be refreshing revelation. His study of the Scriptures and the many years of operating as a prophet is obvious to the reader. This book brings order and clarity of thought that establishes a firm foundation in dimensions of the prophetic for every reader desiring God's voice in their lives and through their lives. I would also encourage you to considering inviting Dr. Naim Collins and Dr. Hakeem Collins to teach and minister. They are cutting-edge teachers of the Word and life-giving prophets whom I love and appreciate.

Apostle Dale L. Mast, Senior Pastor
Destiny Christian Church
Dover, Delaware, USA
Board of Governor for Dr. Bill Hamon
Author of *And David Perceived He Was King,*
Two Sons and a Father, The Throne of David

In *Realms of the Prophetic,* Naim Collins shares the keys to unlocking the prophetic anointing resident in every believer, calling the men and women of this Joel 2:28 generation to a life marked by partnering with Heaven to bring the voice of the Lord to a hopeless and hurting world.

Shaun Tabatt
Host of *The Shaun Tabatt Show*

Realms of the Prophetic has been thoroughly written to recalibrate the prophetic and to reestablish the function, role, ministry, and office of the prophetic for generations to come. Dr. Naim Collins is a genuine prophetic voice in his generation, and I have had the privilege of being his leader when I pastored in Wilmington, Delaware. I'm blessed to have him as a son in the gospel. He is a regular guest, along with his twin brother Dr. Hakeem Collins, on my television show *Greg Davis Live,* which airs weekly on The Word Network. I am very proud of Naim and I highly recommend *Realms of the Prophetic* to all believers who desire to be activated, acclimated, and accelerated in the different facets of the prophetic.

BISHOP GREG DAVIS, Senior Pastor
Celebration Church of Detroit
Detroit, Michigan, USA
Host of *Greg Davis Live* on The Word Network
www.gregdavisshow.com

Realms of the Prophetic is a power-packed, doable book for all believers—from beginners to seasoned vets in the prophetic. Dr. Naim Collins has championed an exhaustive study guide that hits all cylinders, angles, and metrics as it relates to modern-day prophets, prophecy, prophetic ministry, and the current moves of God's Spirit in the twenty-first century. He has masterfully put together a "prophet's manual" that provides language, definition, vocabulary, illumination, and meaning to the prophetic movement, function, and landscape. *Realms of the Prophetic* is a practicum book that will reshape, recondition, and recalibrate each reader's understanding and teaching on the prophetic realm. Dr. Collins serves his generation as a contemporary prophetic voice and catalyst leader called to educate, equip, and train a generation of prophets and prophetic leadership. He has a wealth of experience, knowledge, and wisdom that qualifies him to teach and write on the prophetic with cutting-edge revelatory insight into the things of the Spirit.

Realms of the Prophetic is not an average book on the prophetic subject but a foundational model that will bring leverage to how you see, think, and operate in the power of the prophetic! This well-written literary work will become a compass not just for the prophets but for *all* believers who are ready to move into new realms of the prophetic and the supernatural gifts of the Holy Spirit. I highly recommend and endorse the pages of this groundbreaking book for all who are determined to break mediocrity and supernaturally excel in the *Realms of the Prophetic!*

DR. HAKEEM COLLINS
Champions International
Author of *Heaven Declares, Prophetic Breakthrough*
and *Command Your Healing*
Wilmington, Delaware, USA

As one of Prophet Naim Collins's prophetic foundational mentors, I am honored to relate to you how special this book really is. It takes you from one glory realm to another in the prophetic. It meets the needs of the prophet, as well as prophetic people.

As you are taken on this prophetic journey with every paragraph, take in the knowledge and embrace the heart of Prophet Collins. He has not left one stone unturned. I pray that it ignites the flame of fire that you may have allowed to be snuffed out. I speak that the prophetic in you is stirred up again anew.

As I read the book, it reminded me of how special it is to be chosen as a prophet of the Most High Yah. You can't even imagine the warfare in the atmosphere that Naim had to go through to birth this book in the earth realm. Before you read, ask the Holy Spirit to allow you to be in the sync with the heart of the prophet. Reading this book will bless you; I admonish you to buy a second copy to seed into the life of another prophet or prophetic person. And as a prophet, I declare that you will see a harvest of the extra seed that you seeded into someone else. Get ready to experience the *Realms of the Prophetic.*

RABBI RAYMOND STANSBURY
Prophetic House of Truth Outreach (P.H.O.T.O.)
Natarism Hebraic Assembly
Wilmington, Delaware, USA

Dr. Naim Collins is a right-now voice with a right-now word for anyone who is even remotely interested in the prophetic. He's a naturally gifted writer with a unique way of communicating intricate subject matter. Naim has the distinct ability to take complex material and break it down into easy-to-understand segments, making it more "digestible" for readers.

In this new book, *Realms of the Prophetic*, Dr. Collins takes us on a journey with him into the supernatural with precision and conciseness. He begins with what every well-constructed house is built upon—a great foundation. Like a domicile, this manuscript has been created with solid prophetic architecture, structure, and design in mind. When you finish reading, you'll find yourself with a few more weapons to add to your prophetic war chest than you started with!

Throughout this treatise on the prophetic, Dr. Collins demonstrates that every prophetic realm comes equipped with a revelation. There is an anointing that rests within the pages of this book. The oil will get on you and its residue will stay on you long after you've completed your reading of it. In fact, I can see many referring back to it often, especially those with a prophetic leaning. If you miss reading this book, you'll bypass a tremendous blessing!

Dr. John Veal
Author of *Supernaturally Prophetic: A Practical Guide for Prophets & Prophetic People* and *Supernaturally Delivered: A Practical Guide to Deliverance & Spiritual Warfare*
JohnVeal.org

Could ancient biblical mysteries unlock the prophetic in your life? Dr. Naim Collins says, "Yes," and wants to teach you how to release the gift of prophecy. "Yes," all can prophesy. That is why Paul says in 1 Corinthians 14:1, "…*desire…that you may prophesy*"!

Sid Roth
Host, *It's Supernatural!*

Are you ready to be launched into your prophetic destiny? Do you want to grow in understanding as well as activate the gift of prophecy in your life? If your answers are "Yes," then you've picked up the perfect resource! I believe that *Realms of the Prophetic* has the power to unlock your prophetic potential and release you into the greater glory you are destined for.

Prophet Naim and his brother Hakeem Collins are dear to my heart. I believe in their ministry; the Lord's hand is evidently on their lives. I believe this book will bless your life and Naim's ministry will help equip you to better serve our Lord of glory in your unique, Spirit-filled destiny. We need last-days, prophetic voices on earth—stand up and take your place!

MICHAEL LOMBARDO, Revivalist
Author of *Immersed in His Glory* and host of *Awaken Live*
Life Poured Out International
www.lifepouredoutintl.org
www.facebook.com/michaellombardolpo

Dr. Naim Collins has masterfully penned this manuscript that we deem a work of art. Every thought or question you may have had concerning your prophetic encounters will be thoroughly answered. Each chapter is intrinsically woven with the written Word of God and divinely inspired revelation in such a fashion that it makes you desperate to unveil what he has unlocked in the *Realms of The Prophetic*.

APOSTLE CHRIS WATSON
PROPHETESS KARYN WATSON
Living Waters Christian Center
Suffolk, Virginia, USA

I am astonished at the diversity and depth of information in Dr. Naim Collins' book, *Realms of the Prophetic*. Psalm 45:1, about having the tongue of a ready writer, came to my mind as I read. Dr. Collins has certainly been given a prophetic edge, acceleration, and divine insights as he writes the depths of our Father's heart and instructions in this book. His writing is eloquent, well-worded, and easy to follow as he teaches the depths of God's Word mixed with prophetic revelation from the Holy Spirit. The ease of his writing and depths of revelation will leave both the new and seasoned prophetic person with new revelation, fresh manna to apply to their prophetic destiny, and ease of transitioning into the prophetic realm for the beginner.

Dr. Naim Collins has personally been a prophetic friend and voice to me. I can testify the prophetic words he has spoken over my life are not only confirmed by God—something no one could have known—but I have also seen the manifestation of some of his words in just weeks after being released. He is a dynamic speaker, passionate about the Lord, and humbly lives his life to glorify the Lord while setting on fire and imparting a new breed of apostolic-prophetic voices to advance the Kingdom of God.

KATHY DEGRAW
Kathy DeGraw Ministries
Author of *Speak Out* and *Discerning and Destroying the Works of Satan*
www.degrawministries.org

Both Old and New Testaments describe the value, necessity, and relevance of the gift of prophecy and the ministry of the prophet. The prophetic is an essential ingredient for seeing the church come into the fullness of God's purposes. However, the topic of prophecy is often clouded by confusion, misunderstanding, and controversy. In *Realms of the Prophetic*, Naim Collins does an excellent job of laying biblical foundations for the various dimensions of the prophetic grace and calling. With powerful insights and scriptural teaching, he opens our eyes to the multifaceted nature of prophetic expressions and invites us to know God in a deeper way. As we step into greater realms of the prophetic, we can be used as God's mouthpiece on earth!

JAKE KAIL
Lead Pastor, Threshold Church
Author, *Keys for Deliverance*

Anointed. Visionary. Prophetic. All describe Dr. Naim Collins. I am blessed to endorse his new book, *Realms of the Prophetic*. Dr. Collins is an anointed seer prophet who unlocks and reveals new concepts concealed in Scripture. In this new book he has unlocked revelation contained in Scripture. But the revelation unlocked is not idyllic and utopian; rather, it is practical and powerful. One example is his explanation of the *Office of the Dreamer* in Chapter 5. I have yet to hear anyone share the concept of this biblical office. Understanding the purpose of that office is critical to last-days ministry.

In Acts 2:17, the apostle Peter declares *this is that* regarding the prophet Joel's prophetic declaration, *"And it shall come to pass in the last days, says God, that I will pour out of My Spirit on all flesh; and your sons and your daughters shall prophesy, your young men shall see visions, your old men shall dream dreams."* In Joel 2:23-28, we gain understanding of what those offices, identified in Chapter 5, do—they bring restoration of what has been stolen and eaten by our adversary, satan. Get ready! Your restoration has begun! As you read, I encourage you to understand and apply what is contained in this anointed book—and you shall see restoration take place in every area of your life.

SCOTT WALLIS
Senior Prophet
Author of *Entering the School of the Prophets*,
Plugging into the Spirit of Prophecy, and *The Gospel is Enough*

Realms of the Prophetic is an invaluable asset to deciphering the portals of the prophetic. This book is a must-read primer for those desiring more spiritually. The author gives a message of confidence and strength that will challenge readers to embrace their divine calling and live a purposeful life.

BISHOP-PROPHET ANTOINE M. JASMINE
Choice International Ministries
LaPlace, Louisiana
Author of *How to Dominate the Prophetic Realm*, *Is It Only a Dream?*,
Prophetic Terminology, and *Fathering the Hood*

REALMS

of the

PROPHETIC

REALMS

of the

PROPHETIC

*Keys to Unlock and Declare
the Secrets of God*

NAIM COLLINS

DESTINY IMAGE® PUBLISHERS, INC.

P.O. Box 310, Shippensburg, PA 17257-0310

"Promoting Inspired Lives."

This book and all other Destiny Image and Destiny Image Fiction books are available at Christian bookstores and distributors worldwide.

Cover design by: Eileen Rockwell
Interior design by: Terry Clifton

For more information on foreign distributors, call 717-532-3040.

Reach us on the Internet: www.destinyimage.com.

ISBN 13 TP: 978-0-7684-4867-2
ISBN 13 eBook: 978-0-7684-4868-9
ISBN 13 HC: 978-0-7684-4870-2
ISBN 13 LP: 978-0-7684-4869-6

For Worldwide Distribution, Printed in the U.S.A.

1 2 3 4 5 6 7 8 / 23 22 21 20 19

DEDICATION

This book, *Realms of the Prophetic,* is dedicated first and foremost to my heavenly Father, Jesus Christ my Lord and Savior, and the Holy Spirit who has inspired me and given me the ability to write and scribe this work with the prophetic ready writer's pen. He is my biggest inspiration and support of this book.

Second, this book is dedicated to all of the prophetic fathers and pioneers of the prophetic who have gone before us as forerunners, opening the way for successive generations of prophets and prophetic voices in our generation. I am honored to be graced with unique prophet and seer fathers in the commencement of my prophetic journey: the late, great Bob Jones of Statesville, North Carolina and Dr. Bill Hamon who have created new ceilings for us and strong shoulders for us to stand on. Also, this book is in memory of my Pomeranian dog, Pooh Collins.

Third, *Realms of the Prophetic* is for the present and future generations of prophetic voices, harbingers, prophets, and fathers. I honor, salute, and pay tribute to all of your work, noticed or unnoticed, and pray this book will forever help to pour water on the work of your hands.

> *Render therefore to all their dues: tribute to whom tribute is due; custom to whom custom; fear to whom fear; honor to whom honor* (Romans 13:7 KJV).

> *The one who receives a prophet because he is a prophet will receive a prophet's reward...* (Matthew 10:41 ESV).

Finally, I dedicate this literary work—*Realms of the Prophetic: Keys to Unlock and Declare the Secrets of God*—to you the readers who have invested your resources, time, and trust in this book project. It is my deepest desire and fervent prayer that this spiritual investment will empower, equip, and educate you in the various realms of the prophetic where it will become a key to unlock the secrets of God in your mouth to be a prophetic voice—not only in your life, but in your generation.

DR. NAIM COLLINS
Naim Collins Ministries
The League of the Prophets
Wilmington, Delaware, USA

ACKNOWLEDGMENTS

Mom—to my mother, Paula L. Collins of Wilmington, Delaware. Thank you so much for giving me life and being my biggest supporter. You have been my first example of unconditional love, loyalty, and relentlessness. Your encouragement, love, and voice has molded me into a leader and motivated me to become all that God has ordained me to be. I love you immensely!

Grandmothers—Ruth E. Collins and Mary Guy. Thank you both for your continual love, support, and prayers. Your ageless wisdom and counsel have imparted grace and endurance to remind me of the pedigree and legacy that is within me to carry on. You two women are my rocks and pillars. I love you two more than you know. You are two of the fastest walking grandmothers that my young legs look to follow after and keep up with.

Twin Brother/Wombmate—Dr. Hakeem Collins. Thank you for your unconditional love and continual support during this process. You have set the standard as the first published author in our family as you and I work to make history and a legacy for the Collins's family and brand. God has not made a mistake in electing you to be my twin, wombmate, and eternal friend. I honor and bless you that God has made you my team ministry's James as your John (Sons of Thunder). I love you!

Siblings—Eric Shannonhouse, Damon Daniels, Chantel Shannonhouse, Lakiesha Hargrow, Jasma Collins, and Khadijah Scott. Thank you for your love, support, and faith in me. I love you!

Close Relatives—Apostle Chris and Karyn Watson, Dion Bivens, Evens and Steven Edouard, Jamier "Bonz" Warren (favorite nephew), Jasmin Collins, Zion Cephas, King Carter Collins, Andre Fletcher, Jamar "J.T." Warren, Alijah Shannonhouse, Byron Walker, and Dr. John Veal. I love you all so much. God has ordained our relationship and I thank Him for bringing you into my life at the most critical times. You all are what honor, loyalty, genuine love, and family looks like.

Team of NCM—Prophetess Darlene Tilley (Director of Operations) and Prophetess Sherria Gross (Executive Administrator) of NCM in Philadelphia, Pennsylvania. What can I say about you two phenomenal, beautiful, and powerful women of God? Words cannot describe your unconditional love, support, loyalty, and unwavering accountability to not only the man of God, but to me the man. You both have been with us from the commencement and have sacrificed through it all to stand with me. You have prayed, interceded, prophesied, and even defended the integrity of the ministry by honoring my life and name. I love you both not only as team members but as my beloved spiritual daughters who are my *"daughters of Zelophehad"* who will receive your prophetic inheritance (Numbers 27:1-7).

Spiritual Parents and Mentors—The late Bob Jones, Kenneth and Brenda McDonald, Dr. Bill Hamon, Apostles Dale and LuAnne Mast, Apostle Raymond Stansbury, Bishop Greg Davis, James W. Goll, and the late Reverend Dr. Otis A. Herring. Your voice, influence, spiritual lineage, and legacy has made me into the man of God that I am today. I honor and love you all eternally for believing in my prophetic calling in a time when the ministry of the prophet was not readily received and for developing the man and the prophet in me.

Spiritual Sons, Daughters, Mentees—I love each and every one of you and I thank you for allowing me to cultivate the future in you. You are an extension of my spiritual DNA and legacy on the earth. It is equally an honor to be your spiritual Dad, Papa, Pop, and Senior. I love all of my mentees, both spiritually and professionally. There have been those who were jealous of our relationship and even some have tried to disqualify my presence, place, and position in your life. You have brought me so much joy and I will never stop being a mentor and father to you. I have been born for your voice to be heard and with my very last breath I live for you.

Family and Friends—thank you all for your prayers, personal prophecies, financial support, love, and encouragement over the years. I love all of my brothers, sisters, host of nieces and nephews, uncles, aunts, cousins, close friends, and NCM covenant partners.

Acquisition Agents of Destiny Image: Sierra White, I thank you so much for giving me this incredible opportunity and a prophetic dream come true to become a published author with Destiny Image. I cannot express my love and appreciation to you for discovering me and the timely acquisition of bringing me into the DI fold and family before you moved on to do other things for the Lord. I thank Tina Pugh, my new acquisition agent, who was the lead on this *Realms of the Prophetic* project. I was elated to find out that you were the producer for Sid Roth's *Its Supernatural* when my brother, Dr. Hakeem Collins, and I were guests on his show. Working with you on this project has been an amazing blessing from God. Thank you for believing in me and my message. It has been great to have your expertise and hand on this work. You ROCK!

Destiny Image Publisher—Larry Sparks. I thank you so much for believing in me and welcoming me into the legacy of Destiny Image and believing in my message as an author. You are an amazing theologian, author, and publisher of the prophets. I am honored to have you as my publisher, friend, and co-laborer in the Kingdom. Your leadership and voice are generational.

Destiny Image Publishing Family—John Martin, Eileen Rockwell, Meelika Marzzarella, Cavet Leibensperger, and the entire DI team. Thank you all for being the greatest publishing team on this side of Heaven and working diligently to make this dream of mine come to pass. Your spirit of excellence has pushed me more than you know. I am honored to be part of the DI family.

CONTENTS

FOREWORD

Realms of the Prophetic is a powerful treatment of the prophetic that easily catches one up in prophets' unmistakable frankness. Classic prophetic candor speaks to a diverse readership as a textbook and prophecy guide too. Plainly yet profoundly handling its subject from several angles shows its ability to appeal to all kinds of students and seekers. Despite being prophetic, its teachings book can edify non-prophetic people too who want to understand this medium. Ideally suited prophetic novices and learners, explanations refreshingly communicate the prophets in office. Newcomers to this realm of divine communications and stable prophetics can glean much from its coverage of God's age-old institution. The reason is how well the book blends prophetic thought with its core academic strands. Pedagogic like in its framework, subject matter holds on to the prophets' historic premises, something critical in today's disjointed prophetic climate.

From introductory rudiments to its doable examples, *Realms of the Prophetic's* richly informs its readers methodically and realistically. At the same time it instructs them on prophecy and its messengers' ways, delivering insights and intelligence that come from living and not just learning one's field. Scripture integrations are relevant and connect what follows them to the thoughts anchored to them. Clearly answering why quoted passages fit. That they open each chapter, and preface important discussion points reinforce what prophets are charged to do as God's mouthpiece. That is, remain within Bible prophets' continuum to validate His truths and enable others to do the same. *Realms of the Prophetic* does all this quite well, leaving no room for misunderstandings that take readers and the Lord's people off track. To this end, biblically grounded truths forge vital connections between God's Scriptures and His prophets' words.

I see this work as a sound learning and guiding basis that makes a strong case for prophetic education and its resultant excellence. When it comes to the mature reader, I see it as invaluable to everyday life interactions with the Lord and His world. Reading through it early inspires multifold appreciation for the God of the prophets. Thus, building long overdue trust in the prophetic as an essential connecter of this world to its Maker's. I encourage use of this book as a trainer, Bible study guide, and ministry readiness text most of all. However, it can prove valuable to everyone entering and interacting with God's unseen agents and prophetic messengers. That said, I heartily commend Naim for the solid work he did in writing this book. It is sure to forerun a worldwide prophetic explosion and deal resounding crippling blows to careless prophecies and distorted prophetic practices the Lord's church has endured for far too long. Congratulations,

Dr. Paula A. Price, PhD,
Author of *The Prophets' Dictionary*

INTRODUCTION

In an age and era when the prophetic voice is most needed, more than any other time in history there are opposing agencies striving to push the relevancy of the prophets into extinction or make them absolutely obsolete. The sheer purpose and intent of this book is to forge a new focus and interest in God's sacred ministry of the ages.

The church in the New Testament—frameworked within different segments, circles, streams, denominations, and organizations—have not fully embraced the role, ministry, and function of the prophet, even in our modern epoch. With emerging crises, problems, ideologies, opinions, theories, religiosities, and philosophies, the world, including the church at times, seem to have waged war to silence the prophetic voice.

But, I declare there is coming a resurgence of the prophetic roar that will begin to resound in the earth, and a restoration of the prophet will be unearthed to reinstitute the prophetic in times and seasons when widespread revelation of God is a rarity. I see an unprecedented wave of the Spirit being unleashed upon a rare company of prophets, seers, and dreamers who will redefine the prophetic function in this present age in ways we have not seen before.

There is a prophetic caliber of voices that will carry a special anointing and grace to partner with the thoughts, plans, agendas, and purposes of God for their generation and ages to come. Samuel-type prophetic mantles will help bring greater clarity, definition, and scope to understand various functions in the realms of the prophetic.

I wrote this book to help those who desire a deeper understanding of the different measures, degrees, levels, dimensions, and spheres of the prophetic to find their own prophetic voice. We are beginning to see the spirit of prophecy being poured out upon all flesh—where Christians globally are being moved with inspired utterances. They are seeing visions and dreaming dreams. Moses envisioned a time when there would be a nation of prophets in Numbers 11:29:

> *Then Moses said to him, "Are you zealous for my sake? Oh, that all the Lord's people were prophets and that the Lord would put His Spirit upon them!"*

Since the beginning of the ages, it has been God's heart to communicate intimately and directly with humanity. There have those to whom He has chosen to reveal His secrets, His peculiar friends. These hidden and sacred truths are being unlocked in the treasure of men and women who have ears to hear what the Spirit is communicating.

Realms of the Prophetic introduces to you a world in the prophetic of which many are not aware. The mysteries of the prophetic and the various understandings of the supernatural have been hidden in past ages and in the ancient prophets—until now. God has given keys to some in this generation to unlock His secrets to impart them into this and future generations. In this book you will learn the different dimensions and levels associated with the prophetic. In each chapter you read, you will gain greater depth of understanding of prophetic language, communications, and channels that God uses to speak to us today.

Unfortunately, in this hour there is an entire group of people who teach that the prophetic—the supernatural and signs, wonders, and miracles—is a thing of the past, and that essentially God stopped speaking with the canonization of the Holy Bible. That teaching is against what the Bible instructs us, both in the Old and New Testaments. In truth, there are a vast number of Scriptures through the entirety of the Bible that support and reveal that genuine believers in Christ are prophetic in nature, but may not know it.

You will discover that there is a prophetic anointing resident within every believer. Old and New Testament prophets have provided keys, with their Holy Spirit-inspired penmanship of the Scripture, to unlock for us access into their prophetic realm. And to not only unlock its secrets for us personally, but to help others access the realms of the prophetic as well.

I have found that many today have ignorantly appointed themselves as prophets or prophetesses and some have been ordained as prophets with little to zero understanding of this official office. Many are grossly unaware of the basic terminology and purpose of prophecy—yet carry the title "prophet." This errancy has developed an insatiable discontentment in my heart to thoroughly restore the honor, integrity, and biblical standards to the ministry. I have written this to share and disclose truths that are not often taught in church and for those who have a sovereign prophetic mantle on their lives and need a prophetic sage to help them understand the unseen realm of the prophets.

As you explore each chapter, you will receive an impartation of revelation to comprehend prophetic intelligence and how to access keys to unlock and declare the secrets of God. God has hidden a prophetic anointing in the ancient prophets that will teach you how to break spiritual curses, famine, drought, and depravity. You will discover how to cultivate your own prophetic capacity and learn various dimensions of the prophetic anointing. There is a place for you with space to operate in your prophetic grace. The prophetic is one of the most coveted and powerful gifts that God has endowed you with—and it is time for you to walk into the realm of the prophetic unhindered.

Each chapter of the *Realms of the Prophetic* gives you keys to unlock, operate, and function in each dimension of the prophetic. I do not believe the prophetic is for only the anointed few. Rather, I believe God has poured out His prophetic Spirit upon all flesh so that all His sons and daughters would be prophets. *Realms of the Prophetic* has been written for generations of prophets and prophetic people to understand the academia and the world of prophetic. I wrote this prophetic manuscript for you with 1 Corinthians 14:31 in mind: *"For you can all prophesy one by one, that all may learn and all may be encouraged."*

Realms of the Prophetic gives a prophetic perspective where the prophetic is more than hearing the voice of God and prophecy—it ultimately brings you into prophetic encounters with the Lord Jesus Christ. The greatest key to have in unlocking the prophetic dimension is the Master Key, which is from Christ who is the flawless model and image of the office of the prophet.

My goal in this book is for you to understand the supernatural as it relates to the prophetic; every realm will take you into the greatest revelation of the prophets, which is to see the manifestation of the glory of God in Christ. Some portions of this book may be somewhat of a stretch to understand, but as you continue to read, much clarity will be imparted. The Bible is our ancient textbook written by the prophets of the ages for generations beyond what their physical eyes could see. They wrote spiritually, seeing into the future to reveal, within the letters of the Bible, keys waiting to be used by us to experience the God of the prophets. There are revelatory encounters in these realms that have not been voyaged—yet. This book is your boarding pass to now explore *Realms of the Prophetic!*

PART I

PROPHETIC
FOUNDATIONS

CHAPTER 1

INSPIRED *NABI* PROPHETS

*I will raise up for them a Prophet like you from among
their brethren, and will put My words in His mouth,
and He shall speak to them all that I command Him.*
—DEUTERONOMY 18:18

THE *NABI* PROPHET REALM—THE PROPHET-SPOKESMAN

Nabi is the first and the most generally used Hebrew word for a prophet
found in the Old Testament Scriptures. It is first mentioned in the Book of
Genesis in relation to Abraham:

> *Now therefore, restore the man's wife; for he is a prophet* [nabi],
> *and he will pray for you and you shall live. But if you do not
> restore her, know that you shall surely die, you and all who are
> yours"* (Genesis 20:7).

Nabi is defined as "the inspired man" or "the official prophet," which
in fact could literally be articulated by definition to be the office of the
prophet. In Hebrew, *nabiy* is from a root meaning "to bubble forth, as from
a fountain," hence "to utter." The *nabi* or *nabiy* qualifies as a prophet as
one who is God's mouthpiece, one who with authority conveys God's message to someone as commanded by God. A prophet is simply defined as

an official spokesperson inspired by God who speaks forth the mind, will, original intent, heart, and purposes of God to humankind.

The word "prophet" in Hebrew is transliterated as *nabi* or *nabyi* or *nabiy* according to Strong's Concordance, which occurs 316 times in the Old Testament from the root word (verb) *naba,* which means "to prophesy" or "to speak under inspiration" in prediction or simple discourse. The Hebrew word *nabi* is derived from the verb *naba,* which means "to announce, call a declarer and announcer," according to the New Unger's Bible Dictionary. The primary explanation of a prophet is someone who speaks, utters, announces, and declares a divine communication. Therefore, a prophet is a supernatural communicator, declarer, and announcer.

DEFINING THE INSPIRED SPEAKER

The essential role of a *nabi* is an inspired man who pours forth the declaration of God—an inspired spokesperson, speaking by the inspiration of the Spirit. The prophet is officially the spokesperson of God who has been divinely authorized to speak on His behalf. Nabi prophets are what I call "Masters of Inspired Words"—they are masterful in ministering in the realm of being inspired by the word of the Lord. The word "prophet" appears in the Old Testament more than 300 times and more than 100 times in the New Testament. The following are a few examples of the nabi prophet in Scripture:

Abraham was the first person to be called a prophet directly by God according to Genesis: *"Now therefore, restore the man's [Abraham's] wife, for he is a prophet [nabi], and he will pray for you and you shall live. But if you do not restore her, know that you shall surely die, you and all who are yours"* (Genesis 20:7).

Moses was a prophet who led the children of Israel: *"Since then, no prophet [nabi] has risen in Israel like Moses, whom the Lord knew face to face"* (Deuteronomy 34:10 NIV).

Aaron, the brother of Moses, was given by God as his spokesman: *"Then the Lord said to Moses, "See, I have made you like God to Pharaoh, and your brother Aaron will be your prophet* [nabi]" (Exodus 7:1 NIV).

Jeremiah was called as a prophet to the nations before he was born: *"Before I formed you in the womb I knew you, before you were born I set you apart; I appointed you as a prophet* [nabi] *to the nations"* (Jeremiah 1:5 NIV).

The function of the *nabi* prophet has to do with hearing and speaking on behalf of God as His spokesperson and mouthpiece. Even Malachi the prophet declared that God would send Elijah the prophet—*nabi*—in the last days (Malachi 4:5) in the person of John the Baptist, as Jesus confirms in Matthew 11:7-14.

The following words are synonymous to best describe the nabi prophets:

- inspired
- official prophet
- spokesman
- mouthpiece
- ambassador
- intercessor
- mediator
- interpreter
- herald, town crier, officer
- announcer
- speaker
- oracle
- one who is called
- hearer and declarer of the Word of God

PROPHETIC INSPIRED FLOW

The nabi prophetic flow is described in Psalm 45:1 as a person's "tongue is the pen of a ready writer." The prophetic release out of the mouth of the

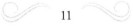

nabi prophet is poured out and words are poetically composed. Their words are released from the heart of the prophet. In other words, there is an overflowing of prophetically engineered and composed words from the Spirit. God put His words in the mouth of His prophets. The heart of the director of music according to Psalm 45:1 is "stirred" or "overflows" with words as he recites his verses he has written down for the king. His tongue speaks likes the pen of a skillful writer. This gives us a deeper understanding of the inspirational aspect of a nabi prophet.

The Word of God is stirred up and overflows in a prophet's heart to speak what God has written verse by verse, line upon line, and precept upon precept. God gave the prophets the "tongue of the learned" (Isaiah 50:4). The tongue of the learned is so they know how to speak a word in season to those who are weary. God awakens the prophet's trained ear to hear as described by Isaiah the prophet. The prophet's ear is just as powerful as his or her mouth waiting to release a supernatural utterance. The language of the prophetic is inspired by the Word of the Lord as a ready writer awaits to arrange the Spirit-inspired composition.

King David, being a prophet, wrote and arranged songs—psalms—by the inspiration of the Spirit and received continual revelation and prophetic foresight into the future regarding the Messiah Jesus Christ (see Acts 2:25-30). The prophetic is inspired words in the mouth of the prophet whose tongue is the pen of a skillful writer.

Nabi prophets speak according to what is stirred from their heart by God who has skillfully written on their innermost being. They release the heart of God. Nabi prophets carry the word of the Lord in their heart and in their mouth. Prophets minister prophetically and poetically where their words flow out with a full measure of skill and precision. There is grace upon their lips (see Psalm 45:2).

WHAT IS THE THEME OF THE LORD?

Oftentimes, when God is speaking and inspiring you to release a prophetic word, He will fill and stir your heart with words to say. Importantly, the key to the nabi dimension of the prophetic is discovered in Psalm 45:1, *"My heart is overflowing with a good theme; I recite my composition concerning the King; my tongue is the pen of a ready writer."* The key to the prophetic is that in the nabi aspect God will give you a word in your heart but that word will come to you in the form of a theme. God revealed this key to me to help others understand how the inspired aspect of the nabi prophetic flow operates in the prophets and inspired believers.

Knowing this will help you recognize when the prophetic is inspiring and moving upon you to speak, intercede, or minister to someone. You do not necessarily have to be a prophet to be inspired to prophesy like the prophets. The inspired word of God will start as a theme in your heart. This is the beginning of the word of the Lord that will "bubble up" from within you. Therefore, you will have to then release what is in the heart of God or what God has written on your heart; your tongue, as you speak from His heart, is the pen of a ready writer.

The word "theme," according the Merriam Webster's Dictionary, means the subject of a talk, a matter, a concern, a piece of writing, a person's thoughts, a topic or a message. In other words, when the word of the Lord comes to a prophet or someone prophetically, God will inspire a theme in the person's heart. This theme will be the subject of conversation that God wants to share with someone. They are the matters of His heart, thoughts, and concerns that need to be communicated or a topic of discussion that the prophet has to convey to the person receiving the prophetic utterance. You will never get a full phrase or paragraph before releasing a prophetic word. God will give you only a word or theme as your starting point to release the word of the Lord.

NATURE OF THE *NABI* PROPHETIC FLOW

The following describes the nature of the nabi prophetic flow, which is to:

- bubble forth or bubble up, as from fountain
- burst forth, burst out or burst open

- gush forth

- well up

- stir up

- boil forth or boil over, like boiling water under heat or fire or like a hot spring (fountain)

- compel

- utter

- burn or to burn with intensity or fervency, burning heart to speak

- flow

- inspire

- speak utterance in an exalted and excited manner by the Spirit of God

The following are some experiential examples of the nabi operating in a believer:

- Cool and heat (burning) type of sensation, feeling or impression in your belly like flowing water.

- Sensation in your stomach, bowel, gut, and torso area that you feel stirring up in your spirit.

- You may feel a sense of nerves or a strong impression to say something welling up inside.

- At times I have had a feeling in my stomach as if I am on a rollercoaster or "gut feeling" that will not subside until I release what I sense in my spirit.

- Words continually coming up in your spirit, mind, thoughts, or heart that you cannot shake. A specific word, person, or thought keeps coming to you.

- It is the intensity within your heart as if the words are trying to burst forth.

- You may feel a strong compelling in your spirit.

- Flowing of thoughts or a flow of words inspired and imparted by the Spirit. A flowing of words as you speak the word of the Lord. Out of our belly, our innermost parts (bosom), are words that flow literally out of you without you thinking beforehand what to say.

ACTIVATING THE *NABI* ANOINTING

The nabi prophetic is activated in a believer or prophet when praying and worshipping in the Holy Spirit. God searches for such who will worship in Spirit and in truth (John 4:23). Praying, worshipping, and singing in the Holy Spirit activates the prophetic in the believer and God will begin to speak and the word of the Lord will inspire you to prophesy. Praying in the Spirit will build up your faith to prophesy and release the Word of the Lord (Jude 20).

Jesus spoke prophetically about the impartation of the Holy Spirit being activated in the New Testament believer. The saints will be inspired by the flow and activity of the Spirit. Out of their innermost parts will flow the prophetic rivers. To be prophetic is to be inspired by the Spirit within us as revealed in John 7:38-39 (NIV):

> *"Whoever believes in me, as Scripture has said, rivers of living water will flow from within them." By this he meant the Spirit, whom those who believed in him were later to receive. Up to that time the Spirit had not been given, since Jesus had not yet been glorified.*

WHAT IS A PROPHET?

> *Now the acts of King David, first and last, indeed they are written in the book of Samuel the seer* [ra'ah], *in the book of Nathan the prophet* [nabiy], *and in the book of Gad the seer* [chozeh]" (1 Chronicles 29:29).

In this and the next two chapters, we will take a closer look at the biblical definition of the English word "prophet" from its original Hebraic roots in the Old Testament Scriptures. It is imperative to do a thorough word study, as we will discover a more definitive and holistic understanding of the prophet. The English definition of prophet is limited in its scope and does not accurately reveal the true essence and nature of the Hebrew prophets.

Defining the word "prophet" from a Hebraic understanding, you will learn that the role, nature, function, and office of the prophet is more extensive and exhaustive than you may have realized. A prophet is simply a spokesperson who speaks on the behalf of God, yet there is more to know.

God speaks and reveals Himself to His prophets in dreams, visions, and other prophetic revelations according to Numbers 12:6: *"Then He said, 'Hear now My words: If there is a prophet among you, I, the Lord, make Myself known to him in a vision; I speak to him in a dream.'"* God does nothing in the earth unless He first discloses His secrets to His prophets; and when He speaks, they are moved to prophesy—as in Amos 3:7-8: *"Surely the Lord God does nothing, unless He reveals His secret to His servants the prophets. A lion has roared! Who will not fear? The Lord God has spoken! Who can but prophesy?"*

There are various job descriptions of the prophet and each is defined by the different types of prophets and realms of prophetic activity. The dominant ministry gift in the Old Testament was the prophet. According to 1 Chronicles 29:29, we see there are three key Hebrew usages in the Old Testament transliterated into the English word "prophet" or "seer": 1) *nabi;* 2) *ra'ah;* and 3) *chozeh.* These are the three major streams of the prophetic, three Hebraic definitive types of prophets in the Old Testament:

1. *Nabi* (official prophet or spokesman—auditory realm)

2. *Ra'ah* or *rō'eh* (seer realm)

3. *Chozeh* or *hozeh* (seer-visionary realm)

ABRAHAM—THE FIRST *NABI* PROPHET

The Book of Genesis in the Bible is regarded as "the book of beginnings." As mentioned previously, the first mention of the term prophet is found in Genesis when God Himself called Abraham a prophet—*nabi*—which best defines the original concept and thought of the word prophet in the mind of God (see Genesis 20:7).

When God called Abraham a prophet, He was revealing the genesis of the prophetic through the lens of the Hebrew word nabi. Abraham was a prophet because he was inspired by God. He heard the voice of God (Genesis 12:1); and at times the Lord would appear and manifest Himself to him (Genesis 12:7). Abraham also was a prophet because he had all kinds of prophetic encounters, visions, appearances, and revelations with God. Abraham is the Bible's prototype of a nabi prophet. Therefore, he became the first prophet of his kind and unlocks for future prophetic ministry, a foundational understanding of the earliest function of a nabi prophet in the Bible.

I believe there are key aspects, components, and elements of the prophetic that are missed when comparing Abraham to our understanding of a prophet in our modern era to God's original idea of His prophets in ancient Scriptures. Abraham is the foundational prophetic example.

PROPHETIC INTERCESSION

It is important to note that the first time we began to hear of Abraham in relation to prophet, it was connected with prayer and intercession. The first function of the inspired *nabi* prophet is in prayer and intercession as we see in the following example of Abraham interceding for Abimelech, the king whose household was barren, in Genesis 20:17-18:

> *So Abraham prayed to God; and God healed Abimelech, his wife, and his female servants. Then they bore children; for the Lord had closed up all the wombs of the house of Abimelech because of Sarah, Abraham's wife.*

One of the key aspects of the prophet is prayer intercession on behalf of God in order to see healing. This is the first place in Scripture that through the prayer of a prophet healing was released. Prophets must have a lifestyle of prayer, which keeps an open channel and frequency with the Lord to be able to hear with much clarity the word of the Lord.

Oftentimes, in today's era of the prophetic, we tend to regard someone as a prophet only if the person is ministering or prophesying the future—or better yet disclosing our names, addresses, or what we ate for breakfast, etc. However, in the first biblical occurrence with Abraham, we see the prophetic revealed in what I call "embryonic stages." Abraham, as a *nabi* prophet, sets the foundation and pattern for what the prophetic would develop into. God introduces us to the basis of the prophetic in the life of Abraham that would become vitally important to all prophets of all time to comprehend. The *nabi* prophets and those who are beginning their journey in the prophetic will start in the Abrahamic stage of prayer and intercession.

MOVED TO PROPHESY

For prophecy never had its origin in the human will, but prophets, though human, spoke from God as they were carried along by the Holy Spirit (2 Peter 1:21 NIV).

The origin of the prophetic does not commence in the will of humanity but through the prophets, though human, spoke from God as they were moved (carried along) by the Holy Spirit. The Holy Spirit moved upon the prophets who were human to speak not of their own wills but the will of God. The Spirit is the origin of the prophetic and the engine that drives the prophets to speak. It is important to understand that no prophetic message ever came from human will, but through people who were under the inspiration, control, and auspices of the Holy Spirit as they spoke the message that came directly from God. The prophets prophesied as they were moved, carried along, or best inspired by the Holy Spirit. The nabi aspect of prophecy is simply to be under the inspiration of God to speak or act on His behalf.

According to the Merriam Webster's Dictionary and Thesaurus, the word "inspire" means to fill (someone) with the urge or ability to do or feel something, especially to do something creative. To be inspired is to be creative. Those who are creative are also prophetic in nature. Some people are inspired to write music, play instruments, create computers, technology, etc. When *nabi* prophets, or inspired people, are inspired by the Holy Spirit to operate on the behalf of God, they are essentially: stimulated, motivated, encouraged, influenced, roused, moved, stirred, energized, galvanized, and incited. This inspiration aspect can be equivalent to: animate, fire, excite, spark, inspirit, and incentivize. All of these synonyms describe the stirring of the Spirit within the prophets when they are moved to prophesy.

INSPIRED WITH FIRE

An "inspired man" is the meaning of an official prophet in the original Hebrew who is by definition an authorized spokesperson. They were described in the scriptural sense of the word as inspired because they were motivated, stirred up, energized, and influenced by the Spirit of God to prophesy on His behalf. I love two of the synonyms describing the inspiration aspect of the nabi prophet as "fire" or "spark." The inspiration of the Holy Spirit upon the prophet was like fire upon him or a spark within his spirit. It is as if God set a fire within the spirit of the prophet or created a spark in the nabi to move. When someone is inspired, the person is ignited or lit on fire. Fire describes the presence and move of the Spirit in a prophet's spirit. The word of the Lord is like fire in the heart and bones of the prophet.

This concept is understood when Jeremiah the prophet says the word of the Lord is like burning fire shut up in his bones. He describes the inspired aspect of the prophetic word in Jeremiah 20:9:

> *Then I said, "I will not make mention of Him, nor speak anymore in His name." But His word was in my heart like a burning fire shut up in my bones; I was weary of holding it back, and I could not.*

The word "fire" described in this passage is the Hebrew word "ash," which means burning, fiery, flaming, and hot. It is better defined as supernatural fire accompanying manifestation. The fire that Jeremiah was experiencing was a manifestation of God activated within him.

This prophetic activity of inspiration is commonly used in the New Testament as an "unction." An unction of the Holy Spirit to prophesy is coined as a "prophetic unction." It is to sense the Holy Spirit moving upon you or within you to speak His mind, will, heart, intent, and purpose that He reveals to someone. An unction of the Holy Spirit inspired the prophets of the Old Testament to prophesy. An unction of the Spirit in the New Testament is the same as being inspired by the Spirit in the Old Testament. The anointing of the Holy Spirit inspiring, flowing, and influencing someone to minister is the unction. Inspiration is the vehicle through which a prophet becomes routinely sensitive and aware of the moves, activities, and operations of the Spirit of God. The Spirit carries the prophet into different realms of the Spirit.

The Spokesperson and Mouthpiece of God

God uses prophets to speak to the people. Yes, we know that God can speak to believers directly by the Holy Spirit within them; however, God has always sent men as His representatives to speak on His behalf. God can speak to people directly through reading and studying the Word of God, the Bible, and also by the Holy Spirit. However, the Scripture does not support the idea or opinion that it eliminated the necessity and role of the prophet today. God, through many passages of Scripture in both the Old and New Testaments, clearly reveals and teaches that He has always and will continue to use people inspired by the Holy Spirit to speak to us directly.

Who Is a Spokesperson?

> *The Lord said to him, "Who gave human beings their mouths? Who makes them deaf or mute? Who gives them sight or makes them blind? Is it not I, the Lord? Now go;* ***I will help you***

speak and will teach you what to say" (Exodus 4:11-12 NIV).

*Now you shall speak to him and put the words in his mouth. And I will be with your mouth and with his mouth, and I will teach you what you shall do. So he shall be your **spokesman to the people**...* (Exodus 4:15-16).

He did evil in the sight of the Lord his God. He did not humble himself before Jeremiah the prophet, **the Lord's spokesman** (2 Chronicles 36:12 NET).

The word "spokesperson," according to the dictionary, means "a person who speaks as the representative of another or others." This person is also called a "spokesman." Moses and Aaron were spokespersons of God who spoke as His representatives. It is important to understand that prophets are representatives of God. They speak on God's behalf. A spokesperson is also a "mouthpiece, speaker, delegate, ambassador, and deputy." A woman who speaks on behalf of another is called a "spokeswoman." Biblically, a spokeswoman is a "prophetess," namely a female prophet.

Scripturally, the English word "spokesperson" in the Hebrew is *dabar*, which means "to speak, to declare, to converse, to command, to warn and to talk (to speak with one another)."

God's prophets are given the capacity to be His spokespeople. He awakens their ears and makes them alert and attentive to His voice and words as disciples of prophecy (Isaiah 50:4). Prophets' ears are trained to hear the voice of God and they are usually "auditory learners." God trains them to speak for Him and to have trained ears to listen attentively for His instructions. He teaches them how to hear His words in order to have the capacity needed to be His spokespeople to help those in need.

Prophets carry a capacity to hear and speak at a heightened and more accurate realm than normal people. They hear and speak supernaturally. They hear and speak with a capacity of authority that makes them distinctively different in their function and operation in the realm of the prophetic. We all can hear and speak for God; but the prophet carries an entirely different capacity of hearing and speaking that is in a class of its own. They prophesy supernatural intelligence and have ears that are privy to secret briefings and details prompted by the inspiration of the Spirit. Their ears are awakened and trained by the Lord to hear at a capacity that is totally supernatural.

The following is an example of the prophet Isaiah declaring the capacity to be a God-inspired spokesperson to help those in need in Isaiah 50:4 (NET):

> *The sovereign Lord has given me the capacity to be his spokesman, so that I know how to help the weary. He wakes me up every morning; he makes me alert so I can listen attentively as disciples do.*

Prophets are commissioned representatives and spokespeople of God. They are under divine protection by the hand of God as official spokespersons and prophets (see 2 Kings 3:15 and Ezekiel 37:1-14). They are sent and commissioned by God to speak on His behalf: *"I commission you as my spokesman; I cover you with the palm of my hand, to establish the sky and to found the earth, to say to Zion, 'You are my people'"* (Isaiah 51:16 NET).

God puts His words in the mouth of His prophets-spokespeople. A spokesperson is also a mouthpiece. A spokesperson and mouthpiece are the same in functionality as prophet. We will learn that God trains and equips His prophets to communicate on his behalf and He uses people to be His mouth, as you will see that Aaron was given to Moses, his brother, as his mouthpiece. A prophet is regarded spiritually as the "mouth" or "mouthpiece." This means that God uses their own mouths filled with His inspired words to articulate on His behalf to people. Let's further examine this function of the prophetic as a mouthpiece.

What Is a Mouthpiece?

> *So he shall be your **spokesperson** to the people. And he himself shall be **as a mouth for you**, and you shall be to him as God* (Exodus 4:16).

A prophet functions as a mouth or "mouthpiece" for God. We can see in this Scripture verse that Aaron was given as a mouthpiece for Moses to speak to Pharaoh, because Moses felt inadequate to speak as a prophet on the behalf of God because of his "slow speech and tongue." Aaron, who could speak eloquently, was chosen to speak on behalf of Moses for God. God gave Moses the direct words and Moses would put those words into the mouth of Aaron to speak technically as a mouthpiece of God to Pharaoh.

JESUS CHRIST AND THE HOLY SPIRIT AS SPOKESMEN OF THE FATHER

Jesus Christ understood the role and function of being a spokesperson speaking on behalf of His Father in John 12:49: *"For I have not spoken on My own authority; but the Father who sent Me gave Me a command, what I should say and what I should speak."*

Jesus spoke what the Father taught Him to say in John 8:28: *"Then Jesus said to them, 'When you lift up the Son of Man, then you will know that I am He, and that I do nothing of Myself; but as My Father taught Me, I speak these things.'"*

The Holy Spirit is also a Spokesperson and Prophet as revealed in the following passage in John 16:13 (NIV): *"But when he, the Spirit of truth, comes, he will guide you into all truths. He will not speak on his own; he will speak only what he hears, and he will tell you what is yet to come."*

A *NABI* PROPHET—GOD'S OFFICIAL MOUTH

God forms the mouth of each of His prophets and gives them the power and the ability to speak for Him (see Exodus 4:11). Moses, in this illustration, was to be as God to Aaron putting His words in his mouth. Therefore, a prophet is one who hears directly from God, His words, in order to stand before the people as His authorized spokesperson.

Jeremiah's mouth was touched by the hands of God to authorize him as His official prophet to speak on His behalf to nations and kingdoms: *"Then the Lord reached out his hand and touched my mouth and said to me, 'I have put my words in your mouth'"* (Jeremiah 1:9 NIV).

Prophets act as God's representatives. It can be even said that prophets act as God's own mouth. The true definition of a mouthpiece is to speak as the very mouth of God before the people. This is very concise with respect to understanding the primary role of being a prophet—spokesperson and mouthpiece. Just as Moses and Aaron spoke to Pharaoh on behalf of God telling him to send the children of Israel out of Egypt, prophets are to speak all that God commands them. One of the primary roles and function of a spokesperson is to speak and communicate precisely all of the words of the person they represent. Two modern examples of a spokesperson is the press secretary of the President of the United States and any country's ambassador to foreign nations.

The press secretary conveys and interprets the President's very words, opinions, thoughts, reactions, intentions, and feelings. Therefore, when the press secretary holds a news or press conference on behalf of the President, everyone expects this spokesperson will never communicate his or her own opinion. In most cases, the press secretary will read the written message of the President to eliminate any room or danger of mistake or misspeaking. The ambassador of nations are appointed to convey and articulate the official decisions, intentions, reactions, and opinions of his or her country, nation, and government to the government of another nation.

Likewise, prophets are ambassadors of God appointed by the government and powers of Heaven to convey the original intent, thoughts, message, and purpose of God on earth.

TAUGHT BY GOD TO BE A PROPHET

> *Then Moses said to the Lord, "O my Lord, I am not eloquent, neither before nor since You have spoken to Your servant; but I am slow of speech and slow of tongue." So the Lord said to him, "Who has made man's mouth? Or who makes the mute, the deaf, the seeing, or the blind? Have not I, the Lord? Now therefore, go, and I will be with your mouth and teach you what you shall say"* (Exodus 4:10-12).

God is with the mouth of His prophets. When prophets speak on behalf of God, they carry His presence with every word. God offered prophetic training on how to speak for Him. Prophets, spokespeople, and mouthpieces are taught in prophetic communications how to be official speakers for God. Their mouths are trained by God. God qualifies the mouth of His prophets and He initiates their training once they embrace the calling.

Moses, due to his speech impediment, felt he could not speak well enough to be a speaker for God. Many people feel like Moses—that they do not have the physical capabilities to speak for God. Or when He calls them to be a prophet and speak for Him, they need to already be an eloquent speaker and fluid communicator. You do not have to be an excellent public speaker and orator to be a prophet—God qualifies His spokespeople and teaches them to speak.

TAUGHT WITH PROPHETIC ACCURACY

God told Moses and Aaron that He would teach them how to speak for Him. He would train their mouths how to release His prophetic words with precision. In Exodus 4:12, God responds to Moses' statement that he could not speak well by saying, *"I will be with your mouth and teach you what you shall say."* The word "teach" in the Hebrew is *yarah,* which means to throw, shoot, cast, or pour. It comes from the Hebraic definition to shoot arrows or to throw water or rain.

In addition, the word "teach" here means to direct, instruct, to point out, and to show. This meaning is powerfully significant to the prophetic and what God was essentially saying to Moses. This Hebrew word *yarah* comes from the primitive root word *yara,* meaning to flow as water or to release as rain. It also speaks of an archer teaching someone how to shoot an arrow by aiming and guiding the finger to accurately hit the target.

PROPHETIC ARROWS WITH SUPERNATURAL POWER

What best illustrates the word *yara* in terms of how God would teach and help Moses to speak His words with accuracy is found in 2 Chronicles 26:15:

> *And he made devices in Jerusalem, invented by skillful men, to be on the towers and the corners, to shoot arrows and large stones. So his fame spread far and wide, for he was marvelously helped till he became strong.*

It is important to understand that God teaches His prophets how to speak for Him. All prophets are called and taught intimately and directly by God. God guided and directed the release of His words in Moses' mouth as an archer is taught how to shoot and release arrows. A prophet is taught by God to flow in the prophetic. The words are released supernaturally. God taught Moses how to flow and release the word of the Lord like water. There is a flow that comes with releasing the word of the Lord—it pours out like rain.

The archer aspect of the prophetic release in 2 Chronicles 26:15 is about Uzziah, who was sixteen years old when he was made king of Judah. He set himself to seek God in the days of Zechariah who instructed and taught him in the fear of God. As long as Uzziah sought the Lord, God prospered him (2 Chronicles 26:5). The key point is that Uzziah was famous for his ability to make war with the Philistines and break through three of their walls and fortresses. God helped him against his enemies.

SUPERNATURAL PROPHETIC RELEASE

Uzziah prepared and equipped the army with shields, spears, helmets, coats of mail, bows, and stones for slinging. He had the skills, gifts, and ingenuity to invent new technologies, weapons, and machines of war to be set on the towers and the corners of the walls to shoot arrows and great stones. His fame spread abroad that he was supernaturally helped until he was made strong.

God gave Uzziah the ability to create new inventions of archery to shoot arrows, stones, and fiery projectiles to hit enemy targets supernaturally with accuracy. It was noticed by all that he was marvelously, supernaturally, helped by God until he grew strong. God helped Uzziah and the army with prophetic precision as they released the arrows. God was guiding and helping to aim the arrows and stones to hit the mark.

Similarly, God teaches prophets how to release His word with prophetic accuracy and precision. God teaches them how to flow in His Spirit and helps them speak supernaturally for Him in order to aim and deliver His messages on target.

Chapter 2

Seer *RA'AH* Prophets

*Formerly in Israel, if someone went to inquire of
God, they would say, "Come, let us go to the seer,"
because the prophet of today used to be called a seer.*
—1 Samuel 9:9 NIV

THE *RA'AH* PROPHETIC REALM—THE SEER-PROPHET

Within the realm of the prophet ministry in the Old Testament, there lies
a distinctive and peculiar prophetic emphasis in the seer realm. The seer
realm is made up of two spheres of the seers, which are the *ra'ah* and *chozeh*
prophets, according to Strong's Concordance. The seer realm functions in
the office of the prophet as those who see into the realm of the spirit. It
describes the nature and frequency of how they receive particular types of
prophetic revelation and impartation. The seer's mode of receiving divine
revelation is distinctly by "seeing" and receiving insight and supernatural
downloads and uploads from God.

The Hebrew word *ra'ah,* according to Strong's Concordance, is the second Hebrew word used in the Scriptures to define the prophet in the Old
Testament. This is the realm that defines the revelatory realm of the seer
and is the second type of prophet mentioned in the Bible. The ra'ah prophet
is commonly regarded today as the seer prophet. Most people are not aware
that there are two types of seers in the Bible. We will define and bring

clarity and distinction between the two—the *ra'ah* and the *chozeh* prophets. *Ra'ah* means a seer, someone who sees. *Ro'eh* is another Hebrew word for the aspect of seeing, which comes from the primitive root word *ra'ah,* which means "to see, look at, inspect, observe, perceive and consider."

The *ra'ah* function of the seer comes out of the realm of the *ro'eh* to see. The *ro'eh* aspect is to see prophetic vision—they can see visions of the future. They have the prophetic vision to see a person in the past, present, and future. This dimension of the seer realm can see into different times, seasons, eras, dispensations, and ages. Simply put, a *ra'ah* prophet is particularly someone who is given revelatory vision from God in the sense of seeing a vision or seeing supernaturally.

There is a navigational dimension to this realm of the seer prophet where they can provide direction, guidance, and insight into finding things that are lost or hidden.

The first mention in the Bible regarding the seer aspect of the prophet is found in 1 Samuel 9:9 (NIV):

> *(Beforetime in Israel, when someone went to enquire of God, they would say, "Come, and let us go to the seer* [ra'ah]*," because the prophet of today used to be called a seer* [ra'ah]*).*

We find in 1 Samuel 9:9 that the *nabi* prophet today was formerly called a seer—*ra'ah*—in the past. Whenever someone would enquire of the Lord, they would search for the seer who is now called a prophet. In other words, they would go to see a prophet who was the seer. The seer was a prophet and a prophet was a seer.

However, it is important to know that not all who see are prophets. Samuel, who was a prophet, identified himself as a seer according to 1 Samuel 9:19:

> *Samuel answered Saul and said, "I am the seer* [ra'ah]*. Go up before me to the high place, for you shall eat with me today; and tomorrow I will let you go and will tell you all that is in your heart."*

Here we can see that the prophetic function of the seer was to tell and reveal all that is in a person's heart. God would give a *ra'ah* prophet visions into a person's life. They can see visions into a person's heart. Samuel was a seer-prophet. He redefined and revolutionized the office of the prophet. Samuel the prophet was known formerly as a seer, but he reestablished the office of the prophet that encompasses both the prophetic and the seer realms. Essentially, Samuel established that a prophet and seer are the same office but with revelatory distinction.

GOD'S PROPHETIC SERVANTS (GPS)

Saul, before being anointed the first king of Israel, was first introduced to the ministry of the seer prophet when he was searching for his father's lost donkeys. The following is an example of those inquiring to use the navigational function of the prophet operating as a seer. Saul's father sends him to look for his lost donkeys in 1 Samuel 9:3: "*Now the donkeys of Kish, Saul's father, were lost. And Kish said to his son Saul, 'Please take one of the servants with you, and arise, go and look for the donkeys.'*"

Saul was advised to seek guidance and direction from Samuel, the seer prophet, in 1 Samuel 9:5-6:

> When they had come to the land of Zuph, Saul said to his servant who was with him, "Come, let us return, lest my father cease caring about the donkeys and become worried about us." And he said to him, "Look now, there is in this city a man of God, and he is an honorable man; all that he says surely comes to pass. So let us go there; perhaps he can show us the way that we should go."

Samuel the seer tells Saul that his father's donkeys have been found and precisely how long they were lost in 1 Samuel 9:20:

> But as for your donkeys that were lost three days ago, do not be anxious about them, for they have been found. And on whom is

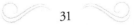

all the desire of Israel? Is it not on you and on all your father's house?

The seer as a prophet has the extraordinary ability to see things that ordinary eyes cannot see. They were able to see in the realm of the Spirit. The *ra'ah* prophet can see with both their natural *and* spiritual eyes. God trains the eyes of His prophets. They are typically those who are usually "visual learners." God trained the spiritual eyes of Jeremiah the prophet to be able to see visions and to interpret what he saw in order to prophesy the revelation. Prophets can see the vision clearly and know what God is about to do:

> *Moreover the word of the Lord came to me, saying, "Jeremiah, what do you see?" And I said, "I see a branch of an almond tree." Then the Lord said to me, "You have seen well, for I am ready to perform My word"* (Jeremiah 1:11-12).

Ra'ah prophets are enabled by the Spirit to see beyond what the natural eyes can see. *Ra'ah* prophets have supernatural vision to perceive things beyond the natural realm, giving them access into the realm of the Spirit.

SEEING THE REALM OF SECRETS

The *ra'ah* prophets have the ability, by definition of their revelatory function, "to see" or "to perceive," which is generally used to describe the seer's ability to reveal secrets. The *ra'ah*—seer—prophet can see secret, hidden, and mysterious things. Though a *ra'ah* prophet will see a vision, what makes this prophet unique in the seer anointing is that he or she sees things that are hidden from the natural eyes of others. They see things that are not easily seen by others and they will see things that others will not see. The seer not only sees visions but sees secrets.

The eyes of the *ra'ah* prophet are piercing and like a key that unlocks the secrets of the human heart. When they prophesy, they unlock what is hidden in us. The *ra'ah* prophet is simply one who reveals secrets, one who envisions. Seers, or *ra'ah* prophets, are *nabi* prophets who were entrusted with the secrets of God. They declare the secrets of God. God reveals His secrets to His prophets who are stewards of revelation and secrets.

Surely the Lord God does nothing, unless He reveals His secret to His servants the prophets (Amos 3:7).

The *ra'ah* (seer) prophets, because of their powerful visions, provided supernatural navigation, direction, and guidance to those who inquired of God. The *ra'ah* prophet's eyes are opened. What the seers see speaks to them prophetically. They see and hear from the Lord when a person comes into their presence. The *ra'ah* prophet sees beyond the natural. They have x-ray and ultrasound vision; and when someone comes into their presence, they tend to perceive, see, and pick up things in their spirit or spiritual vision regarding that person. What they perceive is supernaturally received.

Seer Versus Prophet

The difference between the seer *(ra'ah)* and the prophet *(nabi)* is based solely on the seer's ability to see. A *ra'ah* is a seer and the *nabi* is a speaker. The prophet speaks more and the seer sees more—this is the only distinction between the two functions of prophet and seer. The prophetic dimension and activity of *ra'ah* in the seer means "to see with your eye or to perceive with your mind." The *ra'ah* aspect in seers gives them the supernatural ability by the Spirit to see things with their spirit's eye or in the spirit of their mind. They will see with their natural, spiritual and mind's eyes.

In other words, the *ra'ah* prophets will see and perceive things with their eyes (both natural and spiritual), mind, spirit, vision, and their inner knower. It is important for me to add that the Hebrew word *ro'eh* also means "vision." Therefore, the seer dimension of the prophetic is seeing in the realm of visions and dreams. There is no limitation to the seer's realm. They exercise full capacity of sight.

Ra'ah prophets are what I call "Masters of Sight," as they have the ability to be advisors and counselors of kings and to provide strategies in times of war. The prophet had extraordinary sight and vision in the seer prophetic realm. There are four dimensions of the seer's vision in the prophetic realm:

1. *Prophetic Insight*—the ability to understand the root issues in situations, circumstances, people's motivations, agendas, and plans. They have the keen vision to see into a matter, evaluate the problem, and see in-depth. They have extraordinary insight to counsel and provide wisdom, to bring divinely inspired solutions. Prophets have insight to puzzle and piece together critical, hard, or obscure cases. They are like "spiritual detectives."

2. *Prophetic Foresight*—the ability to see into the future, see things before they happen; see things ahead of time or in advance. They have the visual acuity to predict events, happenings, and pending things in the future.

3. *Prophetic Oversight*—the ability to oversee and understand prophetic context, ecosystems, service roles, functions, and perspectives.

4. *Prophetic Hindsight*—the ability to see things that are in the past. They have the ability to comprehend things that have occurred in someone's past or events that consequently affected the present and could potentially alter the future. Prophets are natural, spiritual historians who understand the pages, books, writings, and literature of history. They have eyes to read the writing on the walls of a person's history. Prophets have a powerful prophetic ability to see and read into someone's personal and spiritual background checks. Their gift of discerning of spirits gives them a higher level of perception to understand someone's spiritual profile.

THE SHEPHERDING PROPHETIC FUNCTION

The Lord is my shepherd [ra'ah]; *I shall not want* (Psalm 23:1).

Prophets have a shepherding function within their prophetic office. The term "shepherd" in the Hebrew is also the word *ra'ah* found in the Scripture passage Psalm 23:1. The term shepherd derives from the original word *ra'ah*, which means to tend to a flock, graze, and to lead with vision—being the eyes of the sheep, to help them to see, *ra'ah*. Prophets are the *ra'ah* of the Lord, leading the sheep onto the paths or in the right direction. They provide guidance, direction, and steering of the flock. The Lord leads His sheep with His eyes through the prophets and seers.

The prophetic seer aspect of this *ra'ah* prophet also has a leading and leadership dimension in their prophetic office according to Psalm 23:2-3:

> *He makes me to lie down in green pastures; He leads me beside the still waters. He restores my soul; He leads me in the paths of righteousness for His name's sake.*

This is the prophetic vision within the pastoral anointing to lead the way. Prophets have the capacity to see through the eyes of a shepherd or pastor. *Ra'ah* dimension within the prophetic realm is to simply see as a shepherd. It is also important to note that shepherds, or pastors, of God's flock have the ability to see in the prophetic. Pastors typically are seers of their local churches. Pastors of local churches are given a prophetic anointing to lead and provide vision for the sheep of God. That is why some may say that they are the "prophet of the house," because they are the visionary leaders who have the vision of where God desires to take them.

Shepherds functions in the seer realm of the *ra'ah* in order to see for the sheep. They are the eyes that lead the sheep in the ways of the Lord. Pastoral leadership in the church is given a prophetic anointing. The prophetic and pastoral anointing work hand in hand. God is restoring the *ra'ah* anointing where the prophets and pastors today will be able to see eye to eye in helping provide the necessary spiritual vision and oversight to lead the church progressively into the future and into their destiny.

Prophets also have the capacity to function in the shepherding grace or operate in a pastoral function. Prophets can be pastors or leaders in the local church. New Testament prophetic ministry should be ordained leaders in the church helping to steer the house toward the purpose of God.

The job description of the *ra'ah* prophet in the shepherding function is to be able to see ahead for the sheep. The role of the prophet is to lead the sheep with the Lord as their shepherd.

NAVIGATIONAL SEERS

The prophet in the *ra'ah* function of shepherding is to see prophetically and lead the sheep as the Lord provides revelation of the way they should go. We can vividly see the *ra'ah* aspect of providing "spiritual navigation" for the sheep in the shepherd's function. It is critically important that pastors are prophetic—that they are able to offer spiritual guidance, direction, wisdom, and counseling for those to whom they have spiritual oversight.

Prophets historically demonstrated the *ra'ah* function in their role as counselors, advisors, and strategists to the kings of Israel as seers. The prophets and seers worked hand and hand within the king's realm, offering the highest level of spiritual intelligence and insight. *Ra'ah* prophets, formerly called seers, were in modern terms coined as "spiritual navigators." Like to us today with our GPS providing vision to show us the way. The shepherding aspect in the prophetic is to lead the way for the sheep and to show the way of the Lord. The prophet has the ability to reveal to the church the way and direction that God is leading the church. Likewise, the *ra'ah* anointing resident in the pastoral and prophetic anointing is "to see the way."

Seers functioned commonly as counselors and advisors to the king within the royal courts. We will see in the following passages of biblical examples of the seer occupying a position in the realm of the kingdom.

Gad the prophet also served as David's seer. Gad functioned in his prophetic office similar to Samuel, as both a prophet and a seer:

> *Now when David arose in the morning, the word of the Lord came to **the prophet Gad, David's seer**, saying, "Go and tell David, 'Thus says the Lord: "I offer you three things; choose*

one of them for yourself, that I may do it to you""' (2 Samuel 24:11-12).

Asaph the seer also functioned in the royal courts of King David as a seer advising kings:

> *Moreover King Hezekiah and the leaders commanded the Levites to sing praise to the Lord with the words of David and of **Asaph the seer**. So they sang praises with gladness, and they bowed their heads and worshiped* (2 Chronicles 29:30).

There is an example in the Scripture that reveals the working relationship of prophets (*nabi*) and seers (*ra'ah* and *chozeh*) in ancient Israel and their position and station as God's official spokespersons:

> *And he [Hezekiah] stationed the Levites in the house of the Lord with cymbals, with stringed instruments, and with harps, according to the commandment of David, of **Gad the king's seer** [chozeh], and of **Nathan the prophet** [nabi]; for thus was the commandment of the Lord by His prophets* (2 Chronicles 29:25).

These examples show Asaph and Gad as seers to King David, but the following Scripture passage shows Nathan serving him distinctively as a prophet:

> *The king said to **Nathan the prophet**, "See now, I dwell in a house of cedar, but the ark of God dwells inside tent curtains." Then Nathan said to the king, "Go, do all that is in your heart, for the Lord is with you." But it happened that night that the word of the Lord came to Nathan, saying, "Go and tell My servant David, 'Thus says the Lord: "Would you build a house for Me to dwell in?"'"* (2 Samuel 7:2-5).

CHAPTER 3

VISIONARY *CHOZEH* PROPHETS

*And he stationed the Levites in the house of the Lord
with cymbals, with stringed instruments, and with harps,
according to the commandment of David, of Gad the
king's seer [chozeh], and of Nathan the prophet; for thus
was the commandment of the Lord by His prophets.*
—2 CHRONICLES 29:25

CHOZEH PROPHETIC REALM—SEER-VISIONARY

The word *chozeh* or *chozah* or *hozeh*, according to Strong's Concordance, is the third Hebrew word for a prophet in the Old Testament. The *chozeh* prophet is the highest level of prophetic in the Old Testament. There is a level of mastery of visions in this aspect of the prophetic that is developed over time in a prophet. This dimension of the prophetic will take some years of development to accurately and properly interpret God's message through visions.

Chozeh prophets "see" divine messages through visual communication. Oftentimes these types of people are what society calls "visual learners" or "day dreamers." God trains their eyes to learn and understand what they see spiritually. He sharpens their "spiritual eyes."

The root etymology of the Hebrew word *chozeh* is to gaze at mentally, to perceive, contemplate (with pleasure). It means specifically to have a vision of, to look, prophesy what is beheld, provide, and to see; to see with the intelligence. More important to note here is that the *chozeh* aspect of the prophetic office is "to see by experience." I called these types "Experiential Seer Prophets." These are the seer prophets who experience their visions or experience through the five senses: taste, touch, smell, hear, and see everything in their dream or vision.

The *chozeh* prophet is also called a seer prophet in the same manner as the *ra'ah* prophet. However, *chozeh* prophets see not only with their eyes but they also see with their spiritual senses. God speaks to them through their five natural senses where they can sense divine or prophetic messages through impressions or inclinations. Essentially, they see the word of the Lord encrypted in anything that God highlights or heightens to their senses.

I discuss more later in this book about the different communications, channels, and conduits of revelations that God speaks to prophets and to us as believers. This is an extraordinary function in the *chozeh* prophetic realm. This dimension of vision is not just for the prophets—its operative and can be activated in believers as well.

DEFINING THE VISIONARY PROPHET

Chozeh means "to gaze at" mentally, to perceive, contemplate with pleasure. Specifically, "to have a vision of," behold, look, prophesy, provide, and see. The *chozeh* function as a prophet is to see as a seer in the ecstatic state. The word "ecstatic" comes from the root word "ecstasy," which means to experience extreme and rapturous emotional excitement. Ecstasy also means to experience euphoria, trance, heaven, and inspiration according to the Merriam Webster's Dictionary. The *chozeh* prophet is caught up into an ecstatic state when encountering a vision of God.

The *chozeh* aspect of the prophetic is experiencing the vision. The *chozeh* prophet is defined as the "beholder of vision." They could be labeled a "visionary prophet" or "vision prophet." Most *chozeh* prophets are taken into their vision whether it is through visions, dreams (night or day visions), open-eye visions, angelic or demonic encounters, trances, being caught up (raptured) in the Spirit, and mental pictorial impressions. The *chozeh* prophetic dimension experiences all aspects of visions. God will take prophets into visions where they are literally seeing and feeling by experiencing the visions. They become characters within the vision in order to gain firsthand and eyewitness accounts of what God is revealing in the vision.

The Old Testament *chozeh* prophets received their prophetic communication through "beholding visions." Ezekiel the prophet experienced the *chozeh* aspect of the prophetic in Ezekiel 1:1:

> *Now it came to pass in the thirtieth year, in the fourth month, on the fifth day of the month, as I was among the captives by the River Chebar, that the heavens were opened and **I saw visions of God**.*

THE VISIONARY PROPHET

The prophets were taken into visions of God. Visionary prophets do not just see a vision, they experience it, equipping them with an experiential revelation for when they interpret and unpack what God is saying in the realm of vision. Prophets who are seer prophets of vision can confirm experiencing physically with their natural sense all of what they are encountering. They encounter and experience much heightened prophetic revelations with God. The *chozeh* prophets are taken into the realm of visions of God. They are very connected to heavenly visions and see into the heavenly or spiritual realm. Ezekiel was able to see that the heavens were open and that give him access into seeing visions of God.

Prophets can see under an open heaven. Prophets who move and operate under an open heaven have their eyes opened to another realm of God. *Chozeh* prophets see visions when the heavens are open; they are ministers of heavenly visions. The *chozeh* prophet functions in the highest prophetic realm of communication. The seer prophetic anointing is evident in the *ra'ah* and *chozeh*, whereas prophets are trained and equipped in all aspects of seeing and visions. Their prophetic ability is groomed and developed over an extensive and intensive process of time. The *ra'ah* and *chozeh* prophets are recipients of heavenly things in visions. They see in the heavenly realms. They are taken into visions of God where they will see from His lens.

Chozeh (seer) has the ability to see things in the realm of the Spirit and interpret the revelation of the visions and images into a message. They are interpreters of the visions of God. In other words, *chozeh* prophets are interpreters of visions. An aspect of their office is to give meaning to what God is saying through the vision of God. Visions of God can come in various forms; but most frequently to a prophet of God is through dreams and vision.

Dreams, as we will discuss in detail later in the book, are "night visions" or "visions in the night." God speaks to His prophets through this method and line of communication. Dreams are very prophetic in nature and we could be overlooking messages of God that need to be decoded. *Chozeh* are decoders of the visions. I call seers *(chozehs)* "Masters of Visions."

THE PROPHET AND SEER REALMS

The operational dynamics and nature of the seer prophet anointing is inclusive of prophetic abilities beyond the inspiration that comes with the *nabi* function of the prophet. The seer anointing in the prophet has the ability to both receive messages through inspired visions and inspired words. The seer prophet can receive revealed messages from God through inspiration as a spokesperson.

Ra'ahs see with their eyes or perceive with their mind. They see by means of visions and dreams and in the spirit of their mind. They see with the mind's eyes. They are given insight into the past, present, and future.

Chozehs communicate the word of God with emphasis on the way he or she received this revelation frequently, that is by beholding and experiencing visions and dreams. A visionary or gazer; one who receives a message in a vision. A beholder of divine visions. One who is given a message in a vision or receives the message in a pictorial mode of revelation.

Nabi prophets are inspired officially by the Word of God to speak supernaturally on His behalf. They are the spokespersons and mouths of the utterance of God to people on earth on behalf of Heaven. They receive revelation by divine inspiration, unlocking and communicating the hidden secrets and mysteries of God and of humans. An authorized spokesperson and messenger for God who receives inspired messages, words, and revelations.

All three types of prophets and seers were acclaimed and accurate voices in ancient Israel history, leaning toward the ear of King David and other kings (godly or wicked) as recorded in the chronicles of the kings. First Chronicles 29:29 says:

> *Now the acts of King David, first and last, indeed they are written in the book of Samuel the seer* [ra'ah], *in the book of Nathan the prophet* [nabi], *and in the book of Gad the seer* [chozeh].

How interesting that all three words for prophet are used in this text:

- Samuel the seer (*ra'ah*)
- Nathan the prophet (*nabi*)
- Gad the seer (*chozeh*)

James W. Goll, in his phenomenal book, *The Seer—The Prophetic Power of Visions, Dreams, and Open Heavens*, definitively brings clarity to the distinction of the offices of prophet and seer when he writes:

> When it comes to prophetic revelation, a prophet is primarily an inspired hearer and then a speaker, while a seer is primarily visual. In other words, the prophet is the communicative dimension, and the seer is the receptive dimension. Whereas nabiy' emphasis the active work of the prophet in speaking forth a message of God, ra'ah and chozeh focus on the experience or means by which the prophet "sees or perceives" that message. The first places emphasis on a prophet's relationship with the people; the second places emphasis on a prophet's revelatory relationship with God.[1]

Nabi prophets bring understanding, relevance, and can both accurately and plainly articulate spiritual things and matters. But the specific difference between a prophet and seer for starters is how they receive revelation from the Lord. *Prophets* are typically and naturally auditory in essence but can still receive visions of God. *Seers* are typically and naturally visionary in essence but can still receive the word of the Lord. This implies that the ability to see alone does not qualify the prophetic function of a seer. Seers have a lot to do with the process of perception and interpretation regarding what is being seen.

The seer dimension in a prophet's ability has to be developed over time, as a prophet is equipped in all aspects of "seeing." There are many aspects of the seer's anointing that cannot be exhausted in this prophetic literary work. Prophets and seers are competent in their ability to speak and see in the realm of the Spirit. They are oracles and seers. They can process what is heard and seen in all kinds of visions, encounters, dreams, open heavens, and angelic engagement for prophetic delivery.

ANGELIC ENCOUNTERS

I almost forgot to add that seers, and prophets more particularly, will have angelic encounters and visitations of seeing in the realm of the angelic. They are able to minister with angels who are also messengers of God. Prophets and seers are messengers of God with supernatural sensitivity to the spirit world.

Elijah was able to see angels in the unseen realm when he prayed for the eyes of his servant to be opened to the realm of the spirit in 2 Kings 6:17-20:

> *And Elisha prayed, and said, "Lord, I pray, open his eyes that he may see." Then the Lord opened the eyes of the young man, and he saw. And behold, the mountain was full of horses and chariots of fire all around Elisha. So when the Syrians came down to him, Elisha prayed to the Lord, and said, "Strike this people, I pray, with blindness." And He struck them with blindness according to the word of Elisha. Now Elisha said to*

them, *"This is not the way, nor is this the city. Follow me, and I will bring you to the man whom you seek." But he led them to Samaria. So it was, when they had come to Samaria, that Elisha said, "Lord, open the eyes of these men, that they may see." And the Lord opened their eyes, and they saw; and there they were, inside Samaria!*

Prophets could see in the supernatural. It was part of their nature to see things that God revealed to them. Elijah wanted his servant to see what he could see that was beyond the realm of the natural—to see supernaturally.

Jesus Christ Himself saw into spirit world in His statement recorded in John 5:19-20:

*Then Jesus answered and said to them, "Most assuredly, I say to you, **the Son can do nothing of Himself, but what He sees the Father do**; for whatever He does, the Son also does in like manner. For the Father loves the Son, and shows Him all things that He Himself does; and He will show Him greater works than these, that you may marvel."*

The following is a list of notable seers who are identified by name:

- Samuel (1 Samuel 9:19; 1 Chronicles 9:22)
- Zadok the priest (2 Samuel 15:27)
- Gad (2 Samuel 24:11; 1 Chronicles 21:9; 29:29; 2 Chronicles 29:25)
- Heman (1 Chronicles 25:5)
- Iddo (2 Chronicles 9:29; 12:15)
- Hanani (2 Chronicles 16:7; 19:2)
- Asaph (2 Chronicles 29:30)
- Jeduthun (2 Chronicles 35:15)
- Amos (Amos 7:12)

The following is a short list of recognized prophets *(nabi)* in the Old Testament:

- Samuel (1 Samuel 3:19 and 9:9,19; 1 Chronicles 9:22; 26:28; 29:29)
- Shemaiah (1 Kings 12:22-24)
- Nathan (2 Samuel 7:2-5; 1 Chronicles 29:29)
- Oded (2 Chronicles 15:8)

Prophets and seers are almost synonymous in light of the Scriptures in terms of their roles and functions, but vary in how they receive revelations from God. The terms "prophet" and "seer" are used interchangeably, as these Scriptures reveal. A prophet and seer are the same in function, role, spiritual authority, and administration of declaring the secrets of God. Certain prophets, according to Scripture, were consistently called by the title prophet or seer, such as Nathan the prophet and Gad the seer. Both are prophets and both are seers respectfully; but to bring clarification and distinction, the frequency of their revelation from God only reveals the capacities and dimensions of how God spoke to them.

The seers did not only see and the prophets did not only prophesy. The prophet and seer both see and hear the word of the Lord by inspiration of the Spirit. Genuinely, prophets are not limited to one way of receiving revelation. Both prophets and seers function interchangeably in the prophetic and seer realms. This is the realms of the prophetic.

The realms of the prophetic embodies and encompasses the office of the prophet and the seer. The title prophet is the prominent title used today, which was reinstated as the official title of the seer in the day of Samuel to speak of both the prophet and seer. The role, function, and ministry office of the seer comes under the title "prophet," which represents the full scope of the prophetic office.

In the chronicles of the kings, we see references to both the prophetic writings of prophets and seers in:

- 1 Chronicles 29:29

- 2 Chronicles 9:29
- 2 Chronicles 12:15

ENDNOTE

1. Jim W. Goll, *The Seer—The Prophetic Power of Visions, Dreams, and Open Heavens* (Shippensburg, PA: Destiny Image Publishers, 2005), 28-29.

CHAPTER 4

PROPHETIC ACTIVITIES
AND OPERATIONS

This chapter is to provide additional prophetic activities and operations that collate and correspond with the realms of the prophetic in the ministry of the ancient prophets. You will find ancient prophetic terminology and etymology that is rooted and has developed over the ages in the mind of the prophets.

SHAMAR PROPHETIC REALM—THE WATCHMEN

The word *shamar* according to Strong's Concordance is another Hebraic word that describes the prophetic nature of the prophet. Although the term *shamar* is not one of the three primary Hebraic words for the prophet, it is imperative to comprehend this term in light of the prophetic office and function of the prophet and seer. The word *shamar* means "watchman." It is also defined as to guard, to keep, to watch, to preserve, to be on one's guard. In addition to being watchmen, prophets are intercessors, warriors and gatekeepers. There are prophets who are "watchmen," "guards," and "protectors," they are commonly regarded as *shamar* prophets.

Naba Prophetic—The Prophetic Release

The word *"naba"* in Strong's Concordance in the Hebrew means "to prophesy"; i.e. speak (or sing) by inspiration in prediction or simple discourse, "to prophesy under the influence of the divine Spirit, in the ecstatic state." It is the influence to prophesy under the inspiration of the Spirit.

Naba is the root word of the Hebrew word *nabi*. This is the spirit of the prophet that makes the official spokesperson who he or she is. The official prophet carried the ability to prophesy *(naba)*. That is the true essence of the prophet to be able to prophesy under the influence of the Holy Spirit. The *naba* anointing is the spirit of the prophet. It is etymology and engine behind what makes a prophet who he or she is.

Massa Prophetic—The Prophetic Burden

The word *massa* in Strong's Concordance in the Hebrew means a burden, specifically tribute, or abstractly porterage; figuratively an utterance, chiefly a doom, especially singing; mental desire. The word *massa* comes from the root etymology in Hebrew *nasa,* according to the Old Testament Hebrew Lexicon, which means to lift up, support, aid, and to assist. *Massa* means to lift oneself or someone up. This aspect of the prophetic is the same in the New Testament, that the purpose of prophecy is to build up, edify, and encourage others (1 Corinthians 14:13). The *massa* aspect of the prophetic is dealing with the burden of the Lord. It describes the anointing and activity in the ancient prophets and prophetic operations. This form of prophetic activity in a prophet is God speaking to the prophet through the burden.

Nataph Prophetic—Prophetic Outpouring of Rain

The Hebraic word *nataph* in Strong's Concordance is used for the word "prophet" but the prominent usage of the word is to "prophesy." *Nataph* simply means to speak the word of God "to fall in drops" or "to open the heavens." This aspect of the prophetic is to prophesy under the inspiration of the Spirit where the word of God that is released out of the mouth of the prophet falls down like dew and rain. *Nataph* represents the activity of the prophets in "prophetic atmospheres, climates, environments, and elements." The operation of *nataph* is atmospheric, climatic, and environmental in function. It deals with things in the heavens. Prophets are powerful stewards and managers of prophetic atmospheres. They have the ability to discern whether the temperature is right for a prophetic release.

Nebuwah Prophetic—Prophetic Forecasting

The word *nebuwah* in Hebrew means "a prediction, spoken or written." It is translated: prophecy. The oral and scribe prophetic anointing is when someone is inspired by the Holy Spirit to predict things in word or writing. This is the aspect of the prophetic that deals with more of a predictive element and future orientation. The prophetic gives a prophet the ability to predict events, occurrences, things, and happenings that are to come to pass in the foreseeable future. The predicative element can be imminent, days, weeks, months, years, and centuries in the future. The ancient prophets were able to predict things that were centuries in the future. They functioned in the realm of "prophetic forecasting" with extraordinary accuracy, especially pertaining to the birth and life of the coming of the Messiah, Jesus Christ. These are Issachar-type prophets and prophetic anointings in discerning and understanding the times and seasons, and importantly what to do in those times or interpreting the signs of the times (see 1 Chronicles 12:32 and Matthew 16:1-4).

NEW TESTAMENT PROPHETIC ACTIVITY

Propheteuo Prophetic—Prophetically Speaking

The word *propheteuō* according to Strong's Concordance is the verb in Greek that means "to foretell events, divine, speak under inspiration, and exercise the prophetic office; to proclaim a divine revelation, prophesy, to foretell the future; to speak forth by divine inspiration; to break forth under sudden impulse in lofty discourse or in praise of the divine counsels." Translated: to prophesy. Prophetic terminology is key to unlocking the full mystery and secrets of God's activity in His ancient vocal ministers who were anointed and authorized to speak on His behalf to humanity. The prophetic operation is to reveal the various characteristics of or relating to a prophet or prophecy. True meaning and essence of the words prophetic, prophecy, prophesy, and prophet give us a perfect language for inspired supernatural utterances and experiences of God through humans.

CHAPTER 5

THE DREAMERS ARE COMING

Then they said to one another, "Look, this dreamer
[master of dreams] is coming! Come therefore, let us
now kill him [Joseph] and cast him into some pit;
and we shall say, 'Some wild beast has devoured him.'
We shall see what will become of his dreams!"
—GENESIS 37:19-20

This chapter reveals the hidden ministry of the dreamers that will emerge on the scene. You will learn that there are three essential prophetic offices: Prophets, Seers and Dreamers. The Dreamers are emerging in the last waves.

There is emerging in the 21st century and beyond an unprecedented movement in the prophetic where there will be the recognition of a new type of prophetic anointing that is not readily understood in our generation. A special prophetic anointing will arise among us in this hour that many have not seen before. The church and the world, to a degree, are becoming more aware and familiar with the ministry of the prophet and even grasping fuller understanding of the ministry and office of the seer. However, I believe strongly that the ministry gift of the dreamer is an entirely different prophetic office and realm that thoroughly needs to be explored with depth and purpose in this generation. There are three essential prophetic offices that I believe the prophecy of Scripture reveals that will emerge fully in the New Testament church according to Joel 2:28 and fulfilled in Acts 2:17-18.

Old Testament Prophecy: Joel the prophet prophesied into an era and generation that God would pour out His prophetic Spirit and Self that will manifest the full expression of the prophetic in three offices: *"And it shall come to pass afterward that I will pour out My Spirit on all flesh; your sons and your daughters shall prophesy, your old men shall dream dreams, your young men shall see visions"* (Joel 2:28).

New Testament Fulfillment: Peter the apostle, in the New Testament, confirms that what people gathered in Jerusalem were witnessing was the commencement and fulfillment of the outpouring of prophecy that was spoken by Joel the prophet:

> *And it shall come to pass in the last days, says God, that I will pour out of My Spirit on all flesh; your sons and your daughters shall prophesy, your young men shall see visions, your old men shall dream dreams. And on My menservants and on My maid-servants I will pour out My Spirit in those days; and they shall prophesy* (Acts 2-17-18).

The prophecy of Joel is revealing three ministry expressions and offices that will fully emerge during the prophetic outpouring of the Spirit through all kinds of people in the New Testament church:

1. Office of the Prophet (Inspired Spokesperson)
2. Office of the Seer (Visionary)
3. Office of the Dreamer (Master of Dreams)

WHAT IS A DREAMER?

Strong's Concordance definition of the word "dream" and "dreamer" in the Hebrew is *chalown,* which comes from the root word *chalam,* which means to bind firmly or to plump or recover. It is to have a vision in the night while the mind is asleep. According to Merriam Webster's Dictionary, the word "dream" is defined as a series of thoughts, images, or emotions occurring during sleep. A dream is a night vision. It is also a strongly desired goal or purpose. A dream can reveal someone's aim, ambition, aspiration, design, intention, plan, or objective. God gives us dreams to disclose His plan, purpose, vision, and intention for our lives.

Dreams reveal God's original design for our lives. Dreams are one of the channels of communication that God uses to speak to us. Someone who dreams more frequently is usually called a "dreamer." A dream is one of God's ways of communicating His plans and purpose to an individual; but a dreamer is one of God's agents of carrying out His communicated plans and purpose to fulfillment. Dreamers are God's prophetic agents who understand how to move from dream concealment to dream fulfillment. Dreams are God's way of speaking and revealing things to us in our sleep. Many of us talk in our sleep because God is talking with us.

Dr. Joe Ibojie defines dreams with such clarity in his book, *Illustrated Dictionary of Dream Symbols: A Biblical Guide to Your Dreams and Visions:*

> God utilizes very individualistic language in communicating to us in dreams. He takes it from our life experiences, specific personal traits, and biblical examples. God also uses events in our lives that no one knows about except Him, and sometimes incorporates these into His communications. So, a person gifted in dream interpretation can help with one's understanding, but correct interpretation must come from the dreamer due to a dream's specific, individualist traits.

> Many people wonder why they do not receive many dreams. Some even claim that they do not dream at all, while others are simply at a loss at what to do with their endless amount of dreams. These puzzles have no simple answers. But everyone needs to understand this incredible form of divine communication. Anyone can have a dream but not everyone is a dreamer.

The Hebrew word *chalowm* translated "dream" reveals three types in the Scriptures:

- Ordinary Dreams (ordinary dreams or non-prophetic) not divinely inspired dreams

- Prophetic Dreams (true prophets) divinely inspired dreams by God

- False Dreams (of false prophets) demonically inspired or self-conjured, false or soulish dreams

The first dreamer in the Bible is when God spoke to Abram in his sleep in Genesis 15:12-13:

> *Now when the sun was going down, a deep sleep fell upon Abram; and behold, horror and great darkness fell upon him. Then He [God] said to Abram: "Know certainly that your descendants will be strangers in a land that is not theirs, and will serve them, and they will afflict them four hundred years."*

Dreams come from God in the form of symbolic or parabolic language or vivid illustrative stories. Mysteries, secrets, and coded messages are enveloped in the form of dreams or night visions. God prophetically opens the ears and conceals His instruction in dreams according to Job 33:15-16: *"In a dream, in a vision of the night, when deep sleep falls upon men, while slumbering on their beds, then He [God] opens the ears of men, and seals their instruction."*

God reveals Himself and speaks to His prophets in dreams as revealed in Numbers 12:6: *"Then He said, 'Hear now My words: If there is a prophet among you, I, the Lord, make Myself known to him in a vision; I speak to him in a dream.'"*

MASTER OF DREAMS

God speaks to His prophets in dreams, but we do not often view the office of a prophet as dreamers. We have embraced the office of the *nabi* (official spokesperson) and the office of the *ra'ah* and *chozeh* (seer and beholder of visions), but not the office of the *chalown* (master of dreams). The *chalown* prophets are dreamers and masters of dreams. There needs to be a new definition of the prophetic office in light of the masters of dreams who will carry a mastery in dream revelation and interpretation of what is being spoken to us in our dreams. The masters of dreams are coming in the new wave of prophets. We will see the ministry of the dreamer emerge with dreams in their mouths.

The purpose of this chapter on the realms of the prophetic is to see the office of the dreamer through the life of Joseph who carried an extraordinary ability as a prophet, who had a gift and mastery and understanding in the realm of dreams, visions, and language of God in the night or while asleep. A dreamer's frequency of revelation from God is tucked away and locked up in the person's sleep. They wake up as interpreters of God's own dreams. They are those prophets in the night who awaken saying, "I have a dream."

The ministry office of the Master of Dreams is not going to come primarily out of a religious experience or a church. The dreamers are coming on the scene by the power and anointing upon their dreams to be catalysts of change in all the world.

In this chapter, we are going to examine Joseph whom God supernaturally caused to emerge into greatness because of his dreams. I share some key components, principles, and processes of this great dreamer of God that will release the anointing, power, and blessing of Joseph upon your life to come forth. There is a Joseph in you that has to emerge. You are one of the dreamers.

EMERGENCE

*If there **arises** among you a prophet or a dreamer of dreams...* (Deuteronomy 13:1).

According to the dictionary the word "emerge" means to rise, come forth, or to come out into view. It also means to arise. We know that Joseph was recognized as the famous dreamer. The Josephs (dreamers) are rising up. They are coming forth. God has Josephs hidden in every generation. Today's Josephs will have dreams that will begin to come forth. We will discover that the dreams that Joseph dreamt caused him to rise to a place of fame, power, and position. This rise to power by Joseph is called the "emergence" of the dreamer. God is releasing dreams in many that will cause them to arise. Dreamers are no longer staying in a place of obscurity—they are coming out into plain view. There is a prophetic awakening happening on earth and dreamers are going to fulfill in the day what they dreamed in the night. Dreamers are going to materialize and manifest what was always in them.

These dreamers of the night will emerge out of sleep with a calling and sense of urgency to do what they see themselves doing in their dreams. They will be revelators in the night and demonstrators in the day. The dreamers will carry the spirit of Joseph upon them that will come forth as dreamers of dreams. The dreamers will no longer stay sleeping giants but will be part of this new awakening.

The dreamers are coming out of hiding. Too long dreams have been locked in the dreamers for generations without a Joseph who will unlock the dreams and go places they can only dream. God is releasing an anointing within dreamers that will stir them up to accomplish unrealistic feats. God gives us dreams to stir our hearts to rise up. Dreams have caused many to emerge and arise to do great things in the world.

Joseph's dreams were the cause of his emergence, and I believe there is an incredible prophetic anointing in dreams to help dreamers fulfill their dreams. Dreams carry an anointing upon them. An anointing is being released from Heaven for every generation to fulfill their dreams. This emerging generation is called the "Joseph Generation."

JOSEPH GENERATION

There is a Joseph in every generation. A generation is emerging that will walk in the spirit and power of Joseph as a dreamer of dreams. This generation of dreamers will possess the same ability as Joseph's to maneuver through obscurity, obstacles, and opposition. As I studied the life of Joseph, I noticed some key components and principles about him that reveal the type of dreamers who are emerging in this age. You are the Joseph in your family, city, region, and nation—and ultimately part of the generation that must arise to bring God's Kingdom to earth. You are the Joseph in your generation who has to manifest your dreams. The Joseph generation will dream dreams—dreams for perpetual future generations to walk in.

GOD CONCEALS HIS INSTRUCTIONS IN DREAMS

> *For God [does reveal His will; He] speaks not only once, but more than once, even though men do not regard it [including you, Job]. [**One may hear God's voice] in a dream, in a vision of the night, when deep sleep falls** on men while slumbering upon the bed. Then **He opens the ears** of men and **seals their instruction....**" [Elihu comments] Behold, **God does all these things twice, yes, three times**, with a man"* (Job 33:14-16,29 Amplified Bible Classic Edition).

In this Scripture passage in the Book of Job, Elihu gives revelatory insight regarding the very nature of dreams and the mode by which God speaks to humans. God gives us sealed instruction in the form of dreams. Dreams are encrypted, divine messages from God that are sealed up and are seldom recognized as being from God. Many people usually do not take their dreams as being important or relevant, and in turn discard them as junk mail instead of hidden messages from God.

Moreover, these verses from Job reveal God's will to us by way of dreams. The dreamers in this hour will carry revelations that are hidden within their heart to perform supernatural things in the earth. God's dreams are parables and mysteries revealed in the night that are symbolic, that provoke the dreamer to seek out the interpretation. Dreams provide dreamers with prophetic markers that guide and navigate them in the right direction to ensure they are on the right course with God.

You can discover your God-ordained purpose in a dream. Dreams disclose the secrets of your future that are revealed for you to fulfill *now*.

THE MANTLE OF THE DREAMER

*Now Israel loved Joseph more than all his children…. Also he
made him a tunic of many colors (Genesis 37:3).*

Genesis 37:3 says that Israel—Jacob, Joseph's father—loved Joseph more
than all his children, because he was the son of his old age. He made him a
colorful tunic—a coat, cloak, outer garment, which can be also known as
a "mantle." The mantle worn by Joseph had many colors, long sleeves, and
distinctly attractive. The tunic was symbolic, representing a mantle of love,
favor, and preferential treatment.

Mantles are worn over the shoulders, which speaks relatively to one
carrying a burden. There was a burden placed on Joseph at seventeen years
of age that partnered him with God to fulfill his God-ordained dreams to
greatness. This mantle became, as the story progresses, a burden that only
few are capable of carrying as a dreamer. I believe this mantle (cloak) was a
mark placed on Joseph as a prophetic sign that he would become someone
great and powerful in the future.

Today's emerging dreamers will carry a mantle of supernatural favor and
provision to fulfill their dreams. These dreamers will sense an incredible
burden of greatness upon their lives to walk into their God-given destiny.
Greatness is the mark of a Joseph whom God is bringing forth on the earth.
Your dreams have been mantles placed with the love of the heavenly Father
to navigate you into your destiny.

Dreamers will sense the love, blessing, and burden of God to fulfill their
purpose. The mantle and favor upon your life may cause strong opposition
or negative reactions from family, friends, and foe. You may be surprised at
those who will not speak well of you and may not even speak to you because
of what they see on your life. Joseph's brothers were so angry they plotted
against him (see Genesis 37:18-22).

The mantle represented the favor of the father upon Joseph. Likewise,
there will be those who see the favor of God the Father on your life and
may initiate warfare: *"But when his brothers saw that their father loved him*

more than all his brothers, they hated him and could not speak peaceably to him" (Genesis 37:4).

The mantle of Joseph was seen by his brothers, which incited hatred toward him. We have to understand that the mantle of the dreamer can cause others to treat us with hatred. Every Joseph will have lovers and haters. That is the life of a dreamer. People will have a revelation of your future by the distinction of what you carry on your life. There is a mantle of the Father's love, favor, and blessing on your dreams.

WHO ARE THE JOSEPHS?

Joseph's name in Hebrew means "Jehovah adds" or "Jehovah increase." Joseph's name gives us prophetic insight into the type of mantle and anointing that he walked in as a dreamer. The anointing upon a Joseph is for increase. Josephs who dream with God will carry a mantle for increase. God adds to Josephs. No matter where a Joseph is placed, God will cause increase. The word "increase" means to become greater and to grow. Increase speaks relatively to growth in capacity. Joseph speaks of someone God is increasing in size, extent, capacity, and influence.

There is a definitive anointing within a Joseph to become greater and grow into something greater. Dreams try to increase your capacity. God is increasing the capacity of the Josephs in this hour to become greater. God wants to impart dreams that will bring increase into the lives of the dreamer. The anointing upon a Joseph will bring supernatural increase. Dreams of Josephs are intended by God to bring them into a realm of increase wherever they go. In this chapter, we will see how Joseph increased supernaturally during this process and emerged in various places.

THE PROCESS OF BECOMING A DREAMER

There are three places where Joseph the dreamer had to be processed in seasons of transition. Every dreamer has to go through the process. All those who have ever had dreams of greatness upon their lives had to be processed and shaped in one or all of these places for preparation, training, and testing. Every prophetic dream from the Lord goes through times of testing. Process can be difficult for many with the mandate to move into greatness.

The three key places that were instrumental in Joseph's emergence to greatness:

1. Pit: Wilderness; empty; place of death; change in appetite and passion. The pit is a place of training, preparation, testing, and opposition.

2. Prison: Place of confinement; limitation; boundaries; walls.

3. Palace: Place of rulership; government; power and authority; kingdom living; fulfillment.

THE PIT EMERGENCE

*Now when they saw him [Joseph] afar off, even before he came near them, they conspired against him to kill him. Then they said to one another, "Look, this dreamer is coming! Come therefore, **let us now kill him and cast him into some pit...**"* (Genesis 37:18-20).

Joseph had a dream and told it to his brothers; consequently, they hated him. Joseph's first dream interpreted that he would emerge as a ruler and reign over his brothers and they would bow down to him (see Genesis 37:5-8). Then Joseph had a second dream that revealed he would not only reign and have dominion over his brothers, but that his entire family would bow down to him one day (Genesis 37:9). His brothers hated and envied him because of his dreams. Even his father rebuked him and questioned his dream (Genesis 37:10).

There will be those in your family who will not believe the kind of dreams God is giving you. Some will even try to rebuke and question if it has come from the Lord. Stand strong. Joseph's dreams caused his brothers to conspire to kill him. Dreamers will cause others to conspire against them to kill their dreams. But God is with the dreamers—He will stand with you.

Dream Killers

We shall see what will become of his dreams! (Genesis 37:20)

Before Joseph came near his brothers, they recognized him from far off and began to conspire to kill him. To "conspire" means to plan secretly an unlawful act and to plot. Likewise, there are secret plots against the dreamers who are coming, who are emerging. Joseph's brothers recognized Joseph from a distance by the distinctive mantle, tunic he was wearing.

Joseph-type dreamers are heading toward a certain place in their destiny, and the enemy is secretly planning attacks against the dreams upon their life. The devil hates dreamers. Dreamers are prophetic—they see the future. The enemy recognizes Josephs from a distance by the mantle upon their life. There are strategic plans launched by the enemy of dreams against the potential that you carry on your life. The pit was the first place Joseph had to experience and then emerge from in order to move closer to where God was leading him.

Hatred, envy, and anger by Joseph's brothers manifested a spirit of murder against his life because of the mantle and his dreams. They wanted to see for themselves what would become of his dreams if they killed him. Assigned to every dreamer is a dream killer. You are carrying your future through the power of your dreams. Your dreams have the potency to alter and save the future and destiny of nations. Therefore, if a dream killer can cut off the dreamer in you before you ever arrive at the place of fulfilling your dream, then he has accomplished his assignment. The dream killer can discern from a distance what you will become by the revelation of your dreams and distinction of your mantle.

Joseph had to deal with opposition in the first stage of his emergence, which was from those in his own household. Some of the fiercest opposition that comes against you is usually from the closest people to you—family and friends. Family can be your greatest support system, but if hatred, jealousy, envy, and anger are thrown into the mix, they can become your worse enemies.

In Matthew 10:36 (NIV), Jesus says to His disciples, *"A man's enemies will be the members of his own household."* Jesus wanted to warn His disciples to prepare for the persecution and even execution because of their ministry. Dreamers will have to endure those who will persecute them, even try to execute them.

The archers shot at Joseph and hated him (Genesis 49:23). This is a type of persecution that dreamers will face in their journey to fulfill the purpose of God. Joseph experienced persecution and hatred by his own brothers. There will be those who will take shots at you because you dare to dream and move into what God has called you to walk. Dreamers are persecuted, attacked, and hated by some. However, Josephs are aimed, focused on their destiny. They can become targets of attacks, opposition, betrayal, persecution, execution, and assassination attempts. But God strengthened Joseph during attacks and opposition (Genesis 49:24)—and He will strengthen you too.

Dreamers' Intercessors

Joseph's brother Reuben overheard his brothers' conspiracy to kill Joseph and plot to cover up the murder. He delivered Joseph out of their hands (read Genesis 37:21-22). Every Joseph needs a Reuben in their life who is placed strategically in certain seasons of our lives to hear the plans of the enemy in prayer against our purpose and destiny, who will intercept, protect, and sway the agenda. God will always place a Reuben presence in the most critical times of your life to help you transition into fulfilling God's dreams.

Reuben became what I call a "prophetic intercessor." Prophetic intercessors stand in the gap on your behalf and protect you in prayer. They will hear, detect, and sense in prayer some hidden attacks brewing spiritually by the enemy against your destiny and future. They will highjack and alter the plans of the enemy in prayer. Every dreamer needs a prophetic intercessor praying and interceding for them.

There are spiritual assassins sent demonically to cut you off before you reach your place of destiny. While the devil has sent spiritual assassins against you, God has spiritual intercessors and angels already stationed on guard on your behalf to protect you, His dreamer. Joseph's brothers changed their murderous plans by the intercession of the eldest brother, Reuben. Rather than killing Joseph, they stripped him of his tunic and threw him into a pit that was in the wilderness (see Genesis 37:21-24). Every Joseph will go through of a season in the pit. The pit in the story of Joseph was his wilderness experience where God was cultivating the greatness upon his life.

The Dreamers' Wilderness Experience

Every great character in the Bible had to experience a wilderness time in their lives. A wilderness is a place of preparation, training, and testing. All of God's prophets must experience a season in the wilderness, which is a classroom for prophets. Moses experienced a wilderness for forty years (Exodus 15:22-27 and Exodus 16). Elijah experience a season in the wilderness being fed by an angel (1 Kings 19:4-8). Jesus Himself was led into the wilderness by the Spirit to be tested by God and tempted by the devil (Matthew 4:1).

The dreamer, too, has to experience this first stage in the process for God to make the dreamer into a person capable to stand in the midst of adversity and not break under pressure. The wilderness of being a family outcast as a Joseph will either make you or break you.

His brothers eventually sold Joseph to some traders in the wilderness who were traveling to Egypt (Genesis 37:28). There will be those in your family who will turn on you. Those who you once trusted may be the ones behind your back coming against you. I call these people "silent killers." On the surface it looks like they are walking with you, but in reality they are digging pits or graves for your demise. Pit experiences reveal those who are for you, against you, and are assigned to kill the dreamer in you.

But pits are only launching pads to shift you into the next dimension of greatness. Dreamers must learn from the pitfalls in their lives. If you can overcome the opposition that comes against you from family, friends, and foes, then you ready for Egypt, the world.

THE PRISON EMERGENCE

Then Joseph's master took him and put him into the prison, a place where the king's prisoners were confined. And he was there in the prison (Genesis 39:20).

The prison is the second place Joseph had to emerge from in order to be released into his destiny. Every dreamer, after emerging from family opposition, must experience the prison. Many dreamers will come to this place in their process as a Joseph in their generation. The prison is a place of confinement, limitations, boundaries, bondage, captivity, and restrictions. God will move dreamers into this place for specific reasons and establish certain disciplines and regulations to be able to function under authority.

God was raising Joseph up to be a man of great authority, but he first had to learn how to operate under authority and within certain restraints, orders, and directives. Joseph, while serving time in prison for a crime he did not commit, tempered the dreams in him. Many dreamers will experience "spiritual prisons."

Prior to Joseph being thrown into prison, the Midianites sold him into slavery in Egypt to Potiphar, an officer of Pharaoh and captain of the guard. Potiphar became his master in Egypt. Egypt, being a symbol and type of the world, the Egyptian master Potiphar, was able to recognize the favor and presence of God on Joseph's life. The key to Joseph's emergence from prison was simply that God was with him. Potiphar saw the presence and favor of God upon his life that would eventually release the blessing of God upon all that Joseph's hands touched in Potiphar's house.

Blessing of the Dreamer

The following two passages of Scripture are examples of the blessing of the Lord within the anointing of Joseph, the Master of Dreams—who was able to prosper wherever he was. We can see the favor of God upon him because God was protecting His dream that was in Joseph.

In slavery:

> **The Lord was with Joseph**, *and he was a successful man; and he was in the house of his master the Egyptian. And his master saw that the Lord was with him and that* **the Lord made all he did to prosper** *in his hand. So Joseph found favor in his sight, and served him. Then he made him overseer of his house, and all that he had he put under his authority. So it was from the time that he had made him overseer of his house and all that had, that the Lord blessed the Egyptian's house for Joseph's sake; and the blessing of the Lord was on all that he had in the house and in the field* (Genesis 39:2-5).

In prison:

> *But* **the Lord was with Joseph** *and showed him mercy, and* **He gave him favor** *in the sight of the keeper of the prison. And the keeper of the prison committed to Joseph's hand all the prisoners who were in the prison; whatever they did there, it was his doing. The keeper of the prison did not look into anything that was under Joseph's authority, because the Lord was with him; and whatever he did,* **the Lord made it prosper** (Genesis 39:21-23).

Temptations of the Dreamer

Joseph was an overseer in the house of his master, Potiphar. Scripture says that *"Joseph was handsome in form and appearance"* (Genesis 39:6), which caused Potiphar's wife to lust after Joseph. The dreamers who are coming will be attractive to the world, which may try to lure them into sinful and lustful activities that do not represent the heart of God. Joseph refused to sleep with her. He did not indulge in activities that would bring a reproach on his name, character, integrity, and promotion. Joseph understood his limits while functioning in the house of Potiphar. He knew that though Potiphar committed all things within his charge, his wife was clearly off limits. Josephs must understand their limits and not cross those lines within their authority and relationship.

Emerging dreamers will understand limitations and boundaries that are set by God. Josephs are men and women of God of extraordinary character and integrity. They will not be easily seduced by tempting offers, compromises, and contracts that would jeopardize their dreams being fulfilled and the blessing and favor of the Lord flowing into their lives. Joseph turned her down. Potiphar's wife tried to cause Joseph's demise because he did not accept her request. Dreamers must be careful of worldly lusts.

Potiphar's wife falsely accused Joseph of rape. As a Joseph, there will be times when the enemy will use people to create false accusations, lies, rumors, and speculations through gossip against you to discredit your name. This is one of the oldest yet effective strategies and tricks of the enemy to hinder, slow down, stop, and ultimately kill the dreamer from emerging and rising into a higher place. Every dreamer of God will experience false reports, news, and allegations about them in the public eye. The enemy—anyone who is an adversary—will try to taint your name through means of defamation of character, integrity, and value. Enemies of your destiny will stir up controversy to restrict, limit, and block your ability to move into your God-given purpose.

Some people in the world, and even in the church, will try to seduce you to fall into sin, sexual immorality, scandals, controversy, and foolishness that will taint the anointing and keep the dreams of God in you from coming forth.

Sin places limitations and bondages on us that minimize our ability to fulfill our dreams. Dreamers must be cognizant of the reality that the devil intends to seduce and tempt them into lustful activities that bring shame, guilt, and a bad reputation. But—Josephs will rise up in truth and innocence during times of false allegations, charges, and claims against them.

Because of Potiphar's wife's false accusation, Joseph was put in the prison where the king's prisoners were confined. However, Scriptures reveal a pattern in the life of Joseph—wherever he was placed, God was with him and the favor of God was evident to everyone and everything that came under his authority.

The Dreamer's Power and Prophetic Anointing

Joseph is a fruitful vine, a bough, whose branches run over the wall (Genesis 49:22). Dreamers are fruitful and productive. Jesus declared that He is the true vine (John 15:1-8); therefore, dreamers are connected to the anointing. The vine characterizes power, anointing, and release. The fruitful vine has the ability to rise and climb over walls. The anointing of Joseph cannot be contained inside walls.

Dreamers cannot be limited by human limitations and boundaries placed on them. They have in them the power to continue to rise above circumstances, situations, obstacles, oppositions, and mountains. The anointing upon Josephs will not stay in the same place; they have an overcoming anointing to rise over things in their way.

The prison was a place to confine Joseph. The word "confine" means to hold within a location, to keep within limits, to inhibit, control or restrict, according to the dictionary. A place of confinement can be anything that encloses such as borders, fences, boundaries, lines, ceilings, or walls. Dreams go through a season of imprisonment and confinement. All dreamers may feel in their journey that they are not getting anywhere. This feeling of confinement actually develops into a breakthrough anointing upon a Joseph whose name epitomizes the capability to grow, extend, and enlarge in the midst of a place that is limited.

Josephs possess within them an anointing upon their dreams to go forth and break barriers, walls, and limitations. They have an anointing to grow out of places because their dreams are too great to be confined to one place, location, or way of thinking. Dreamers are forward thinkers and they have a vision for greater. One important thing to note is that gifts are cultivated, released, discovered, and unlocked in prison.

Supernatural Power to Interpret Dreams

While Joseph was in prison, two of the king's officials were put in prison and both had a dream in the same night. They were perplexed and sad because there was no interpreter. Joseph's gift to interpret dreams was manifested in prison, which consequently released and restored the chief butler to his position in the king's palace. Unfortunately, the chief baker was hung after Joseph interpreted and prophesied that he would be executed by the king. Joseph's extraordinary gift to unlock the mysteries hidden in the dreams of the chief butler and the chief baker prophesied their fates.

Dreamers are coming to unlock the future destinies of those in high places that will open doors and bring them into the presence of leaders. Dreamers are not sleepwalkers, they are dream-walkers. They walk in the fulfillment of their dreams and cause others to do so. Dreamers will bring a restoration in leadership on all levels. God caused Joseph's gifts to open doors to the palace. Gifts are discovered in the prison that will open palaces to the dreamers, Josephs in their generation.

THE PALACE EMERGENCE

> *Then Pharaoh sent and called Joseph, and they brought him quickly out of the dungeon; and he shaved, changed his clothing, and came to Pharaoh* (Genesis 41:14).

Acts 7:9-10 summarizes Joseph's process from the pit to the palace in all of Egypt:

> *And the patriarchs, becoming envious, sold Joseph into Egypt. But **God was with him and delivered him out of all his troubles, and gave him favor and wisdom** in the presence of Pharaoh, king of Egypt; and he **made him governor over Egypt** and all his house.*

Testing of the Dreamer

The palace was the third and last place of emergence where Joseph rose to become second to only Pharaoh. When Pharaoh's strange dreams could not be interpreted by the Egyptian magicians, wise men, and royal experts, the butler remembered Joseph, who was summoned to the royal courts of the king. Before appearing before the king, Joseph needed a royal makeover. God was supernaturally changing his entire lifestyle in a day.

God shows a dreamer the end of a thing, but it is up to the dreamer to walk through the process to get to that place. Oftentimes, it will look the opposite of what God said or revealed in the dreams. However, it is critical that the dreamer hold on. God's prophetic word came to pass in Joseph's life, and it will in yours too. Every dreamer goes through seasons of testing.

The prophetic word, anointing, character, integrity, and life of Joseph the dreamer had to be tested. Psalm 105:19 (Amplified Bible Classic Edition) says: *"Until his word [to his cruel brothers] came true, until the word of the Lord tried and tested him."* God gave Joseph the dreams of emergence to become a ruler, and he revealed the prophetic dream to his brothers, which initiated the trying and testing of that dream. His dream needed to be battle-tested.

Dreamers go through tremendous warfare before their dreams come to pass. They will face fierce opposition while their names are being thrown in the mud—the pit. It may feel like you are going nowhere, as if you are in prison, but remember that it is only a test to cause you to discover the dreamer inside you that needs to emerge for God to give you the keys to the palace.

Joseph endured the process that led him from the pit to the palace. Through it all, he held on to the prophetic word that God had shown him in a dream. Joseph held on to the word of God while in the pit and in the prison until that word came true. As a dreamer, you cannot give up on your dreams. Do not give up on your word from God. Do not give up on your future. Hold on to your prophetic dream until you see it come to pass in your life.

Keys to the Palace

No one could interpret the dreams of Pharaoh (Genesis 41:8). Then Pharaoh heard of Joseph and the special gifting and ability to interpret the dreams of his chief butler and baker. Likewise, there will be people in high places who will hear your name. As a result, Pharaoh sent for Joseph and he shaved and changed his clothes to prepare himself to stand before royalty. Joseph went from the pit to the prison in thirteen years, which gave him the keys to the kingdom. The palace is a place of power, authority, and dominion. This move to the palace fulfilled his dream that he would rise to a place of rulership. During the process, God changed Joseph's appearance. People will not recognize where you have been after God changes your life. Your dreams will bring you into a different way of living. Your dreams will change your lifestyle from pit and prison living to kingdom living.

Joseph was thirty years of age when he stood before Pharaoh, the king of Egypt (Genesis 41:46). God caused thirteen years to pass during the process for Joseph to receive his keys to the palace. Dreams in certain seasons provide you with keys to your next season. Joseph rose to power in the palace after interpreting Pharaoh's dreams of severe famine and providing Pharaoh with a strategy that saved Egypt and other nations. Joseph emerged to become a father to Pharaoh and saved his posterity. Posterity refers to future generations. Your dreams are for the future, which have the prophetic power to save not only your life but also those dreaming and rising up behind you.

The Scriptures say that Joseph recognized his brothers, but they did not recognize him. Joseph recognized his brothers when Egypt and surrounding areas were experiencing severe famine and they had to come to Egypt to buy food from him in order to survive. They found themselves before Joseph who had power over all of Egypt (see Genesis 41:37-46). Joseph understood in the end that it was not his brothers who sent him to the palace, but God who made him a father to Pharaoh and ruler throughout all the land of Egypt (see Genesis 45:5-8).

Dreamers must know that it is God who is ultimately bringing them forth. Joseph never wavered in his faith and trust in God—even though the process took many years. Those who think that their dreams are not relevant will come to a place where they will see their dreams coming to fruition. There are future generations waiting for an awakening of the dreamers to come forth and give them hope.

Generations in the future are counting on your dreams to come forth, bringing God's Kingdom to earth for their benefit. You are their future. They will see the dawning of a new day and era emerging when they will say to their generation, "Look, the dreamers before us reached their destiny and we can continue their work as dreamers as well!"

Part II

Dimensions of the Prophetic

CHAPTER 6

PROPHETIC DIMENSIONS AND REALMS

[That you] may be able to comprehend with all saints what is the width and length and depth and height— to know the love of Christ which passes knowledge; that you may be filled with all the fullness of God.
—EPHESIANS 3:18-19

And God raised us up with Christ and seated us with him in the heavenly realms in Christ Jesus.
—EPHESIANS 2:6 NIV

As we gain a greater understanding into the world of the prophetic, there must be a grassroots comprehension that the prophetic gift is one of the supernatural gifts of the Holy Spirit. Therefore, those who operate in the prophetic are also people of the supernatural. Prophets and prophetic people live not only in the realm of the prophetic but also equally in the realm of the supernatural. Prophets are men and women who speak supernaturally. They are spiritual in essence, and how they operate in the realms of the supernatural becomes difficult to explain to those who are carnal or nonspiritual.

God is raising up prophetic voices that will grasp and comprehend spiritual concepts and realities that are beyond their finite limitations.

Supernaturally they will, by faith, move progressively and exponentially into various dimensions, realms, measures, and dominions in the prophetic as they grow in grace.

For starters, the prophetic is a supernatural gift—a gift that can be learned, desired, explored, developed, and imparted. There are endless discoveries in the supernatural world of the prophetic. From prophetic novices to seasoned prophets, the Scriptures provide believers with basic, prophetic concepts that can be easily understood. There are different classes, levels, measures, and degrees of walking in the supernatural.

Studies on the supernatural are extremely broad; therefore, it is my objective in this chapter for readers to understand the supernatural and its many facets, realms, and dimensions—and narrow the focus more specifically as it relates to the prophetic. Understanding the prophetic and its many dimensions of revelatory encounters is essential to unlocking the mysteries of the supernatural.

The supernatural is a world in the spiritual realm. As we engage in our study into the prophetic, it is paramount to be familiar with the terminologies defined in this chapter and book, which will aid in gaining a better grasp of spiritual and prophetic concepts that are often used interchangeably.

DIMENSIONAL PROPHETS

Prophets operate in various dimensions of the prophetic that help the church comprehend prophetic dimensions of the supernatural. Within the realms of the prophetic, there are dimensions that need to be explored, learned, and revealed. Prophets help to unlock the realms of the prophetic that are made up of multiple dimensions. There are revelations of the supernatural that prophets are given keys to that will better equip the church to acquire dimensional knowledge that ultimately brings us into the love of Christ. Next we will discuss five types of prophets that will expand and sharpen your prophetic edge.

These five dimensions of prophetic types add various capacities and volumes to our lives prophetically. I call these five dimensions of prophets

"Dimensional Prophets." I coined this phrase because I believe different prophets add various things to our lives that will increase our mental, spiritual, and prophetic capacities. Prophets who walk in the office of the prophetic may function in one or more dimensions depending on their ministry assignment; but for the most part, those who walk in the prophetic office function in all five. You may function interchangeably to one person in one dimension and to someone else in another.

What Is a Dimension?

According to the Merriam Webster's Dictionary, the word "dimension" means the physical property of length, breadth, or thickness. It is the range over which or degree to which something extends. It speaks relatively of a scope. In other words, a dimension is the extent, magnitude, degree, measure, proportion, size, or scope of a thing.

For example, a single slice of your favorite pie is a dimension of the whole pie. The pieces to a puzzle or each side of a box or every part, organ, bones, tissue, etc. are dimensions of the whole.

Spiritually, people have a supernatural dimension to their existence. As it relates to prophetic dimensions, when you align with a certain prophet, he or she can add a quality to you that is an extension or scope of your being. There are multiple dimensions, facets, aspects, elements, and scopes within the supernatural realm that correlate directly with the realms of the prophetic. Each dimension of the prophetic make up the *Realms of the Prophetic* that I highlight in each chapter of this book.

Dimension brings definition to the width, breadth, length, depth, height, volume, and the extension of a specific realm. When measuring a thing, usually a measurement is taken all of the dimensions just mentioned. Each dimension provides a different scope, view, or understanding. For example, someone who is tall can see things different from someone who is short. Get my point? Dimensions distinguish the scope of a complete element.

Dimensional prophets release upon the body of Christ five dimensions of the prophetic: 1) prophetic width and breadth; 2) prophetic length; 3) prophetic depth; 4) prophetic height; and 5) prophetic volume.

There are five dimensional types of prophets who are given to the church:

1. Prophets of Width and Breadth—prophets who add width and breadth

2. Prophets of Length—prophets who add length

3. Prophets of Depth—prophets who add depth

4. Prophets of Height—prophets who add height

5. Prophets of Volume—prophets who add volume

Let's examine each of these dimensional prophets more closely.

1. Prophets of Width and Breadth

Prophets of Width and Breadth will expand the place where you are. These types of prophets are prophetic educators who have schools of the prophets and they expand and enlarge your understanding in prophetic schools of higher learning. They open and expand your mental capacity. When you are under the prophetic mantle of a master (senior) prophet, the prophet will help you gain knowledge of a dimension of mastery to be fully equipped and trained to flow in various degrees, measure, and scope.

These prophets add a dimension of width and breadth for you to become not just a student of the prophetic but a son or daughter of the prophets. Students are given their teacher's information, but children have their father's impartation. The Prophets of Width and Breadth impart wisdom into their children and students to increase their space for expansion.

> And the **sons of the prophets** said to Elisha, "See now, the place where we dwell with you is **too small for us**. Please, let us go to the Jordan, and let every man take a beam from there, and let us make there a place where we may dwell." So he answered, "Go" (2 Kings 6:1-2).

God opens our understanding so we can comprehend the Scriptures.

> *And He* [Jesus] *opened their understanding* [minds], *that they might comprehend the Scriptures* (Luke 24:45).

Prophets of Width and Breadth will open your mind to understand the Scriptures in ways that others cannot understand. You will be able to comprehend the mysteries, hidden things, secrets, parables, riddles, and codes of the Kingdom of God. You will be a wise person—a thinker, theologian, Bible scholar, and philosopher of Scriptures prophetically.

2. Prophets of Length

Elijah stretched his full-length body on the child who had died and interceded for his life. God heard the voice of the prophet and the child revived. Prophets of Length will stretch you in the supernatural and intercession. These prophets function in a realm of the supernatural that will stretch you in length to continue to intercede and pray until you see revival. They add a dimension of importunity in prayer and intercession. Prophets of Length have an anointing to stretch you in the things of God. They will stretch your prophetic voice so God will hear you and answer with miracles, signs, and wonders.

> *And he* [Elijah] *stretched himself out on the child three times, and cried out to the Lord and said, "O Lord my God, I pray, let this child's soul come back to him." Then the Lord heard the voice of Elijah; and the soul of the child came back to him, and he revived* (1 Kings 17:21-22).

Elisha, Elijah's successor, was stretched to do the same in raising the dead. Elisha, as a Prophet of Length, was able to impart a prophetic voice (mouth), prophetic vision (eyes), and prophetic power (hands) to raise a dead child. A Prophet of Length will stretch your voice, vision, and power as an apprentice or budding prophet. Prophets of Length will impart a dimension of their prophetic voice, vision, and anointing so you can emerge. In these two biblical examples, the dead children were under the weight, the glory, of the prophet who imparted prophetic life, because of the length of their mantle.

> *When Elisha came into the house, there was the child, lying dead on his bed. He went in therefore, shut the door behind the two of them, and prayed to the Lord. And he went up and lay on the child, and put his mouth on his mouth, his eyes on his eyes, and his hands on his hands; and he stretched himself out on the child, and the flesh of the child became warm* (2 Kings 4:32-34).

3. Prophets of Depth

Prophets of Depth have the capacity to teach you and provide a different strategy of how to do things. In Luke 5, Jesus, a carpenter, tells seasoned and career fishermen how to fish. He added a different approach, a different dimension, to their fishing that day that was not traditional. Aligning with Prophets of Depth will launch you out into realms and places that you may not be familiar with or have not been seen or done before.

When they followed His instruction, they caught so great a number of fish that their net was breaking. He taught them a different way of doing something that may not have made sense to them, but it did to God. These prophets will teach you to obey the Word of the Lord, even if it goes against the grain or how you are used to doing it. New technology and strategy are added in this dimension of the prophet.

> *Then He* [Jesus] *got into one of the boats, which was Simon's, and asked him to put out a little from the land. And He sat down and taught the multitudes from the boat. When He had stopped speaking, He said to Simon, "Launch out into the deep and let down your nets for a catch." But Simon answered and said to Him, "Master, we have toiled all night and caught nothing;* **nevertheless at Your word I will** *let down the net." And when they had done this, they caught a great number of fish, and their net was breaking* (Luke 5:3-6).

Prophets of Depth will call you into deeper things in God. They will release a dimension where you want to search for revelation. They are diggers of truth in the Word of God. When you align with this type of prophet, they will add a dimension of depth so that you will minister with extraordinary insight into the written Word of God. You will minister with revelatory depth in your teaching, preaching, and prophesying. People will be amazed at your pearls of revelation ministry. Shallow or surface words of revelation is not your level. Prophets of Depth will challenge you go deeper and launch out farther. They will teach you how to swim in revelatory knowledge.

> *Deep calls unto deep at the noise of Your waterfalls; all Your waves and billows have gone over me* (Psalm 42:7).

4. Prophets of Height

Prophets of Height will not reject you and will not judge you according to former ways things have been done. When you align with this type of prophet, they will add a dimension of height where you will look at the heart when prophesying and releasing the prophetic anointing. You will not prejudge with your natural eyes or through the traditions but through the heart and eyes of God as a prophet or prophetic voice. These prophets will raise you up and add a dimension of height in order to see from God's perspective, view, and scope. These prophets will give you eyes to measure and see the heart of a man.

> *But the Lord said to Samuel, "Do not look at his appearance or at his physical stature* [height], *because I have refused* [rejected] *him. For the Lord does not see as man sees; for man looks at the outward appearance, but the Lord looks at the heart* (1 Samuel 16:7).

Prophets of Height will increase you in the areas of wisdom, status, and favor with God. They carry a prophetic anointing upon their lives that will cause you to grow up and mature in the things of God. When you align with this type of prophet, they will add spiritual status, stature and a dimension of spiritual wisdom. With their prophetic reputation, you will grow with influence with God and people; and like Samuel you will be established in the prophetic and your ratio of prophetic acuity will be recognized because God will be with you (1 Samuel 3:19).

> *And Jesus increased in wisdom and stature, and in favor with God and man* (Luke 2:52 NIV).

5. Prophets of Volume

Prophets of Volume cause you to walk in the will of God and in every prophetic word spoken or scribed, or written, concerning you. When you align with and hear these prophets minister, they will stir you up to walk in the volume of the book God has written about you. These prophets will prophesy from out of the scroll of your book written in the Lamb's Book of Life that is in heavenly realm (Revelation 21:27). They will add a dimension of volume to your life to walk in the fullness of what God has for you. Prophets of Volume have anointing to provoke you to accomplish all of your prophetic words. They release a prophetic anointing upon you to walk in everything that is the will of God for your life. You will carry an anointing to do the will of God.

> *Then I said, "Behold, I have come—in the volume of the book it is written of Me—to do Your will, O God"* (Hebrews 10:7).

> *Then I said, "Behold, I come; in the scroll of the book it is written of me"* (Psalm 40:7).

SUPERNATURAL REALMS

> *And God raised us up with Christ and seated us with him in the heavenly realms in Christ Jesus* (Ephesians 2:6 NIV).

The word "realm" in Hebrew, according to Strong's Concordance, means a kingdom; an area or range over or which someone or something acts, exists, or has influence or significance. A realm is also a sphere or domain. In other words, a realm is the area, place, or domain where a king, ruler, or someone of authority acts, lives, operates, and exercises influence, power, and authority, according to the dictionary.

THE HEAVENLY REALMS

The term "heavenly places" or "heavenly realms" (NIV) is used in several Scripture references in the Book of Ephesians that reveal a world in the realms of the spirit that many are unaware of, yet exists in and around them. The phrase "heavenly realms" is translated from Strong's Concordance as the Greek word *epouranios,* which literally means "the heavenlies." The phrases the heavenly places, realms, or heavenlies speak of "the sphere of spiritual activities." Too many Christians are not able to comprehend realities in dimensions that are outside of the earthly realm.

There are three realms of the heavens (Genesis 1:1):

1. First Heaven—The earthly or terrestrial realm or domain, skies above, firmament, planets, the moon, stars, galaxies, and the expanse of the heavens (Genesis 1:9,20).

2. Second Heaven—The invisible or celestial realm of angels and fallen angels (demons) principalities, powers, rulers of the darkness of this age, spiritual hosts of wickedness in the heavenly places (Genesis 1:8 and Ephesians 6:12).

3. Third Heaven—The God realm, the abode of God, Heaven, highest heavens, Paradise, realm of God, Glory habitation (2 Corinthians 12:1-4).

DEGREES, MEASURES, AND LEVELS OF THE PROPHETIC

There are eight dimensions in the realms of the prophetic that I discuss further in the following chapters that help to expand our understanding of the prophetic. As we examine each of these eight dimensions, not only will it broaden our prophetic perspective and scope in the different levels, streams, channels, dimensions, and realms of the prophetic, but more importantly teaches us how to activate, function, and operate spiritually in each.

It is my goal in the following eight chapters to not just provide information but an impartation. I want to share with you the eight keys that will unlock doors for you to move into multiple dimensions of the prophetic, that will help you understand the world in the prophetic. Each key provides access to a door that opens different dimensions in the prophetic realm. My intent is to expand your perspective, paradigm, theory, grid, and comprehension of the different degrees, measures, and levels associated with the prophetic.

The following are the eight dimensions in the realms of the prophetic that we will examine extensively in Chapters 7, 8, 9, 10, 11, 12, 13, and 14:

1. Spirit of Prophecy (Prophetic Spirit and Atmosphere)
2. Gift of Prophecy (Prophetic Gift)
3. Prophetic Anointing (Prophetic Power)
4. Prophetic Mantle (Prophetic Covering)
5. Prophetic Presbytery (Prophetic Eldership)
6. Office of the Prophet (Prophet Office or Seat)
7. Office of the Prophetess (Prophet Office or Seat)
8. Prophecy of Scripture (Prophetic Scripture)

CHAPTER 7

THE SPIRIT OF PROPHECY

The First Dimension of the Prophetic Realm

And I fell at his feet to worship him. But he said to me, "See that you do not do that! I am your fellow servant, and of your brethren who have the testimony of Jesus. Worship God! For the testimony of Jesus is the spirit of prophecy."
—REVELATION 19:10

The first, basic, and grassroots dimension of the prophetic is the "spirit of prophecy." The spirit of prophecy is the beginner's stage in the prophetic realm. This degree of the prophetic makes it possible for all desiring Christian believers to flow in the prophetic. It is important to understand that there are levels of the prophetic, and this level will whet your appetite and develop a hunger in you to move into higher dimensions and realms of the prophetic that will unlock doors of ancient-inspired utterances in you by the Holy Spirit.

Prophetic Scriptures will help you understand the spirit of prophecy from the lens of the prophets. They reveal ancient secrets and we will start with the first door to the realm of the prophetic—the spirit of prophecy.

PROPHETIC ATMOSPHERES, CLIMATES, AND ENVIRONMENTS

The spirit of prophecy is the introductory level that speaks to spiritual atmospheres, climates, and environments. The spirit of prophecy is the canopy and or the umbrella of the prophetic. This degree in the prophetic has a lot to do with unlocking the atmosphere for the prophetic to operate and flow into a meeting. A corporate anointing is associated with this measure of the prophetic that is accessible to all Christian believers, including those who are sinners, unbelievers, and unchurched. All believers who are worshippers of God in Jesus Christ function to some degree in the spirit of prophecy.

According to Revelation 19:10, the spirit of prophecy is activated when you worship God in private or corporately. All believers, including nonbelievers in a corporate setting of worshippers, will come under the umbrella of prophecy that empowers all to prophesy.

The spirit of prophecy represents the following:

- Prophetic worship
- The testimony of Jesus Christ
- The canopy and umbrella of prophecy
- Unlocking prophetic atmospheres, climates, and environments

The spirit of prophecy is the testimony of Jesus Christ. This dimension of the prophetic is connected to worshipping God as we see in the following verse:

> *I fell at his feet to worship him. But he said to me, "Don't do that! I am a fellow servant with you and with your brothers and sisters who hold to the testimony of Jesus. Worship God! For it is the Spirit of prophecy who bears testimony to Jesus"* (Revelation 19:10 NIV).

THE TESTIMONY OF JESUS CHRIST

The angelic being in Revelation 19:10 tells John the apostle to worship God for the testimony of Jesus is the spirit of prophecy. John, the writer of the Book of Revelation, was caught up in a prophetic vision and encountered an angel of God in the heavenly realm. Angels are heavenly beings accustomed to being in the presence of God; they understand culturally the atmosphere of Heaven. Because John the apostle was in the heavenly realm in a vision, the angel of the Lord had to admonish him about the spirit behind the conduciveness of the atmosphere, climate, and environment of Heaven. The atmosphere of Heaven is an atmosphere of worship. Worship is the culture of Heaven.

Angels are not only messengers of God, they are worshippers of God. This is the key element to the spirit of prophecy. Therefore, prophets and prophetic people must understand that you are not only divine messengers—but first worshippers of God (John 4:24). That is the reason the angel corrects John's posture of worshipping angels (see Revelation 22:8-9) for he is also a fellow servant, his brother who has the testimony of Jesus Christ.

UNLOCKING THE SPIRIT OF PROPHECY

The angel releases a key to John that unlocks the atmosphere of Heaven—the key is simply to worship God. Worshipping God opens the door to the spirit of prophecy. When we worship God, we are unlocking and opening the first dimension of the prophetic. This is the first door to accessing the realms of inspired utterance. Worship embodies the spirit of prophecy, which testifies and bears witness through spoken words, songs of adoration, and ministering the song of the Lord. Any form of worshipping of Jesus Christ—through singing gospel music or singing personal ballads to the Lord—is testifying of Him. Heaven is the atmosphere where the spirit and presence of prophecy operates. Angels worship in the very presence of God in Heaven.

Therefore, worship essentially invokes the presence of the Lord so Heaven comes into our environment and the testimony of Jesus Christ, through the spirit of prophecy, is released. All believers in Jesus Christ are born again to worship the Father as His witnesses speaking for the testimony of Jesus Christ. One of the ways believers witness of Jesus is through worship, which is demonstrated through the spirit of prophecy in an atmosphere of worship. The key to understanding the realm of the prophetic is to know that all Spirit-filled believers in Christ Jesus have the spirit of prophecy imparted to them at their conversion and new birth.

PROPHETIC LIMITATION OF THE SPIRIT OF PROPHECY

The limitation of the spirit of prophecy in this level of prophetic utterance will be limited to the testimony of Jesus Christ through activation by faith, worship, and the meditating, preaching, and teaching of the Word of God—just to name a few. This does not mean that a person is a prophet who prophesies in the spirit of prophecy. The spirit of prophecy can fall like a blanket upon anyone, both believers and non-believers alike, and they will commence to prophesy. We will explore some Old Testament Scriptures to reveal the power behind this level of the prophetic. The spirit of prophecy is a corporate prophetic spirit. Corporate prophetic anointing is released during corporate worship in a service. God releases the spirit of prophecy over an entire body of believers, groups of people, and in some cases blankets all, even children, enabling and empowering those who do not have a "gift of prophecy" to prophesy.

We are seeing blanketed outpourings of the prophetic upon every tongue, tribe, and nation. The spirit of prophecy does not discriminate, segregate, or isolate. It is not racist, sexist, bigoted, or elitist. The spirit of prophecy is an equal opportunity employer, employing all with the opportunity to prophesy at this level of the prophetic. It is the prophetic that testifies and bears witness of the very presence of God and Christ in a place and what He has done, is doing, and will do. Those who prophesy under this spirit become immediate witnesses and messengers of His presence—the very presence of Jesus Christ among us in the Spirit.

POWER OF PROPHETIC WITNESSES

Jesus declares in Matthew 18:20, *"For where two or three are gathered in My name, I am there in the midst of them."* This statement by the Lord Jesus was prophetic, saying essentially that when at least two or three believers in Him assemble together for the purpose of worshipping and calling on the name of the Lord in worship, He will come and manifest Himself in their midst. When the assembly of believers gather together to worship God, it is an invocation of Jesus Christ to manifest His very presence among His people. A prophetic gathering is a place where an atmosphere of Heaven for the presence of God is created. The spirit of prophecy lives in a place of worship. That is the purpose of our worship of God—that His presence would manifest among us.

Essentially, Jesus prophesied that the spirit of prophecy, through the baptism of the Holy Spirit coming upon believers, will empower them to be His witnesses in diverse places:

> *And being assembled together with them, He [Jesus] commanded them not to depart from Jerusalem, but to wait for the Promise of the Father, "which," He said, "you have heard from Me; for John truly baptized with water, but you shall be baptized with the Holy Spirit not many days from now"* (Acts 1:4-5).

Supernatural witnesses through the power of the Spirit will testify of Jesus Christ actively alive and working in the life of all believers as they minister to Him in all types of places. Power is the "birthmark" of the witnesses of Christ. Power is the signpost of every believer of Jesus Christ. They will witness and testify of Jesus Christ and His gospel with confirming, attesting, and accompanying miraculous signs (Mark 16:19-20).

IMMERSED INTO THE MIRACULOUS

The early church was infused with the power of the Spirit to witness to Jesus in various places:

But you shall receive power [miraculous ability] *when the Holy Spirit has come upon you; and you shall be witnesses to Me in Jerusalem, and in Judea and Samaria, and to the end of the earth* (Acts 1:8).

When believers are baptized in the Holy Spirit, they receive supernatural abilities to witness for Christ. Believers receive power after the Holy Spirit has come upon them. This power is supernatural and prophetic. The term "power" in the Greek is *dunamis,* which means literally miraculous power or residing supernatural force. They were immersed in the power of prophecy. All believers are given the spirit of prophecy and are able to testify of Jesus Christ as witnesses.

There are four geographical spheres where God will send prophetic witnesses and prophets to release the spirit of prophecy. Prophetic witnesses carry the spirit of prophecy into these four different spheres and territories. There are prophets who are given jurisdictional and geographical authority in four key places. The following are four key geospheres where the spirit and power of the supernatural prophetic will operate according to Acts 1:8:

1. Jerusalem—cities
2. Judea—regional or national
3. Samaria—multicultural, multiracial, and subcultures
4. Ends of the earth—global sphere, international, and through the worldwide web

PROPHETIC LEADERSHIP

Then the Lord came down in the cloud and spoke with him, and took some of the power of the Spirit that was on him and put it on the seventy elders. When the Spirit rested on them, they prophesied—but did not do so again (Numbers 11:25 NIV).

The Holy Spirit is a prophetic spirit (see John 16:13). In Numbers 11:24-30, the seventy elders of Israel all began to prophesy when God took the prophetic spirit that was on Moses the prophet and placed it upon them. Some portion of Moses's prophetic spirit was transferred upon the leadership who would assist him so that Moses would not bear the weight of responsibility alone. The spirit of prophecy came upon the seventy elders; and as soon the Spirit came on them, they prophesied. These seventy were given the same spirit of their leader in order to share some of his prophetic responsibility to lead the people.

PROPHET BURDEN OF RESPONSIBILITY

> *So the Lord said to Moses: "Gather to Me seventy men of the elders of Israel, whom you know to be the elders of the people and officers over them; bring them to the tabernacle of meeting that they may stand there with you. Then I will come down and talk with you there. I will take of the Spirit that is upon you and will put the same upon them; and they shall bear the burden of the people with you, that you may not bear it yourself alone"* (Numbers 11:16-17).

It is interesting to note that as soon as the Spirit rested on the eldership they prophesied, but they did not continue prophesying. They could not continue flowing in this dimension because the spirit of prophecy is temporary. It was not residential then as it is today in the New Testament. Some have been known to prophesy only when the spirit of prophecy is upon them.

It was important for these elders to assist Moses as leaders to help him bear the load and carry the prophetic burden. Likewise, today, it is important for those who are assistant or associate pastors, elders, and ministers under senior leadership to help carry the same spirit of their leader. It was immediately evident that those set apart, consecrated, and ordained as leaders prophesied as soon as the spirit of prophecy that was on Moses rested on them.

Under the influence of the Holy Spirit, they will prophesy with the same spirit that is upon the leader in some measure, degree, level, or capacity.

For example, if someone is aligned and under the leadership of an apostle, bishop, pastor, prophet, or man or woman of God who has a healing ministry and anointing, then that healing anointing will rest upon them too, empowering them to heal and flow in that spirit.

Those ordained under their leader should carry the same spirit as their leader to undergird the ministry. A prophet will have a spirit of prophecy. An evangelist will have the spirit of evangelism. A business owner will have an entrepreneurial spirit. What is on the set man or woman of God should be evident and visible in all of the leadership. There should be clear signs or indicators that the same spirit of the prophet or leader rests upon their leadership.

The ancient spirit of the prophecy releases the following:

- Prophetic leadership
- Prophetic impartation
- Prophetic power and authority

Prophets can see the mantle and spirit of the prophet upon the candidates for spiritual sonship, leadership, and apprenticeship. The company of the prophets saw the same spirit of Elijah resting upon his spiritual successor, Elisha the prophet, in 2 Kings 2:15:

> Now when the sons of the prophets who were from Jericho saw him, they said, "The spirit of Elijah rests on Elisha." And they came to meet him, and bowed to the ground before him.

PROPHESYING OUTSIDE THE FOUR WALLS

Two of Moses's elders, Eldad and Medad, communicated the prophetic power of Moses outside the tabernacle and also prophesied in the camp of the Israelites in the wilderness:

> A young man ran and told Moses, "Eldad and Medad are prophesying in the camp." Joshua son of Nun, who had been Moses' aide since youth, spoke up and said, "Moses, my lord,

stop them!" But Moses replied, "Are you jealous for my sake? I **wish that all the Lord's people were prophets and that the** **Lord would put his Spirit on them!"** (Numbers 11:27-29 NIV)

When Joshua wanted Moses to stop Eldad and Medad from prophesying, Moses's response reflected his desire and vision for all of God's people to have the Spirt of prophecy—he envisioned a nation of prophets.

The elders received an impartation of the Spirit based on their alignment to Moses. Proper alignment brings proper impartation.

One of the ways that activate the prophetic in a person is to serve, align, and connect with a prophet, preferably in a prophetic house under the covering of a prophet, and or connect in a network and company of prophets. Eldad and Medad were prophesying in the camp even though they were not in the same place where the other sixty-eight elders were receiving the impartation. The reason Eldad and Medad also received the impartation of the spirit of prophecy was due primarily to them being aligned and connected to Moses.

These two leaders were not even present at their ordination at the Tabernacle with the other sixty-eight elders, but the spirit of prophecy still came upon them and they began to prophesy. There will be those like Eldad and Medad with a prophetic anointing who will prophesy outside the four walls of the church. Their prophetic anointing is not limited to a local church. The prophetic is not just for the church; I believe it is for the church without walls. They will prophesy outside the box, the norm, the religious circles, and human limitations. The Eldads and Medads will be a type of team ministry that will take the prophetic anointing and spirit of prophecy beyond traditional boundaries.

The spirit of prophecy is not limited to a geographical location. When someone is truly connected and under prophetic covering, it does not matter where you are located. You do not have to be in the same city, region, or nation of your spiritual covering to receive an impartation. A prophet and those who are connected, aligned, and under the covering of the prophet could be in different territories and will still receive a portion of the anointing of the prophet. The spirit of prophecy will track, locate, and find you to rest upon you.

PROPHETIC JURISDICTION— UNDER PROPHETIC ARREST

> [Saul] *sent men to capture him* [arrest David]. *But when they saw a group of prophets prophesying, with Samuel standing there as their leader, the Spirit of God came on Saul's men, and they also prophesied. Saul was told about it, and he sent more men, and they prophesied too. Saul sent men a third time, and they also prophesied* (1 Samuel 19:20-21 NIV).

Saul himself discovered the power of the spirit of prophecy when he went into the jurisdiction of the prophet Samuel where the spirit of prophecy was operating. Saul also came under the influence and spiritual arrest of the Spirit of God. Samuel, as the leader over that atmosphere, had prophetic jurisdiction in Naioth. Therefore, Saul, though the king, was out of his jurisdictional authority to arrest David because of the prophet's (Samuel) mantle. You can see in the following example that Saul stepped into a prophetic habitation of the prophets. It was a prophetic hub, atmosphere, and environment conducive for prophets. Anyone who crossed over that threshold turned into a different person.

> Then he [Saul] *himself went to Ramah and came to the great well that is in Secu. And he asked, "Where are Samuel and David?" And one said, "Behold, they are at Naioth in Ramah." And he went there to Naioth in Ramah. And the Spirit of God came upon him also, and as he went he prophesied until he came to Naioth* [dwellings or habitation] *in Ramah. And he too stripped off his clothes, and he too prophesied before Samuel and lay naked all that day and all that night...* (1 Samuel 19:22-24 ESV).

Prophetic Habitation

King Saul sent messengers with a warrant to arrest David in order to kill him. David ran to Ramah in the town of Naioth where Samuel the prophet and the company of prophets lived. He ran and hid from Saul in Naoith. "Naoith" in Hebrew is *naviyth,* which means habitations. It was a dwelling place of the prophets in the time of Samuel. Today, it would be a gated community of prophets where they lived, ate, and breathed the prophetic. It was conducive for prophetic habitation—the presence and spirit of the prophets rested and inhabited that place.

This is where David chose to hide himself, under the jurisdiction of the prophets. He came within the jurisdiction of the prophetic that was under the prophetic governance of Samuel, the master, or senior prophet. The prophetic was airborne within that jurisdiction. Anything that came even remotely close to it was immediately induced and under the influence of the spirit of prophecy that rested in that dwelling place of prophets. The prophetic was contagious. The messengers of Saul discovered that reality when they came into contact with an atmosphere where the spirit of the prophetic was the air the prophets breathed. Prophecy was literally in the air.

In other words, there was an atmosphere of worship to God. Worship is the spirit of prophecy. The messengers of Saul entered an environment where the prophetic was flowing heavily with Samuel standing as the appointed leader over the company of prophets. In that place, Samuel the prophet had jurisdictional authority over the spiritual atmosphere, climate, and environment. The messengers of Saul had no authority in that place that was governed by the presence of God and the power of the prophetic. It was a safe haven for David to hide. David understood spiritual jurisdiction and Saul had no power to make an arrest in that domain, or realm, of the prophetic. David was safe under the leadership of the prophet Samuel, and he told Samuel all that Saul intended to do to him.

PROPHETIC COVERING AND CONCEALMENT

The spirit of prophecy protected David under Samuel's spiritual authority. Samuel was a "temporary" protection or restraining order from Saul's
intent to kill David. David was under Samuel's prophetic protective custody
because of the spirit of prophecy resident in that place. According to the
Merriam Webster's Dictionary, a "covering" is something that protects and
or conceals. David hid in Naioth under the leadership, covering, of Samuel
the prophet. It is important to see what the spirit of prophecy provided
David under that canopy of prophecy within the jurisdiction of Naioth
in Ramah.

First, the prophetic covering of Samuel, as the appointed leader who was
set governmentally and spiritually over the area, protected David from three
attempts by Saul's messengers and soldiers to arrest and kill him. Once
they stepped within the prophetic jurisdiction of Israel's judge and prophet
Samuel, the messengers of Saul were arrested by the spirit of prophecy in
the habitations of the prophets. They were subjected to the spiritual and
prophetic climate among the prophets. The Spirit of God overruled and
served them notice that Saul's arrest warrant did not have authority in the
sphere of the prophets. The spirit of prophecy came upon (messengers and
soldiers of Saul) and they prophesied among the prophets because of the
flowing prophetic atmosphere.

We cannot, as New Testament believers, underestimate the first dimension of the realms of the prophetic. The spirit of prophecy turned them
from messengers of Saul into messengers of God. Whoa! No enemy can
stand a chance against the power of prophecy.

The enemy has no authority against the prophetic anointing upon your
life. The prophecy over your life will protect you against every assassination
attempt and attack of the enemy. David was anointed to be the next king
of Israel—Saul's replacement—therefore, God's prophetic word over him
covered and protected him from premature death.

Second, while in Naioth under the spirit of prophecy, David hid; under
the prophetic covering David was concealed. David knew that he could

hide there because of the covering that he was under in the place. The prophetic anointing is a safeguard to hide and conceal you until the time of your manifestation. The spirit of prophecy can hide you from spiritual attacks. In the realm of the spirit, there is spiritual jurisdiction that protects us from seen and unseen attacks when we come under the anointing and mantle of a prophet.

TURNED INTO ANOTHER MAN

Saul first encountered the spirit of prophecy coming upon him when he was anointed king. Samuel prophesied that Saul would be turned into another man after the spirit of prophecy came upon him.

> *After that you shall come to the hill of God where the Philistine garrison is. And it will happen, when you have come there to the city, that* **you will meet a group of prophets** *coming down from the high place with a stringed instrument, a tambourine, a flute, and a harp before them; and* **they will be prophesying.** *Then the* **Spirit of the Lord will come upon you, and you will prophesy with them and be turned into another man** (1 Samuel 10:5-6).

Saul comes into contact with the spirit of the prophecy that was operative in the company of the prophets and was temporarily prophesying among the prophets. The spirit of prophecy will give you the temporary ability and capacity to prophesy:

> *When they came there to the hill, there was a group of prophets to meet him [Saul]; then the Spirit of God came upon him [Saul], and he prophesied among them. And it happened, when all who knew him formerly saw that he indeed prophesied among the prophets, that the people said to one another, "What is this that has come upon the son of Kish? Is Saul also among the prophets?"* (1 Samuel 10:10-11)

CHAPTER 8

THE GIFT OF PROPHECY

The Second Dimension of the Prophetic Realm

*If I have the gift of prophecy and can fathom all mysteries
and all knowledge, and if I have a faith that can move
mountains, but do not have love, I am nothing.*
—1 CORINTHIANS 13:2 NIV

The second dimension of the realm of the prophetic is the "gift of prophecy." This realm of the prophetic is for believers who have moved into a higher level of prophetic activity. It is beyond the realm of the testimony of Jesus Christ, which is the spirit of prophecy. The gift of prophecy is one of the nine gifts of the Holy Spirit (1 Corinthians 12:7-10). This realm of the prophetic is active in believers who have personally developed the ability to flow in the gift of prophecy even when the spirit of prophecy is not necessarily present. They do not need the spirit of prophecy to prophesy.

The gift of prophecy is not a temporary function—it is a permanent function. It is a resident gift. Unlike the spirit of prophecy, which is more reliant on atmosphere and worship to operate, the gift of prophecy can be activated by the believers themselves. The gift of prophecy does not need to rely on a prophetic atmosphere or the spirit of worship or even to be in the company of prophets for their gift to operate.

The *spirit* of prophecy is the lowest dimension of the prophetic realm and any believer who simply yields and opens themselves up can flow in this level of prophecy. However, the *gift* of prophecy in the believer can be stirred up or activated according to Paul: *"Therefore, I remind you to stir up the gift of God which is in you through the laying on of my hands"* (2 Timothy 1:6).

This gift of prophecy requires only activation. To "activate" means to spur into action, make active or reactive. Activate means to spark, trigger, charge, actuate, crank, and turn on. Believers in this dimension can turn on this gift without any external or outside assistance from the Spirit. It is a gift of the Spirit imparted to them at their new birth in Christ Jesus. These individuals have learned how to exercise and develop this gift before God, even in a setting of people they can simply "stir up the gift" that is within them—they activate the gift of Spirit.

Paul the apostle urges Timothy, his spiritual son, to maximize the use of the spiritual equipment given to him for ministry. While the Scripture example (2 Timothy 1:6) does not specify the gift per say, Paul's use of the Greek word "charisma" implies a distinct manifestation of the Holy Spirit bestowed upon him through the laying on of hands by the apostle and others through the presbytery.

Paul reminded Timothy to stir up (turn on) the gift that was in him through the power of the impartation at his ordination. He was to keep the fire alive. Timothy was not to allow his spiritual gift to be deactivated due to disuse.

> *And though I have the gift of prophecy, and understand all mysteries and all knowledge, and though I have all faith, so that I could remove mountains, but have not love, I am nothing* (1 Corinthians 13:2).

What Is the Gift of Prophecy?

The gift of prophecy according to 1 Corinthians 13:2 is the supernatural ability to understand all mysteries and all knowledge. This is the primary ability of the prophets who operate in the realms of unlocking the mysteries and knowledge of God. Prophets utter by inspiration plainly the mysteries, secrets, and hidden thoughts of God to humans. Prophecy is a sign for the believer in the same manner as speaking in different kinds of tongues is a sign for unbelievers (1 Corinthians 14:22).

The supernatural inspiration of the gift of prophecy is simply the ability through inspired utterance to speak plainly in the native language or tongue the words of God. In other words, it is the supernatural utterance or speech in the native tongue. It is a miracle of divine utterance, not conceived by human thought or reasoning. The gift of prophecy typically does not have a foretelling element, rather it has a forth-telling flow to it.

WHAT IS THE PURPOSE OF PROPHECY?

The purpose of prophecy in the New Testament is to build up others. The gift of prophecy is a building gift. Prophetic words released out of the mouth of those who prophesy in the dimension of the gift of prophecy are limited in their ability, authority, and scope. All prophecy is intended to build. Period. This is a very important foundational truth to grasp if you are to minister in the realm of the prophetic. The purpose of the prophecy in the beginner stage is only to serve and build up others in the local church.

The gift of prophecy is the divine communication of God through people to people. Prophecy is for the purpose of speaking directly to build up people according to 1 Corinthians 14:3. The scriptural definition of prophecy, the purpose of prophecy, and the general job description of those who prophesy within its limitation is found in the following biblical example:

> *But the one who prophesies speaks to people for their strengthening, encouraging and comfort* (1 Corinthians 14:3 NIV).

Those who are not called and proven to the ministry office of the prophet or office of prophecy should operate only within the realm, boundary, and limitation of the gift of prophecy, which is *"strengthening, encouraging, and comfort"* or from the New King James Version, *"edification, exhortation, and comfort."* Let's look at how this threefold limitation of the gift of prophecy is to be ministered according to 1 Corinthians 14:3.

1. *Edification* is the Greek word *oikodome* which means to build up, the act of building. The root word is edifice, which means building. Therefore, there is a building aspect to prophecy. Prophetic words are intended to edify the church, to build up others, to promote another's growth in Christ. When we edify through prophecy, we are essentially promoting growth. We speak as promoters of others to announce what they will become in God. God is our greatest supporter, cheerleader, and fan. He loves to promote and brag on His children, and prophecy is the means He uses to speak to us to reveal how proud He is of our growth and maturity. God always desires to promote and build up His people through prophecy.

2. *Exhortation* is the Greek word *paraklesis,* which means solace, entreat, consolation, admonition, imploration, or comfort, according to Strong's Concordance. It comes from the root word *parakaleo,* which means to call near or call to one's side to help. It means also to address or speak to in order to encourage and strengthen by consolation. It simply means to help through words of refreshment and comfort. *Paraklesis* is related to the word *parakletos,* meaning Comforter, a name for the Holy Spirit who comes alongside us as believers as a Helper. The Holy Spirit uses prophecy to comfort believers and to exhort them to a holy lifestyle, love, hope, faith, prayer, humility, giving, serving, and much more.

3. *Comfort* is the Greek noun *paramuthia,* which means consolation. This is a different aspect of comfort in term of ministering to those who are suffering or struggling in their walk or faith.

PROPHETIC FUNCTION

The function of prophecy is to build up the church and the believers. The gift of prophecy is one of the nine manifestation gifts of the Holy Spirit. The gift of prophecy unlocks the prophetic realm. It is a visionary prophetic gift. An outpouring of this gift is prophesied in Joel 2:28 and Acts 2:17-18 and shows that early Christians believed this prophecy was fulfilled on the day of Pentecost. As a manifestation of the Spirit, the gift of prophecy is to bring forth an inspired utterance. That is, the Holy Spirit reveals the heart of God through a thought, vision, audible voice, or an impression.

PROPHETIC WARFARE

Apostle Paul in the following verse charges Timothy to use his greatest weapon in his spiritual arsenal—prophecies. The prophetic is our most powerful weapon against the enemy. We simply use the prophecies spoken over us to remind ourselves—continually speaking and declaring it in a season of tremendous warfare—that what God has spoken will come to pass. Open your mouth and wield the word of the Lord in battle.

> *This charge I commit to you, son Timothy, according to the prophecies previously made concerning you, that by them you may wage the good warfare* (1 Timothy 1:18).

The prophetic words spoken and imparted into our lives can be used as weapons to navigate us in the right direction and declare victory in times of spiritual attack and warfare. Paul reveals that there is prophetic warfare. He tells Timothy, his spiritual son in the gospel, how to wage a good warfare, which is simply to use his prophecies, given to him through prophecy and laying on of hands, as weapons. Every word spoken by God can become a defensive shield of faith for the believer and a sword of truth, offensively. The prophetic will initiate and at times instigate spiritual warfare that comes at you unwarranted. This allows you to understand how serious the powers of hell, demonic forces, and satanic operations take the word of the Lord that has been spoken over your life. It is a powerful revelation that one of the engagements of war is prophecies.

Every prophetic word will arm you to prosper and succeed in seasons of warfare. There will be times when you feel the opposition and attacks, you will become discouraged, overwhelmed, depressed, and exhausted, just to name a few. Timothy was charged by Paul to use the prophecies, that had been imparted during his ordination, and personal impartation as weapons and fuel to continue to press forward no matter the opposing forces. In doing this, Timothy would be fully equipped for supernatural ministry.

Paul metaphorically likened his contest with the difficulties that opposed him continually in the discharge of his apostolic duties as warfare. He endured an onslaught of warfare as an apostle. Timothy was to grasp that level of warfare that was awaiting him in his ministerial career and campaign apostolically. His greatest spiritual weapon was the prophetic. Timothy received the impartation of spiritual gifts through prophecy and by the laying on of hands, which is similar to receiving actual physical weapons for military service.

THE GIFT OF PROPHECY—THE REALM OF GOD'S LOVE REVEALED

The keys to operating in this realm of the prophetic and increasing your capacity to function in higher prophetic activities is to first seek and pursue love, and desire for spiritual gifts, but with a greater emphasis to prophesy according to apostle Paul: *"Pursue love, and desire spiritual gifts, but especially that you may prophesy"* (1 Corinthians 14:1).

Love is the premise and foundation to unlocking the gifts of the Holy Spirit. Love is the prerequisite of the prophetic and it represents the very nature of God. First John 4:16 (NIV) says, *"And so we know and rely on the love God has for us. God is love. Whoever lives in love lives in God, and God in them."* Love is God, and those who minister in love are true ministers of God. This love refers to *agape* love that naturally releases God to flow through the Holy Spirit who is God in us and has given us the gift of love.

In some versions of the Bible, the word "gifts" in 1 Corinthians 14:1 is italicized, meaning it was not written in the original Greek text and manuscript. The words printed in italics in the King James Version are for emphasis. The use of italics is a device used to draw attention to the words added by the translators to convey and bring clarification of meaning. Therefore, the correct way to read 1 Corinthians 14:1 regarding the word spiritual gifts is "Pursue love and desire spiritual, but especially that you may prophesy." The Greek word for "gift" is *charisma,* which means "favor that one receives without any merit of his own, a gift of grace, an undeserved favor, a grace-endowment to edify the Church." The English dictionary defines *charisma* as "a divinely conferred power or talent." The prophetic gift is a building gift.

The word "spiritual" in 1 Corinthians 14:1 relates to the supernatural. What Paul was trying to emphasize in the verse is to desire supernatural gifts. However, when it is rephrased in the original Greek text, he was essentially encouraging believers to desire the supernatural. The supernatural is the nature and activity of the saints. We have been given supernatural abilities, endowments, and powers, especially prophetic powers. This is critical to understanding that being a believer means being supernatural and not to ignore that reality.

The word "desire" means to burn with zeal, to be zealous for, to lust after, to covet, to strive after, to envy, to pursue ardently and to desire eagerly, passionately or intensely. The root word of desire means to ardor in embracing, pursuing and defending. This term gives you the charge by God today through the letters of Paul to zealously embrace, pursue after, and defend the spiritual gifts—especially the supernatural powers to prophesy.

There are enormous numbers of believers who do not operate in the supernatural and relegate it to the past and not for today. Yet, Paul is encouraging us to desire spiritual gifts especially that you may prophesy. The prophetic is one of the gifts that should be emphasized and most manifested among the saints. The gift of prophecy is an exceptional, remarkable, and strikingly powerful and important gift to build up the church. It would behoove all believers to begin functioning in this ancient but relevant gift.

LOVE UNLOCKS THE REALM OF PROPHECY

> *If I have the **gift of prophecy** and can fathom all mysteries and all knowledge, and if I have a faith that can move mountains, **but do not have love, I am nothing** (1 Corinthians 13:2 NIV).*

It is important to realize that even if we have the gift of prophecy as believers in Christ and have supernatural abilities to fathom all mysteries and all knowledge, clearly without love we are nothing. Paul set love as the standard and as a prerequisite for operating in all of the manifestation gifts.

Apostle Paul provides us with a description of what love genuinely is when functioning in the manifestation of the Spirit, especially the gift of prophecy. In 1 Corinthians 13, Paul reveals definitively what is the nature of those operating in the love of God. I believe knowing this will prompt every believer to first do a heart check-up before representing the love of God in our ministry, gifts, and office as sons and daughters of God. In 1 Corinthians 13:4-8, Paul describes what love is and what love is not:

Love is:

- Patient
- Kind
- Rejoicing with the truth
- Always protective
- Always trusting
- Always hoping
- Always persevering
- Never failing
- Forever and eternally lasting

Love is not:

- Envious
- Boastful
- Proud
- Dishonoring of others
- Self-seeking
- Easily angered

- A recorder of wrongs
- Delighted in evil

BE EAGER TO PROPHESY

We are encouraged as believers to covet to prophesy in the following example: *"Therefore, my brothers and sisters, be eager to prophesy, and do not forbid speaking in tongues"* (1 Corinthians 14:39 NIV).

First Corinthians 14:39 helps us understand fully that God desires us to prophesy. The prophetic is clearly a supernatural gift that is the most coveted and the only gift above all other gifts to eagerly desire.

The gift of prophecy should be one of the most sought-after gifts. Those who prophesy are greater than those who speak in tongues. Yet, some have chosen to "major" in speaking in tongues and "minor" in prophesying. The Corinthian church elevated tongues over all of the other spiritual gifts. Paul had to set the record straight—tongues is the lesser gift, because those who speak in tongues are not understood by others unless there is an interpreter. Moreover, those who speak in tongues only edify and build up themselves spiritually—those who prophesy build up the entire church spiritually.

The gift of prophecy is greater than the gift of speaking in tongues as Paul expresses the distinction in function and impact in 1 Corinthians 14:5 (NIV):

> *I would like every one of you to speak in tongues, but I would rather have you prophesy. **The one who prophesies is greater than the one who speaks in tongues**, unless someone interprets, so that the church may be edified.*

It is vital to the growth of the local church, even universal, to over-emphasize the importance of prophecy, and for those who function in the realm of the prophetic to seek to excel in it:

> *Even so you, since you are zealous for spiritual gifts, let it be for the edification of the church that you seek to excel* (1 Corinthians 14:12).

PROPHETIC IGNORANCE

> *Now about the gifts of the Spirit, brothers and sisters, I do not want you to be uninformed* [ignorant] (1 Corinthians 12:1 NIV).

Paul, in 1 Corinthians 12:1, is teaching against ignorance of spiritual gifts—he wants believers to be informed and aware of spiritual gifts. The word "gifts" in the New King James version is italicized; as we discussed previously that means it was not in the original Greek manuscript, therefore the emphasis is on not being ignorant of the spiritual. There are two concerns that Paul points out—he does not want us to be ignorant of: 1) the supernatural and 2) gifts. I agree with Paul that we should not be ignorant or uninformed of the gift of prophecy, which describes prophetic ignorance.

IMPARTATION OF PROPHECY

The gift of prophecy, along with other spiritual gifts, can be imparted and implanted through the laying on of hands and prophecy as Paul reveals the power of impartation:

> *Do not neglect the gift that is in you, which was given to you by prophecy with the laying on of the hands of the eldership* [presbytery] (1 Timothy 4:14).

> *Therefore I remind you to stir up the gift of God which is in you through the laying on of my hands* (2 Timothy 1:6).

> *I long to see you so that I may impart to you some spiritual gift to make you strong* (Romans 1:11 NIV).

GRACE OF PROPHECY

Those functioning in the gift of prophecy or the prophetic will manifest special divine abilities that will distinguish their prophetic ability. Those who possess the gift of prophecy will have a grace connected to the gift of prophecy that will make their prophetic flow different from others who function in the same gift. This grace is best defined as someone's "gift distinction" or "ministry distinction." It is coupled with your spiritual gifts that makes your gift unique that God has given you by the Holy Spirit. Some have a grace in certain areas. Every office prophet has a grace distinction or ministry distinction, which gives them their specialty. Grace is your space in a special area. It can be your *gift specialty*. In other words, some prophets have a grace to function in stronger gifts of revelatory knowledge so they can prophesy and minister with forensic, explicit accuracy and detail concerning your life.

There are different levels of prophetic gifting, which means *prophetic grace*. There is a *grace of prophecy* that measures out the different levels and capacities in which we all can prophesy:

> *Having then gifts differing according to the grace that is given to us, let us use them: if prophecy, let us prophesy in proportion to our faith; or ministry, let us use it in our ministering; he who teaches, in teaching; he who exhorts, in exhortation; he who gives, with liberality; he who leads, with diligence; he who shows mercy, with cheerfulness* (Romans 12:6-8).

RATIO OF PROPHECY

We can prophesy according to the proportion of our faith. The word "proportion" refers to a ratio or measurement. This proportion or ratio of faith gives a believer the faith to prophesy to one person, while to another person the faith to prophesy to ten or more people, and to another the faith to prophesy to more than one hundred people at a time. I have a prophetic ministry along with my twin brother Dr. Hakeem Collins who is a bestselling author of the book *Heaven Declares*—and we are recognized widely as the "Twin Prophets." We travel individually as well as together as a team ministering prophetically. People are amazed at the uniqueness and rarity of twin prophets, but importantly the grace and faith in which my brother and I are able to prophesy accurately to people one-on-one at a ratio of a hundred people or more at a time in some of our meetings. We have heard people say that we have "prophetic rivers" in us.

All believers have been given a grace from God. This grace is what makes your gift different or unique. Someone may not have been called to the office of the prophet, but God will give an individual a prophetic grace to flow and operate in the prophetic mantle as a prophet for a specific reason. He may put a special grace upon people that causes them to be a specialized type of prophet. I believe God will anoint prophets for a season, reason, or a lifetime depending on when their ministry is needed the most.

Grace is God's boundary and His ability in the believer to function. A prophetic grace is available for all believers to prophesy; however, not all believers will prophesy with the same grace or at the same level. We can all prophesy, but all will not have the capacity to operate in the highest dimension and realm of the prophetic grace—the office of the prophet. There are different levels, measures, dimensions, and realms in the prophetic. It is important to discover your *prophetic space* or *prophetic grace* or *prophetic place*. Your prophetic grace is your prophetic space, which is your prophetic place.

MANAGERS OF GRACE

> *As each one has received a special gift, employ it in serving one another as good stewards* [managers] *of the manifold grace* [charis] *of God* (1 Peter 4:10 New American Standard Bible).

In 1 Peter 4:10, we are exhorted to *"employ"* the gifts that have been given to us in serving each other. If we do not become good stewards of the gifts that God has given us, He will give them to someone who will use them responsibly. Many of us do not employ or work our spiritual gifts in serving others as good stewards or managers of the variety of grace. For many of us, our special gifts are unemployed. Therefore, we should strive continually to keep our special, spiritual, and or prophetic gifts and graces employed. The angels of the Lord hearken to the voice of the Lord (Psalm 103:20) and many of our angels are unemployed because we fail, refuse, or are afraid to prophesy. Angels hearken—listen and obey—to the voice of God's word. Prophets are the voices of God on earth uttering His word.

Each believer has been given at least one special gift to employ for the purpose of serving others as a good manager of the various grace of God upon their lives. The spiritual gifts are within us. The word "steward" in the Greek is the word *oikonomos*. Strong's Concordance defines it as the manager of a household or of household affairs; the one who is a house distributor or overseer. God has made us managers over His manifold grace.

Therefore, as a manager of grace it is important to ensure that each special gift is used properly and to employ it to do exactly what it is intended to do. For example, if I have been given the gift of prophecy, it is my responsibility to be a good manager over it and to put it to work, to prophesy words of edification, exhortation, and comfort to others. If I have been given the gifts of healings, likewise it is my duty as an overseer to minister and employ different types of healings to serve those who are sick, diseased, or hurting with all kinds of aliments and proclivities.

When we employ and work the grace of God that is in us to serve others with our special abilities, then God is glorified through us in Jesus Christ. The manifestation of the glory of God is released when we release the grace of God within. Do not allow your God-given grace to go unemployed. There is a need for what is upon your life. We are ministers of grace.

> *If anyone speaks, let him speak as the oracles of God. If anyone ministers, let him do it with the ability which God supplies, that in all things God may be glorified through Jesus Christ...* (1 Peter 4:11).

GRACE OF OPERATION—GOD'S SPACE TO OPERATE

We as believers serve God with our spiritual gifts. Therefore, it is understood that each one in the body of Christ receives a measure of grace in which to function.

Grace is God's limit of space in us to operate. God measures out in each of us a space in which He will work and display His ability. There is a grace for the space. In other words, you are limited by the amount of grace you receive from God. The grace of God is the realm of space out of which we can function. The realm of the prophetic is the limited space that God gives to us. Every believer should operate in the realm or space of the prophetic in one or more levels of prophecy. We should seek to move into greater measure of the prophetic realm.

PROPHECY IMPARTS GRACE

It is important to know that prophecy has the unbelievable power to impart grace to those who hear:

> *Let no corrupt word proceed out of your mouth, but what is good for necessary edification, that it may **impart grace to the hearers**. And do not grieve the Holy Spirit of God, by whom you were sealed for the day of redemption* (Ephesians 4:29-30).

Those who operate in any level of prophecy has the ability to impart grace to those over which they are speaking prophetic words. Though those who operate in the gift of prophecy are limited to edification, exhortation, and comfort, you can also impart grace to those you minister to. The gift of prophecy, though being a higher level of prophecy than the spirit of prophecy, can still impart into others. In fact, all levels and realms of prophecy have the power of impartation. Those with the spirit of prophecy have the capacity to impart faith.

The spirit of prophecy testifies of Jesus Christ and imparts saving grace in Christ but the gift of prophecy through edification, exhortation, and comfort imparts strength. Prophecy is the vehicle to impart grace supernaturally by speaking into someone's life. We use the phrase "speaking into someone's life" when prophesying over someone personally, which can be interpreted best as imparting grace through prophecy or prophetic communication. Prophets have the ability to impart grace through their prophetic words. Sitting under a prophet or in a place where prophecy is being released has the ability to cause those who hear to become strengthened and encouraged by the grace imparted by the inspired words.

I have been in many meetings where prophecy was being uttered and spoken corporately over the entire congregation, and I can recall feeling encouraged, strengthened, and supernaturally empowered to accomplish anything or the impossible.

CHAPTER 9

THE PROPHETIC ANOINTING

The Third Dimension of the Prophetic Realm

*Also you shall anoint Jehu the son of Nimshi as king
over Israel. And Elisha the son of Shaphat of Abel
Meholah you shall anoint as prophet in your place.*
—1 KINGS 19:16

The third dimension of the prophetic realm is the "prophetic anointing."
This realm of the prophetic is accessible to all believers and is one of the
key dimensions in which prophets in both the Old and New Testaments
operated. The prophetic anointing is a much higher degree of the prophetic.
This is the power behind the prophetic gift that brings change. The prophetic anointing is the power of prophecy. The prophetic anointing makes
flowing in the gift of prophecy and the prophetic easy. The anointing of
prophecy makes the difference in ministering in the prophetic or the gift of
prophecy compared to someone who is not anointed or gifted by the Spirit
to prophesy.

All believers in Christ carry a measure of the prophetic anointing, but
most are not quite aware of it. Oftentimes we think that only the ancient
prophets carried the prophetic anointing and were the only ones able to
access it by the Spirit. However, this powerful anointing resides in all Spirit-
filled believers. The prophetic anointing is residential. It lives permanently
inside all believers.

I believe that God desires all believers to move into higher levels in the prophetic. The prophetic anointing is a higher realm of the prophetic—up from that of the spirit of prophecy, gift of prophecy, and prophetic grace. This dimension of the prophetic realm is important as we understand how to embrace and fully operate in higher degrees of prophetic operation. This is a powerful dimension in the prophetic realm that will unlock the power of prophecy in your life.

You will learn that there is an anointing on your life to prophesy. When the anointing is activated and tapped into, when you begin to speak in whatever level of the prophetic, you will begin to see manifestation of the Spirit in your life and those to whom you minister. The "prophetic anointing" is the anointing of revealing prophetically: identification, consecration, affirmation, ordination, and sanctification. The prophet has the "oil"—the anointing—to reveal who is God's election for a specific calling, purpose, assignment, appointment, and ministry.

The oil, anointing, is the agent of revelation that God sends His prophet to pour out upon the crowns of the heads of His chosen. There is anointing resident in the prophet's office to be able to spiritually see the oil of God on a person's life for a calling. For example, the physical oil only represents in the spirit the appointment to a specific calling, position, assignment, and purpose. The oil is the indicator or sign of what position one was anointed and appointed for.

The prophet has the ability to see spiritually the oil, anointing, upon a person's life. The prophet can see various anointing and graces upon a person's life, which makes it easy for the prophet to see and identify with their calling, office, and position sanctioned by God. The oil (olive oil and aromatic herbs) represents the setting apart and setting in of offices of a person.

WHAT IS THE ANOINTING?

Old Testament

The word "anointing" in the Old Testament in Hebrew is *mashah*, which means to smear or rub with oil, typically as part of a religious ceremony. It means to anoint for the purpose to consecrate, set apart, appoint into sacred office or position. Anointing is the act of rubbing, smearing, spreading, and/or painting a substance such as oil on someone to identify a calling of God or a setting apart for special work.

The word "anointing" appears twenty-three times in the Old Testament. Various words used are anoint, anointest, and anointed and are used more than 150 times in the whole Bible. The Hebrew word *mishchah* or *moshchah* is derived from the primitive root *mashach* that often means to "smear or spread a liquid."

New Testament

The New Testament meaning of the "anointing" and "unction" are taken from the same Greek word *chrisma*, which means an unguent or smearing, act of smearing with oil. It speaks of a special endowment, *chrisma*, of the Holy Spirit. The anointing, unction, or *chrisma* comes directly from the Holy Spirit. He gives us an anointing or unction. The endowment is a gift of the Holy Spirit imparted to believers. It is God's special ability and power within us to accomplish and finish His work. The unction of the Spirit gives us the power of God. It is our supernatural equipment to complete the assignment that God has anointed us for. One of the catch phrases used to describe the anointing—*the unction to function.*

It is important to understand that there have been given a realm of special endowment of the Holy Spirit. Just as there are diversities of gifts, *chrisma*, distributed to each believer by the Spirit according to 1 Corinthians 12:4, there are also diversities of anointing and unction, chrisma, that are given with those gifts.

In others words, if I have the gift of prophecy or I function in prophetic gifts, there will be a prophetic unction, an anointing, on that gift for me to function. There are times when I can simply stir up and activate my prophetic gifts to serve the church, but there are also times when I receive a prophetic unction to operate. The Holy Spirit activates and influences me to minister. There is something special that prompts or moves me to minister in the prophetic, which is the prophetic anointing.

There is something special that comes on or empowers the prophetic gifts or supernatural gifts in a believer. The anointing is not limited to any specific gift; but typically, we identify the anointing simply by the manifestation of the Spirit that is operating. What I mean is, when a person is operating in a prophetic anointing, there are endowments and gifts of the Spirit that are functioning when the anointing of the Spirit is flowing. The anointing is described as the Holy Spirit moving upon you and the gifts of God to partner with Him to do the will of the Father. Today we are able to identify ministry, a calling, grace, and office by the anointing that is upon a person's life. They are identified by their anointing. The anointing is the Holy Spirit.

ANOINTING OF KINGS, PRIESTS, AND PROPHETS

There is a prophetic flow to the anointing. When priests, kings, and prophets were anointed, the anointing oil was poured on the head of the person being anointed (Exodus 29:7). The anointing flows from the head downward to the feet. Kings were consecrated through the ceremony of anointing that was performed by a prophet.

The Old Testament records examples of the anointing by a prophet of God, Samuel was sent to anoint Saul as king (1 Samuel 15:1), and Elijah was to anoint Jehu (1 Kings 19:16). Moses a prophet, poured the anointing oil on Aaron's head and anointed him, consecrating him into his priestly office (Leviticus 8:12; 21:10-12).

The following illustrates the flow of the anointing over Aaron, the high priest, in Psalm 133:1-3:

> *Behold, how good and how pleasant it is for brethren to dwell together in unity! It is like the precious ointment upon the head, running down on the beard, the beard of Aaron, running down on the edge of his garments. It is like the dew of Hermon, descending upon the mountains of Zion; for there the Lord commanded the blessing—life forevermore.*

CLASSES OF ANOINTING

The anointing was applied primarily to three classes of people: prophets, priests, and kings. A prophet who is anointed would be carrying a "prophetic anointing." Priests who were anointed carried a "priestly anointing" upon their life. Kings who were installed and inaugurated into their royal position were those ruling with a "kingly anointing."

There were three types of anointing or anointed ones in the Old Testament:

1. King—the anointing to reign, rule and govern with absolute power and authority.

    You prepare a table before me [King David] *in the presence of my enemies. You anoint my head with oil; my cup overflows* (Psalm 23:5 NIV).

    But David said to Abishai, "Do not destroy him [King Saul]; *for who can stretch out his hand against the Lord's anointed, and be guiltless?"* (1 Samuel 26:9).

2. Priest—the anointing to teach, train, make atonements for sins, and minister to God.

    And you [Moses] *shall take the anointing oil, pour it on his* [Aaron the high priest] *head, and anoint him* (Exodus 29:7).

3. Prophet—the anointing to be God's special spokesperson, mouthpiece, and messenger. Prophets were sent to anoint kings, priests, and even prophets. Also, prophets were anointed with oil. Elisha, the successive prophet, was anointed with oil by Elijah the prophet, his predecessor.

    Also you shall anoint Jehu the son of Nimshi as king over Israel. And Elisha the son of Shaphat of Abel Meholah you shall anoint as prophet in your place (1 Kings 19:16).

Elisha was anointed by Elijah to be a prophet after him. He was anointed and set apart into his office and ministry. This is the only place in the Scripture where a prophet was anointed by another prophet. It took another prophet to identify the prophetic anointing, or oil, on another prophet's life. Prophets can identify the oil, the anointing, upon a person's life. God told Elijah to anoint Elisha to be a prophet. The anointing released upon Elisha was a prophetic anointing.

By the Holy Spirit, all believers are given supernatural, miraculous faculties, endowments which are the anointing:

> *But you have an anointing* [unction] *from the Holy One, and you know all things* (1 John 2:20).

> *But the anointing which you have received from Him abides in you, and you do not need that anyone teach you; but as the same anointing* [unction] *teaches you concerning all things, and is true, and is not a lie, and just as it has taught you, you will abide in Him* (1 John 2:27).

ANOINTED FOR THE ASSIGNMENT

The prophetic anointing has limitations. We are not anointed for everything and we are not anointed to do everything. The limitation of the anointing is within the boundaries of the position, special assignment, and ordination for which we are set apart. The anointing is limited to the assignment for which you are called. There is an anointing for each person's particular calling. We are all anointed with a special mission, assignment, mandate, and commission. For example, if you are anointed to be a prophet of God, there is a corresponding anointing that is given by God as equipment to work in that specific ministry.

Every prophet is given a residual anointing that serves as their spiritual equipment and tools to complete their assignment to which they were ordained. The prophetic anointing is limited to and works in conjunction with the particular gift, grace, and assignment on a person's life. We all are anointed for a specific work or assignment. The appointees were anointed and ordained by prophets in the Old Testament, just as believers today can also be anointed and ordained appointees by prophets and the Holy Spirit in the New Testament. There is no power in the physical oil itself. The oil is symbolic to represent the Holy Spirit coming upon a person to set them apart for a holy work of God. The Spirit of the Lord represents His partnership in the anointing with the person.

All believers are given anointing and unguent from the Holy Spirit to fulfill their God-ordained calling. The anointing from the Holy Spirit signifies that all believers are set apart, holy unto God, consecrated and anointed as kings and priests. We have been made a kingdom of priests. We carry by right of the anointing of the Holy Spirit, a kingly, priestly, and prophetic anointing.

There is a realm of anointing in every believer to accomplish his or her own work of ministry. All believers are called by God to accomplish a work that He has ordained for them. For many are called but few are chosen (Matthew 20:16; 22:14). The limitation of the anointing on a person's life is predicated on their specific assignment. God anoints us for the assignment. That assignment can be temporal, seasonal, or generational. Anointing is typically time sensitive.

There are times when I am ministering when I sense a strong anointing on me to do something by faith. I can also sense that God has provided a period of time, a window of time, an "opportunity" of time to get it done. In other words, if God has put an anointing of healing on me in that moment, then it is important for me to pray and release that anointing upon all who are ill.

There is a special anointing to accomplish the impossible. God's anointing upon our lives will empower us to do things that we are not capable of doing in our own natural strengths and abilities. The anointing of God is simply God's ability upon us to finish His work. The anointing on us is the tangible presence of God merged with the power of God. The anointing is the presence and power of the Holy Spirit upon and within believers. There is a reserve, a reservoir of unlimited access to the supernatural supply of miraculous power. The emphasis of this chapter is to focus on the "prophetic anointing," but for fundamental purposes I want to explain that each believer has the power to prophesy by the anointing of the spirit of prophecy resident in every follower and disciple of Jesus Christ.

REVELATION IS IN THE ANOINTING

There are Scripture examples of prophets being used in the anointing, setting apart, consecration, and sanctification of priests, prophets, and kings. The prophetic anointing resident in the prophet provided the revelation and insight into a person's calling, spiritual gift, grace, anointing, and ministry offices. There is a pattern where prophets were regularly used as vehicles of ordination and established the offices of the king, priest, and prophet.

Many times God would command His prophets to fill his flask or horn with oil for the purpose of anointing those God had divinely selected into their office and position. Prophets carry an anointing upon their lives to announce prophetically who God has chosen for a specific calling, position, office, and purpose. Just as the prophets naturally filled their horn with the anointing oil of setting the next king, priest, and prophet, spiritually they carry an anointing within their prophetic function to identify and ordain men and women into their God-ordained offices and ministries.

THE ANOINTING OF THE PROPHETS

The anointing was an act or spiritual ritual executed to represent an office occupied by a person who would be used by the Spirit to carry out an assignment. As long as the anointing and Spirit of God was upon a person, it demonstrated God's approval and endorsement. If the Spirit of God left a person, it could mean that their assignment in that role was completed or terminated. David prayed that God would not take His Spirit from him.

The Spirit of God left Saul. Though he was still in position as king of Israel, God had already found another one, David, who was better:

And as Samuel turned around to go away, Saul seized the edge of his robe, and it tore. So Samuel said to him, "The Lord has torn the kingdom of Israel from you today, and has given it to a neighbor of yours, who is better than you" (1 Samuel 15:27-28).

Therefore, Samuel was instructed to go to Jesse's house to anoint the next king of Israel. Saul was still in position, but God was no longer with him. The oil, anointing, that was in the horn of the prophet had David's name written all on it to rule as king. Kings are anointed to rule, reign, and have dominion. God always sent prophets with oil to anoint God's chosen. The prophetic anointing can see who is chosen. Also, the anointing is symbolic to represent those who have been chosen by God to a position of power and authority. The anointing of the Spirit represents God's power and authority operating in your life and that God is with you just as He was with the anointing of David by Samuel the prophet.

ANOINTING OF GOD'S CHOICE

Now the Lord said to Samuel, "How long will you mourn for Saul, seeing I have rejected him from reigning over Israel? Fill your horn with oil, and go; I am sending you to Jesse the Bethlehemite. For I have provided [seen for] *Myself a king among his sons"* (1 Samuel 16:1).

Samuel's prophetic anointing chose the one God provided for Himself:

And Samuel said to Jesse, "Are all the young men here?" Then he said, "There remains yet the youngest, and there he is, keeping the sheep." And Samuel said to Jesse, "Send and bring him. For we will not sit down till he comes here." So he sent and brought him in. Now he was ruddy, with bright eyes, and good-looking. And the Lord said, "Arise, anoint him; for this is the one!" Then Samuel took the horn of oil and anointed him [David] *in the midst of his brothers; and the Spirit of the Lord came upon David* [with power] *from that day forward. So Samuel arose and went to Ramah* (1 Samuel 16:11-13).

INCREASE IN THE ANOINTING

David was first anointed king in his house among his brothers, while still tending to the sheep of his father Jesse. His second anointing was as king over Judah. David grew into being king over a tribe of people; and last, he was anointed king in Hebron over the entire nation of Israel, all twelve tribes. He went from king in a house, to over a tribe, and then the nation. You, too, can grow into the anointing or measure of rule, authority, and power that God designed for you.

Your anointing is connected to your assignment. Therefore, as your assignment increases in capacity and those who are under your influence grows, there will be an increase in the capacity of your anointing. As defined previously, the anointing means to spread. It is safe to say that as your sphere of influence increases, your anointing will spread out over larger territories, places, regions, tribes, and even nations.

David had three realms of anointing that increased in capacity:

1. House—Father's house among his brothers (1 Samuel 16:1-13)

2. Judah—Tribe group of people (2 Samuel 2:4)

3. Nation—Nation or nations of people (2 Samuel 5:3)

There are those who carry anointing for different groups of people. The anointing can be limited to your specific assignment or geographical location. Some carry anointing for a specific place or geographical area. Prophets are called and anointed to first serve in the house of God before He trusts them with more. He will measure our faithfulness in His house among our brothers and sisters in the Lord before He entrusts us with nations. The anointing is often developed in the local church among the body of believers. That is where your anointing is developed, cultivated, and groomed. The Bible says, *"...you were faithful over a few things, I will make you ruler over many things..."* (Matthew 25:21). Faithfulness is the key to increasing the anointing of God on your life.

We can see the principle of faithfulness taught by Jesus to His disciples in Luke 19:17 (New Living Translation): *"Well done!' the king exclaimed. 'You are a good servant. You have been faithful with the little I entrusted to you, so you will be governor of ten cities as your reward.'"*

THE WORD OF GOD

How do you increase in the prophetic anointing? When we find ourselves bound or oppressed or beaten into submission by the enemy, we can grow in the prophetic anointing by increasing in the words of God in our lives. The word of God is a very important element in the prophet's ministry. The anointing of the prophetic increases as he or she increases in the knowledge of the Scriptures, both Old and New Testaments. Prophets' anointing is in their mouth and when they teach, preach, and prophesy to the people they receive and are fed from the word of the Lord that is released. People grow under their prophetic ministry as they feed on the Word from the man or woman of God.

It is the responsibility of the prophet to know the written Word of God in order to be an official speaker, spokesperson, mouthpiece, and oracle of God. Without the Word of God, you cannot be a true spokesperson of God. Some prophets believe there is little to zero reason to study or learn the Word of God because they can just flow prophetically and receive revelation. That belief is misguided. Prophets who do not study or know the Scriptures are dangerous and extremely susceptible to error and falsehood. They are candidates to become false prophets. The Word of the Lord must be in the mouth of His prophets.

Ezekiel's prophetic anointing increased as he ate the whole scroll of the Word of God:

> *Moreover He [God] said to me [Ezekiel], "Son of man, eat what you find; eat this scroll, and go, speak to the house of Israel." So I opened my mouth, and He caused me to eat that scroll. And He said to me, "Son of man, feed your belly, and fill*

your stomach with this scroll that I give you." So I ate, and it was in my mouth like honey in sweetness (Ezekiel 3:1-3).

CHAPTER 10

THE PROPHETIC MANTLE

The Fourth Dimension of the Prophetic Realm

He [Elisha] *also took up the mantle of Elijah*
that had fallen from him, and went back
and stood by the bank of the Jordan.
— 2 KINGS 2:13).

The fourth dimension of the realm of the prophetic is the "prophetic mantle." This realm of the prophetic is for believers who have moved into a realm of prophetic power and authority. The mantle of the prophetic opens a portal to access the power and authority that rested upon the ancient biblical prophets. It gives believers who God is calling into the prophetic ministry to be able to wear this power as a mantle upon their lives. The mantle of the prophetic represents the realm of supernatural power that God invests in His spokespersons and mouthpieces. Believers whom God has summoned into the prophetic ministry and office of the prophet will be able to operate in greater levels of power, authority, and strength in the realm of the prophetic.

The prophetic mantle is a dimension of "prophetic power and authority." The mantle of prophecy is a dimension of power and prophetic anointing that gives someone who has matured in the lower levels of the prophetic an opportunity to grow in gifting, grace, anointing, and now power to walk in prophetic ministry or the office of the prophet.

In this dimension of the prophetic, you will discover the ancient power behind the mantle of the prophet and how God's anointed spokesperson operated in the realm of power and authority to declare the secrets of God on earth. The prophet of God carried a mantle that identified with the measure and capacity of power the prophet walked in the supernatural. The mantle was the symbol of prophetic power that the prophet carried on his or her life.

There is a mantle of the prophetic that God is releasing in this hour for all believers to access in order to walk in a realm of extraordinary power of the prophets. The prophets of God were able move in the realm of power in the prophetic in this dimension. God desires for all believers, sons and daughters, in His church to prophesy, but importantly that we may all prophesy with power.

THE MANTLE OF PROPHECY

The prophetic mantle is the "mantle of prophecy" that every believer can function in through the mantle of the Holy Spirit. This mantle of prophecy is the residual anointing that resides in those who are called particularly to the prophetic ministry or office of the prophet. This degree of prophetic operation is for those who are assigned, called, and appointed to a greater scope, brevity, and authority in that realm.

This is not the spirit of prophecy, the gift of prophecy, or the prophetic anointing that we previously discussed, this is the mantle of prophecy that rests upon people's lives permanently, that empowers them to function at any time in their prophetic ministry or office. They do not have to wait for the spirit of prophecy or the prophetic anointing to operate. They have been given spiritual authority by the Lord Jesus Christ to exercise in this realm of power whenever there is an opportunity to witness, minister, and release the love, power, and glory of God to others. This realm of the prophetic is activated through sheer spiritual authority.

The mantle speaks relatively of the prophetic authority that is invested in a person's assignment.

When God places a mantle upon your life, it is the authority and reinforcement of Heaven that will reinforce your inspired utterance, words, intercession, and decree. It empowers you to prophesy not just by revelation but by authority. It is the ability to exercise spiritual authority as a law enforcement officer enforces the law. The mantle of prophecy gives you the ability to police, reinforce, and execute spiritual laws in the prophetic realm.

This is operating with the authority of a prophet. This is not functioning in the limitations of the testifying of Jesus Christ (spirit of prophecy), edification, exhortation, and comfort (gift of prophecy) and/or the prophetic anointing (power to prophecy). The mantle of the prophetic is not primarily prophesying but more governing, establishing, binding, loosing, nullifying, prohibiting, creating, legislating, and executing. This prophesying is more governmental in essence and more happens in the realm of the spirit first before it is manifested in the realm of the earth.

It is important to understand that the prophetic mantle does more in the realm of the spirit than prophecy: it gives the prophetic the spiritual authority that causes what they speak on earth to be reinforced by angels. The angels hearken to the Word of the Lord (Psalm 103:20). Jesus understood this dimension of spiritual authority that was invested in Him by the weight of the mantle that He carried. He revealed that whatsoever we as believers bind on earth shall be bound in heaven (Matthew 18:18). The prophet's mantle is recognized first in the heavenly realm and reinforced in the earthly realm. Therefore, wearing the spiritual mantle of the Holy Spirit gives the prophet authority in both Heaven and on earth. Mantles are not for Heaven, because God has no need for them there—they are needed on earth by humans.

Because the mantle is given by the Lord Jesus Christ, it gives the prophet access into the realms of the prophetic, empowering him to function in the highest level of spiritual authority. There are realms in the prophetic where only those with prophetic mantles can operate. Satanic, demonic, and diabolical spirits and entities recognize mantles in the spirit. They are easily able to recognize if someone is walking in the office of the prophet because of the prophet's mantle (Acts 19:15).

THE PROPHET'S UNIFORM

A mantle is a prophet's uniform or garment worn for a specific job, work, or calling. By a person's physical uniform, we can quickly identify someone in the United States Armed Forces—whether in the Marine Corps, Navy, Air Force, Coast Guard, or Army. The prophetic mantle is recognized in the realm of the spirit from the ministry offices of apostle, evangelist, pastor, and teacher. The mantle represents a uniform of authority that a prophet wears that identifies his or her spiritual authority, power, and rank. It is similar to a coat that a police officer, FBI agent, or firefighter wears that identifies the office or organization they represent. The office of the prophet wears a mantle to identify his or her calling as an officer of God.

There are different mantles, clothing or garments, that also reflect what rank of authority someone carries. For example, apostolic mantles represent the power and authority of an apostle, a sent one. Apostolic and prophetic offices are the highest degrees of spiritual authority in the church. Therefore, this gives us an understanding of the weight upon those who carry apostolic and prophetic mantles of God. All authority is ordained of God (Romans 13:1). A mantle represents ordained authority by God. Spiritual mantles reflect spiritual authority. All believers function out of the spiritual mantle of Jesus Christ who gives us a measure of authority over the powers of the devil. Every believer carries spiritual authority out of the mantle of the Holy Spirit imparted and sent by the Father and Jesus Christ.

To fully comprehend the function of the prophetic coat, cloak, and covering, the prophetic mantle is a mantle of power that empowers us to prophesy with greater strength, depth, and authority. When you prophesy with a prophetic mantle, you are essentially prophesying with a cloak of the powers of the ages before you. You prophesy out of a portal of power where you will literally see the word of the Lord become flesh. God is moving us into a realm of speaking things into existence by the manifestation of the word of the Lord being released out of our mouths.

The ancient mantles unlock the true essence and power of the prophetic that give us the ability to carry that same power and greater into the future. Ancient mantles that were locked up, preserved, and hidden in former ages are coming upon believers today to walk heavy in impartations of the prophets. The mysteries behind the mantles are being revealed today by the New Testament prophets who are decoding and unfolding the mantles of the Old Covenant prophets for us to release that same thrust of prophetic power in our generation and generations to come. I believe there are greater mantles to be released out of Heaven for the prophets, prophetic people, prophetic churches, and prophetic generations of leadership to do greater work.

MANTLE OF RESPONSIBILITY

Mantles are worn on the shoulders of the bearers as signs of carrying burdens and the weight of responsibilities. When a mantle is given to someone, it is a sign that the person has the ability and strength to shoulder responsibilities, tasks, assignments, heavy loads, and work. Mantles are not given to those who are incapable of carrying such a mandate from God.

A prophetic mantle can signify the responsibility, grief, distress, persecution, attacks, and all that encompasses the calling of the prophet. The prophet is able to endure and carry all of what comes against him or her because of the mantle on his or her life. There are various types of prophetic mantles that collate with the prophet's assignment, mission, anointing, and jurisdictional authority. Prophet have specific assignments and mantles upon their lives. The nature of the office and ministry is indicative of the mantle that they carry.

The mantle of Jesus Christ was governmental according to Isaiah the prophet: *"For unto us a Child is born, unto us a Son is given; and the government will be upon His shoulder"* (Isaiah 9:6).

What is upon a prophet's shoulder becomes part of his or her mantle. What your burden and area of calling is represents the mantle on your life. If you have a burden for healing, then essentially a "healing mantle" rests upon your life to see people healed. You will eat, sleep, and rest with a mantle of healing—it becomes part of your life's mission. The mantle and the bearer become one. You must become one with your mantle.

WHAT IS A MANTLE?

To understand the power of the prophetic mantle, the secret is hidden in its definition. A mantle was worn for a purpose; however, there is spiritual revelation that needs to be grasped if we are going to operate in realms of the prophetic. The ancient mantle is more than just a piece of cloth worn by the prophets. A mantle is far more significant in the spirit realm than what is understood in the natural realm. The prophetic mantle gives a prophet, or person functioning in this dimension operational, capabilities extending beyond the basic functions of the spirit of prophecy, gift of prophecy, prophetic grace, and prophetic anointing. It is important to examine what the prophetic mantle entails compared to the other dimensions of the prophetic. Prophets in the Old Testament operated minimally in the gift of prophecy versus how they operated and functioned primarily in their spiritual mantles.

There are various meanings of mantle in the Bible, but the main idea is that of a covering such as a cloak, robe, or other article of clothing. In biblical times, an ancient mantle was typically described as a large, loosely fitting garment made of animal skin, probably sheepskin. Several people are mentioned as wearing a mantle, including Job (Job 1:20) and Ezra (Ezra 9:5). Women also wore mantles (Isaiah 3:22).

The prophet Samuel's mantle was torn by King Saul as a symbol that God was tearing the kingdom away from him. Mantles represent a realm of authority, as in the tearing of Samuel's mantle in 1 Samuel 15:27-28: *"And as Samuel turned around to go away, Saul seized the edge of his robe [mantle], and it tore. So Samuel said to him, "The Lord has torn the kingdom of Israel from you today, and has given it to a neighbor of yours, who is better than you."*

Elijah cast his mantle upon his anointed successor Elijah as a sign of a prophetic call to the office of the prophet in 1 Kings 19:19: *"So he departed from there, and found Elisha the son of Shaphat, who was plowing with twelve yoke of oxen before him, and he was with the twelfth. Then Elijah passed by him and threw his mantle on him."*

These Scripture passages show that prophets were known for wearing mantles as a sign of their calling from God (1 Kings 19:19). Samuel wore a mantle as a prophet (1 Samuel 15:27). The prophet Elijah *"threw his mantle"* on Elisha as a symbol of Elijah's ministry being transferred on to Elisha. The transference of the mantle from Elijah to Elisha signified the passing of prophetic responsibility and the power of God resting upon him. The prophet's mantle was indicative of God's ordained authority and responsibility as God's chosen spokesperson (2 Kings 2:8). Elisha understood clearly what Elijah was doing when the prophetic mantle touched his life.

The mantle also served the practical purpose of keeping people warm and protecting them from the outside elements. It also served a symbolic purpose, in the case of the prophets, showing they were wrapped in God's authority and protective aspect against demonic attacks.

Prophets were identified by their mantle. The prophetic mantle was their spiritual identification in the realm of the spirit. Saul perceived it was Samuel when he sought a medium to summon Samuel to inquire of the Lord regarding his death:

> *So he [Saul] said to her, "What is his [Samuel's] form? And she [a medium] said, "An old man is coming up, and he is **covered with a mantle**." And Saul perceived that it was Samuel, and he stooped with his face to the ground and bowed down.*

MANTLE OF AUTHORITY AND SPIRITUAL COVERING

A mantle was an outer cloak used for additional covering and warmth, especially at night. The mantle was essentially the only blanket or protective covering the person had, so even when used or borrowed as a pledge, the law of Moses explicitly required it be returned before bedtime (Exodus 22:26-27). From the idea of a covering in the natural, a mantle can easily be seen to represent a spiritual covering. Just as Elijah served as a spiritual covering for Elisha, mantles usually refer to spiritual authority and covering. Though the focus in this chapter is on the prophetic mantle, it important to understand that there are also mantles for business, media, arts, entertainment, science, education, government, medicine, etc.

A prophetic mantle or mantles, generally speaking, is simply defined as spiritual garments of authority that endow the wearer with supernatural abilities, grace, and an anointing of God to establish and accomplish the assignment and appointment. Each mantle depicts a differing of divine election in the Kingdom and authorization of that calling required for operation. The prophetic mantle gives those who are called to carry the mantle of the prophet with the prophetic power and authority to access higher realms of the prophetic than the spirit of prophecy and the gift of prophecy. The mantle of prophecy is for those who are called to operate in prophetic ministry or the office of the prophet. Ancient mantles were distinct in description, the earliest were made of animal skin. Elijah and John the Baptist wore mantles of "fur" or "hairy mantles" indicating a similar nature and type of prophetic ministries.

> So they answered him, "A hairy man wearing a leather belt around his waist." And he [King Ahaziah] said, "It is Elijah the Tishbite" (2 Kings 1:8).

> Now John himself was clothed in camel's hair, with a leather belt around his waist; and his food was locusts and wild honey (Matthew 3:4).

In ancient times, a mantle revealed everything about a prophet and a person. An individual's authority, office, gender, education, vocation, social and economic rank and status were ascertainable in just one glance with the distinction of their mantle. Priestly prophets wore royal or priestly mantles (1 Samuel 2:18). Prophets and kings wore mantles of fur, distinguishing them from common folk. These were ancient mantles. The mantle worn by Elijah is the Hebrew word, in Strong's Concordance, *adderet,* a cloak that could be made of animal hair and a garment of distinction worn by kings and especially by prophets.

The prophetic mantle activated in a believer will have the following effects:

- The level of operation increases in the sphere of the local church, where continual and progressive use of the gift of prophecy and prophetic anointing is recognized by leadership with maturity.

- Leadership recognizes a prophetic calling.

- Gifting and anointing are recognized, nurtured, and commissioned by the leadership for the primary ministry function in the local church.

- More ministry occurs in the prophetic anointing than in the simple gift of prophecy of edification, exhortation, and comfort.

- A greater level of commitment is displayed in devotion to a prophetic lifestyle and call to the full development, preparatory, training, and equipping to function as a mature and seasoned prophet.

- The height, width, depth, breadth, and scope of the prophetic gifting broadens in its usage to include words concerning people, places, situations, events, issues, and activities.

- There is an increase in gift, grace, anointing, faith, wisdom and revelation, character, accountability, authority, and stewardship of the secrets and mysteries of God.

- A higher frequency of dreams and visions are unlocked, and prophetic utterance are more directive and insightful.

- Prophetic senses are trained and exercised (Hebrew 5:14).

- There is greater revelation and understanding of the Scriptures in both the *logos* and the *rhema*.

CHAPTER 11

THE PROPHETIC PRESBYTERY
The Fifth Dimension of the Prophetic Realm

Neglect not the gift that is in thee, which was given thee by prophecy, with the laying on of the hands of the presbytery.
1 TIMOTHY 4:14 KJV

The fifth dimension of the realm of the prophetic is the "prophetic presbytery." This realm of the prophetic is for believers who have moved into a realm of spiritual ordaining, identifying, establishing, and setting into ministry gifts, callings, and offices. Those who move into this higher degree of prophetic operation have been chosen with a higher perceptivity of identifying spiritual gifts, ministry callings, assignments, and offices. There is a prophetic dimension that releases the mind, will, and intentions of God through the prophetic where it reveals God's secrets concerning an individual's future.

The prophetic presbytery is the realm of God unlocking and disclosing His will, purpose, and predestination in the heart of a person. The prophetic presbytery has the capacity of leadership in the local church to legally set and establish people in their gifts, ministries, and offices. The ancient spirits of the prophets rest upon the prophetic presbyters to make known the plans of God to individuals, churches, ministries, future leaders, heads of states, and world changers.

The prophetic presbytery carries a cluster of anointings to reveal, affirm, confirm, make strong, and set in motion what is the prophetic trajectory of a person's purpose in God. This realm within the prophetic operation is for those who are selected, inclusively by local church leadership, with prophetic authority and anointing to activate, ordain, consecrate, announce, and launch believers into their calling. The prophetic presbytery has a responsibility through the means of prophetic wisdom and revelation to recognize who the Holy Spirit has called and set apart for the work of ministry.

The prophetic presbytery at the church at Antioch commissioned Barnabas and Paul as sent ones:

> *Now in the church that was at Antioch there were certain prophets and teachers: Barnabas, Simeon who was called Niger, Lucius of Cyrene, Manaen who had been brought up with Herod the tetrarch, and Saul. As they ministered to the Lord and fasted, the Holy Spirit said, "Now separate to Me Barnabas and Saul for the work to which I have called them." Then, having fasted and prayed, and laid hands on them, they sent them away (Acts 13:1-3).*

Those who are elected to participate in this realm of the prophetic have an enormous responsibility as the primitive mouthpieces of God to unlock in others the secrets of God. We will further examine this realm of the prophetic that will increase and accelerate the gift, anointing, calling, and power of God in those who experience this powerful ministry function in the church. I believe that as we look further into this we will discover, as I have in my studies and experience in the prophetic presbytery, that this ministry function is needed more than ever today, and will release greater identity to individuals, ministries, and churches.

The prophetic presbytery is one of the highest dimensions of prophetic utterances that carries the weight and brevity of establishment, impartation, and ministry release. This is an establishing anointing in the prophetic realm that spiritually certifies, licenses, endorses, brings notoriety, and signatures a person's ministry as God reveals it. I call the prophetic presbytery in the realm of the prophetic the "council of prophecy."

WHAT IS PROPHETIC PRESBYTERY?

Do not neglect the gift that is in you, which was given to you by prophecy with the laying on of the hands of the eldership (1 Timothy 4:14).

Strong's Concordance definition of the word "presbytery" comes from the Greek word *presbyteros,* which means an order of elders, body of elders, senate, or council. The presbytery consists of a body of leaders within the body or assembly of Christians or a Jewish eldership. It is important to note that spiritual gifts, graces, and empowerments are given to us through prophecy and the laying on of hands by the body of elders in the church. Paul is revealing to Timothy, his spiritual son, not to neglect that reality. This phenomenon will exponentially expand your anointing to function in heightened operations in the spirit realm. The impartation will release a supplement of special endowments when the eldership lays their hands on you that will equip you to walk worthy in your spiritual vocation.

The prophetic presbytery is one of the highest channels for prophetic ministry for impartation of gifts. The reason the presbytery is named "prophetic presbytery" is because one of the key components of impartation is through prophecy. Prophecy is the primary role in releasing a prophetic word and speaking into the life of believers. The two primary roles and functions of the prophetic presbyters is: 1) prophecy and 2) the laying on of the hands.

The word "neglect" in this verse (1 Timothy 4:14), defined by Paul means to be careless of, to make light of it and take no regard. In other words, Paul the apostle was telling Timothy not to take lightly the gift that was given to him through prophecy and the laying on of hands by the presbytery. He was revealing to him that what was imparted spiritually is weighty and it must be regarded with care. He wanted him to understand the gravity of what happened during that sacred moment and to realize he needed to take care of and steward the gift. There must be an attitude of gratefulness and care for God's gift in us.

Unfortunately, there are those in the church who either ignore, are ignorant of, or simply are careless about the gift of God in them. Sadly, many could care less. Prophets and apostles are very interested in the development of the gifts of the Spirit; and what Paul is essentially telling Timothy is to care for and develop the gift in him. There is a responsibility of the bearer of the gifts of the Spirit to cultivate, develop, and grow in grace, gifting, and anointing. It was given by the prophetic presbyters, but it is Timothy's responsibility to nurture it as a parent takes care of their newborn child.

Gifts that are neglected are underdeveloped, leading to immature ministry gifts in the church due to spiritual negligence and lack of stewardship to grow and sharpen their gifts. The prophecy that is uttered through the prophetic presbyter is a discourse emanating from divine inspiration and declaring the purposes of God, whether by reproving and admonishing the wicked, or comforting the afflicted, or revealing things hidden in someone or foretelling and unfolding future events, plans, and strategies of God. Presbyters represent the prophetic faculty in the local church or body of Christ. They carry the utterance of the prophets.

PROPHECY AND THE LAYING ON OF HANDS

The hands of the presbytery are a means or instrument symbolic of God's might, activity, and power. In other words, the hands represent the instrument and means by which the might, activity, and power of God is transmitted. This is where the power of impartation is realized and understood. The laying on of hands by the prophetic presbytery is symbolic to represent the power of God coming upon someone. I bring this to your attention to help you understand the spiritual significance behind Paul's admonishment to Timothy not to neglect what has taken place in the realm of the spirit and that he has a responsibility to cultivate that impartation. The impartation of the prophetic presbytery I picture as farmers planting the seed or seeds into a person's spiritual soil. The prophecy is the seed and the hands represent implanting the seed.

Paul understood the power of impartation and implantation of spirituals gifts through the laying on of hands in the following Scripture passages:

> *Therefore I remind you to stir up the gift of God which is in you through the laying on of my hands* (2 Timothy 1:6).

> *For I long to see you, that I may impart to you some spiritual gift, so that you may be established* (Romans 1:11).

Therefore, the prophetic presbytery is not just imparting, they are implanting. When a seed is planted in the ground, it is critical that it is properly and continually watered for it to grow. The function of apostles and prophets is to plant and water. The word "implant," according to the Merriam Webster's Dictionary, means "to set firmly and deeply; to fix in the mind or spirit and to insert in the living tissue (as for growth or absorption)." The word "implant" is synonymous with embed, entrench, ingrain, and to root.

This gives you an idea of what is happening during the prophecy and the laying on of hands by the prophetic eldership of the church. It is as if God is taking the gift of the Spirit and using the prophecy and hands of the presbyters to implant it deeply inside your spirit for it to grow. The gifts of the Spirit are spiritually embedded in the hearts and souls of every believer. In retrospect, apostles and prophets serve as those who impart and implant gifts. Some will have a function in your life to impart gifts and others will come to help develop your spiritual faculty.

The point I am making is that God has given fivefold ministry gifts to the church for equipping and training purposes, which we will discuss later in this book. But for the purpose of this chapter and the prophetic emphasis, we will focus on understanding that imparted gifts, graces, anointing, and endowments must be cultivated.

As a side note, God is not raising up "doom and gloom prophets" who will pronounce judgment over you. He will send and align "groom and bloom prophets" who will be instruments and means of your spiritual investment, development, and growth. This is key to your maturation and matriculation through the prophetic realms. It will take a concerted effort and personal investment in your own spiritual growth to labor with those whom God has aligned your destiny with key mantles to unlock things in you to see you prosper and succeed. God will send you senior prophets with mantles with unusual mastery, expertise, experience, and encounters to equip you. We need not only prophetic teachers but prophetic trainers as well.

Now let me get back to the importance of having leaders impart and implant in the dynamic of prophetic presbytery. The prophetic presbytery serves to plant and water supernaturally those whom God wants through prophecy and laying on of the hands. Prophecy and the laying on of hands are ways we can impart and implant spiritual things in the life of the believers.

Look at this following example of Paul revealing a spiritual truth regarding the agricultural aspect of the function of the apostolic and prophetic:

> For when one says, "I follow Paul," and another, "I follow Apollos," are you not mere human beings? What, after all, is Apollos? And what is Paul? Only servants, through whom you came to believe—as the Lord has assigned to each his task. I planted the seed, Apollos watered it, but God has been making it grow. So neither the one who plants nor the one who waters is anything, but only God, who makes things grow. The one who plants and the one who waters have one purpose, and they will each be rewarded according to their own labor (1 Corinthians 3:4-8 NIV).

In Dr. Bill Hamon's book *Prophets and Personal Prophecy Volume 1*, on page 54 he provides us with four functions the prophetic presbytery serves regarding various sets of qualifications both in the presbyters and in the candidates receiving prophetic presbytery:

1. Prophetic revelation and confirmation of those called to leadership ministry in the church.

2. Ordination to the fivefold ministry. This is the laying on of hands for authorization and recognition as an ordained minister of God.

3. Confirmation and activation of membership ministries in the body of Christ.

4. Progress in Christian maturity.

The practice and act of the laying on of hands in the New Testament is the fourth of the six doctrines of Christ that people must experience in their spiritual maturation:

> *Therefore, leaving the discussion of the elementary principles of Christ, let us go on to perfection, not laying again the foundation of repentance from dead works and the faith toward God, of the doctrines of baptisms, of laying on of hands, of resurrection of the dead, and of eternal judgment* (Hebrews 6:1-2).

PROPHETIC PRESBYTERY POWER

A prophetic presbytery is composed of a council or group of presbyters (elders) of a local church who are made up of apostles and prophets who have at least the resident gift of prophecy. It is at best composed of an eldership of prophets or prophetic leaders with prophetic anointing and prophetic insight. The nature of prophetic presbytery is held by the leadership of the church during set times of ordination or seasons for the presbyters to lay hands on and prophesy over selected believers to speak the mind, will, and secret plans of God over them, impart gifts, and graces, and to release them into their membership ministries. The presbyters do not have to necessarily be from the local church where the presbytery is being conducted; leaders can call in qualified and trusted prophetic presbyters from other churches and ministries to conduct the presbytery.

THE PROPHETIC PRESBYTERY VS. THE OFFICE OF THE PROPHET

It is important to note that the prophetic presbytery does not replace or eliminate the necessity for the individual office of the prophet. Both the prophetic presbytery and the office of the prophet are equally valuable in the realm of the prophetic, but their strength and functionality cannot be ignored or brushed over in terms of when the prophetic presbytery is needed and when is the time and season for the summoning of the prophet. The prophetic presbytery and the office of the prophetic are higher degrees of prophetic function; but without question, the strength, weight, caliber, and scope in the office of the prophet is in a class of its own.

The office of the prophet is the master in the realms of the prophetic. This office is indisputably full of God's most trusted conduits and ancient ministries of ordination, coronation, and inauguration of His anointed. All ministers and others in church leadership, whether they are apostles, evangelists, pastors, teachers, ministers of the gospel, deacons, etc., can exercise their faith and speak a word of prophecy over individuals while functioning as a presbytery team member. However, only a prophet can minister and function heavily in that prophetic realm and dimension ordained and set apart for the office of the prophet. In other words, the prophet has within the power and authority to ordain and set someone into their membership ministry and office. The office prophet is the prophetic presbytery in one person.

The prophet's mantle and ministry are, in truth, divinely authorized to function in all the realms of the prophetic presbytery for starters, as well as to fulfill the ministry office of the prophet in the New Testament. We will discuss this further in the chapter regarding the highest dimension in the realms of the prophetic—the office of the prophet. The prophet is an automatic qualifier to be a presbyter, by right, as one of their functions in the office. He or she can participate as one of the presbyters or they can do it singlehandedly. Prophets are anointed to do on an individual basis all that the prophetic presbytery does as a team.

One distinct variable in function, however, is that the prophetic presbytery is given the honor of extending formal and final ordination to a ministry or church. What do I mean regarding the distinction in function of the prophetic presbytery and the office prophet? The office prophet, mouthpiece, and oracle of God may reveal a person's call to fivefold ministry, and lay his or her hands on the person to anoint him or her for it; however, the ordination aspect is performed by the presbytery. The prophetic presbytery is called in for special and formal ceremonies and ordination. Yes, a council of prophets is part of that ceremony, but it is done as a team and not by a single prophet.

The prophetic presbytery is when two or more prophets and or prophetic ministers lay hands on and prophesy over individuals at a specified time and place. Dr. Bill Hamon defines the purpose and reasons "prophetic presbytery" are conducted in the followingr:

- Revealing a church member's membership ministry in the body of Christ.

- Ministering a prophetic rhema word of God to individuals.

- Impartation and activation of divinely ordained gifts, graces, and callings.

- Revelation, clarification, and confirmation of leadership ministry in the local church.

- "Laying on of hands and prophecy" over those called and properly prepared to be ordained fivefold ministers.

God Himself, in the beginning before He created man in His own image, took council with Himself. He created man, ordained him, and blessed him. He said, *"Let Us make man in Our image."* This was a type or picture of a prophetic presbytery of Adam and Eve being ordained with dominion by the Godhead Presbytery or Divine Council of Prophecy.

> *Then God said, "**Let Us make man in Our image**, according to Our likeness; let them have dominion over the fish of the sea, over the birds of the air, and over the cattle, over all the*

earth and over every creeping thing that creeps on the earth."
*So **God created man in His own image; in the image of
God He created him; male and female He created them.
Then God blessed them**, and God said to them, "Be fruitful
and multiply; fill the earth and subdue it; have dominion over
the fish of the sea, over the birds of the air, and over every living
thing that moves on the earth"* (Genesis 1:26-28).

CHAPTER 12

THE OFFICE OF THE PROPHET

The Sixth Dimension of the Prophetic Realm

And He Himself [Christ] *gave some to be apostles, some prophets, some evangelists, and some pastors and teachers.*
—EPHESIANS 4:11

The sixth dimension of the realm of the prophetic is the "office of the prophet" or "office of prophecy." The office of the prophet is the highest realm in prophetic function and operation. This realm of the prophetic is for believers who have moved into the highest measure, degree, and dimension of prophetic activity that is beyond the realms of the spirit of prophecy, gift of prophecy, and prophetic anointing.

The office and ministry of the prophet encompasses all of the prophetic dimensions in the person of the man or woman of God. The office of the prophet is for those who are called and summoned by God to this ministry. It is a special and sovereign calling and commission to the office of prophecy. The office of the prophecy is not just a function—it is lifestyle. A prophet is who they are and not just what they do. A prophet is a mouthpiece, spokesperson, oracle, and voice of God who speaks by divine inspiration and authority to edify, build up, encourage, and strengthen the body of Christ.

It was the zeal of Moses prophetically that all of God's people were prophets: *"But Moses replied, 'Are you jealous for my sake? I wish that all of the Lord's people were prophets and that the Lord would put his Spirit on them!'"* (Numbers 11:29 NIV).

The office of the prophet carried the greatest anointing, authority and responsibility in the realm of the prophetic. A prophet has a stronger utterance and has the grace to go beyond the realm of edification, exhortation, and comfort. This office is a gift extension of Christ Himself as the Prophet. The office of the prophet is anointed and authorized to operate in a higher realm than the one who is endowed with the Holy Spirit's gift of prophecy and operates on the level of the prophetic Spirit. Because the prophetic ministry is often in the spotlight and highly coveted due to the extraordinary gifting and anointing and attraction, there is an overwhelming tendency in the body of Christ to exalt this gift above the other ministry gifts cited in Ephesians 4:11.

Due to this tendency, there has been an increase of deception, abuse, manipulation, doctrinal error, mismanagement, and miseducation regarding the practice of the prophetic today. There has been an elevation of people who function in the ministry of the prophet and a celebrity-type nature that is now associated with the prophetic office over the other gifts—that is a critical error. All of the gifts are needed to bring clarity, truth, power, balance, equipping, and maturity to the body of Christ.

There are three major prophetic offices in the Bible:

1. Prophet—*Nabi,* official prophet and spokesperson (1 Samuel 9:9 and 1 Chronicles 29:29)

2. Seer—*Rō'eh, Ra'ah,* seer realm; *Chozeh,* seer-visionary realm (1 Samuel 9:9)

3. Dreamer—*Chalown,* night visionary realm (Genesis 37:19 and Acts 2:17)

Key Functions of the Office of Prophecy

The following is a list of a few of the key functions and facts about the office of the prophet and prophecy in the New Testament:

- Prophets are only called by God and the office is a special governmental position given by Christ's gift (Ephesians 4:7-12 and 1 Corinthians 12:28). This is a specialized calling by Christ, the head of the Church, not a developmental spiritual gift given by the Holy Spirit. The gift of prophecy is not the same as the office of the prophet or office of prophecy. It is a sovereign calling. Having the gift of prophecy does not make someone a prophet; but those who are called to the office of the prophet will function in the gift of prophecy.

- Prophets are foundational ministries and they are instrumental in building upon the foundational truths of the Church and Jesus Christ (Ephesians 2:20-22 and Ephesians 3).

- Office prophets have been recognized by the church and have authorization by God through the affirmation of the leadership (eldership) of the church to engage in public ministry.

- They have gone through extensive training and multiple encounters with the presence of God.

- They have a proven creditability in the prophetic, which has been established with a proven track record of ministering accurate and seasoned prophecies, wisdom, and the purposes of God in steering the body of Christ.

- They will be ministers of the supernatural where they move into greater realms of hearing God, speaking things into existence or manifestation and being His mouthpiece and spokesperson.

- They call and gather believers to prayer and intercession.

- Prophets in this realm of the prophetic will see into the motives of people's hearts, the secret or hidden things, identify spiritual gifts, ministry callings, graces, mantles, and the purposes of God.

- These prophets have the authority and latitude to give direction or steering, correction, alignment, adjustment, and rebuke to churches; while in the process, they build up the body of Christ. Prophets are spiritual builders.

- Prophets will equip the church for supernatural ministry and their primary function is to equip believers in the prophetic. They will release the grace that is upon them onto others to function and operate in the gifts of: prophecy, word of knowledge, word of wisdom, and discerning of spirits, which are the revelatory gifts of the prophet out of the manifestation of the Spirit.

- Prophets will speak to churches, communities, cities, regions, and nations.

- A prophet's words will be heard by those in authority— church leaders, presidents, prime ministers, heads of states, kings, and governmental officials, politicians.

- Their words will be accompanied by signs and wonders in the realm of healing miracles, signs of the supernatural presence, and the glory of God.

- Prophets will equip the church in spiritual warfare and release strategies that will bring spiritual breakthroughs and victory over the demonic, diabolical, and demonic and satanic attacks. They will teach the church how to *shamar,* guard against spiritual attacks.

- The office of the prophet is local and trans-local, para-church ministry. They are itinerant and travel to different churches, cities, territories, regions, and nations according to their specific ministry assignment and commission.

NEW TESTAMENT DEFINITION OF PROPHET

The English word "prophet" in Strong's Concordance comes from the Greek *prophetes,* or *profetes,* which signifies, in classical Greek, one who speaks for another, especially one who speaks for a god, and so interprets his will to man; hence its essential meaning is "an interpreter." The New American Standard New Testament Greek Lexicon, according to the Bible Study Tools online definition of the word "prophet" in Greek writings, is an interpreter of oracles or of other hidden things. One who is moved by the Spirit of God as His spokesman, hence His organ who solemnly declares what he has received by inspiration, especially concerning future events, and things related to the Kingdom of God and to human salvation.

The word "prophesy" in the Greek is *propheteuō* and means "to foretell events, divine, speak under inspiration, exercise the prophetic office; to proclaim a divine revelation, prophesy, to foretell the future; to speak forth by divine inspiration; to break forth under sudden impulse in lofty discourse or in praise of the divine counsels." Prophet both in the Old and New Testaments were called and sent by God.

In the New Testament example, Jesus mentions sending prophets and apostles by the wisdom of God in Luke 11:49: *"Therefore the wisdom of God also said, 'I will send them prophets and apostles, and some of them they will kill and persecute.'"*

NEW TESTAMENT PROPHETS

In the New Testament there were prophets who were key and instrumental to the church. The ancient ministry of the prophet took on a distinctive role in the New Testament of expanding the Old Testament's ministry of building, edifying, encouraging, training, equipping, and steering the church. The following is an example of New Covenant prophets who exhorted and strengthened the believers and the churches by many words, teaching, and preaching the Word of the Lord, such as Judas and Silas:

> *Now Judas and Silas, themselves being prophets also, exhorted and strengthened the brethren with many words....And he went through Syria and Cilicia, strengthening the churches* (Acts 15:32,41).

There were prophets in the New Testament who foretold and unfolded things of the future. We can see an example of foretelling in the prophetic ministry of Agabus the prophet who saw in the Spirit that Paul would be bound by the Jews at Jerusalem:

> *And as we stayed many days, a certain prophet named Agabus came down from Judea. When he had come to us, he took Paul's belt, bound his own hands and feet, and said, "Thus says the Holy Spirit, 'So shall the Jews at Jerusalem bind the man who owns this belt, and deliver him into the hands of the Gentiles'"* (Acts 21:10-11).

Prophets were functioning and operating in the office of prophecy. This role and function of the office of prophet was a very active part of the local church. The following is an example of one of the active roles of the prophet in the New Testament with respect to identifying, setting, ordaining, releasing, and commissioning apostolic and prophetic ministries to which they are called by the Spirit.

Note: The Holy Spirit in the New Testament is instrumental in calling His fivefold ministry gifts. The fivefold ministry is regarded commonly today as "Post Ascension Gifts of Christ" according to Ephesians 4:7-11. Christ calls these ministry gifts directly by the Holy Spirit as the church recognizes and affirms it. Certain prophets in the New Testament were instrumental in appointing or setting apart Barnabas and Saul who were called to apostolic ministry at the church at Antioch:

> *Now in the church that was at Antioch there were certain prophets and teachers: Barnabas, Simeon who was called Niger,*

Lucius of Cyrene, Manaen who had been brought up with Herod the tetrarch, and Saul. As they ministered to the Lord and fasted, the Holy Spirit said, "Now separate to Me Barnabas and Saul for the work to which I have called them." Then, having fasted and prayed, and laid hands on them, they sent them away (Acts 13:1-3).

APOSTOLIC AND PROPHETIC TEAMS

In the Acts 13 example, we see a separation and sending out by the Holy Spirit for team ministry. The prophets in the church at Antioch were ministering to the Lord and fasting, and the Holy Spirit instructed these prophets and teachers who were presumed to be part of the prophetic presbytery in establishing Barnabas and Saul's apostolic ministries. We can see that they laid hands on them and sent them away by commissioning them to do the apostolic work. In Acts 13:1 and 2, the prophets and teachers together were given divine direction concerning Barnabas and Saul.

In most of the New Testament ministry, men moved in apostolic team ministries. Jesus our Lord Himself sent His twelve disciples out two by two and gave them power over impure spirits (Mark 6:7) and the "seventy two" in Luke 10:1 (NIV) when it says, *"After this the Lord appointed seventy-two others and sent them two by two ahead of him to every town and place where he was about to go."*

According to these verses, we can see that even in the gospel the prophetic blueprint by Christ was fully executed in the early church by Paul who moved in apostolic teams. Team ministry was a great emphasis of apostle Paul with respect to his apostolic mission. The majority of his apostolic ministry was with his ministry companions and team of prophets. This apostolic and prophetic ministry was a very powerful team in the Book of the Acts of the Apostles. Barnabas and Paul were sent out of Antioch together, inspired by the Holy Spirit. This was the mind of God with regard to the apostolic work and mission. The apostle and prophet, being a foundational ministry, were necessary for the advancing, mobilizing, and building of the church of God.

We know that Paul was an apostle, and we are led to believe that Barnabas was a prophet in the early church; but many believe that both Paul and Barnabas were apostles, but Barnabas had more of a prophetic function as a prophet. He would be considered in some streams as a prophetic apostle or an apostolic prophet.

Barnabas's name suggests that he was a prophet with an apostolic function in Acts 4:36: *"And Joses, who was also named Barnabas by the apostles (which is translated Son of Encouragement), a Levite of the country of Cyprus."*

The King James Version says, *"And Joses, who by the apostles was surnamed Barnabas (which is, being interpreted, The son of consolation), a Levite, and of the country of Cyprus."*

Barnabas' name means son of encouragement and consolation, which is indicative of the prophetic ministry that is to encourage and to console. Barnabas's name was given by the apostles who interpreted his name to accurately mean "son of prophecy" that spoke relatively to the prophetic ministry. By this we are led to concede that Barnabas was the prophet and Paul was the apostle on the team. They went out together as apostle and prophet, ministering as a team in establishing, encouraging, strengthening, and building local churches. There were times when Silas, a prophet, would be chosen by Paul to join his apostolic team because of the recommendation of the brethren and the grace of God on his life to assist in confirming the churches (see Acts 15:40-41).

Prophets are prophetic to the bone as evidenced in 2 Kings 13:20-21:

> *Then Elisha died, and they buried him. And the raiding bands from Moab invaded the land in the spring of the year. So it was, as they were burying a man, that suddenly they spied a band of raiders; and they put the man in the tomb of Elisha; and when the man was let down and touched the bones of Elisha, he revived and stood on his feet.*

The foundational ministries of apostles and prophets are aligned perfectly with Christ our Cornerstone in the church, where He has laid the foundational ministry blueprint of the apostle and prophet. Jesus Christ set what the apostolic and prophetic ministry is in the body of Christ. The office of the prophet and prophecy is a foundational ministry of the church. God has set and appointed them in His church according to 1 Corinthians 12:27-28:

> *Now you are the body of Christ, and members individually. And God has appointed these in the church: first apostles, second prophets, third teachers, after that miracles, then gifts of healings, helps, administrations, varieties of tongues.*

THE 5G's FIVEFOLD HOUSEHOLD MINISTRY FUNCTION

The following is a brief overview of the governmental offices in the church. Included is a short description of the roles in the body of Christ, giving understanding and assistance in receiving their ministry into our lives. The functions and role of the fivefold ministry of apostle, prophet, evangelist, pastor (shepherd) and teacher in the building process of the household of God:

1. Apostles Govern
2. Prophets Guide
3. Evangelists Gather
4. Pastors Guard
5. Teachers Ground

ROLE OF THE NEW TESTAMENT PROPHET IN THE CHURCH

Prophets are set permanently in rank and divine order in the New Testament church according to the following:

- Prophets are set and appointed in a position, office, and order in the church.

- Prophets are second in rank and order in the church.

- Prophets are governmental ministries.

And God has appointed [set] *these in the church: first apostles, second prophets, third teachers, after that miracles, then gifts of healings, helps, administrations, varieties of tongues* (1 Corinthians 12:28).

God has chosen to build His church by using apostles and prophets as the master builders, who we would call general contractors today (see 1 Corinthians 3:10). God has "set" apostles first in rank and second, prophets. Prophets are the second highest-ranking officers in His church and this setting is primarily in God's divine order of government.

The word "set" refers to permanence, to set as concrete; immutable and unchangeable. God set this ministry gift in His church permanently and He has not changed the order of His governmental offices. Some today dismiss the role, function, and relevancy of the ministry of the apostles and prophets. However, God's inspired Holy Scriptures refute and rebuke such a claim; and as long as there is the church of Jesus Christ, the vital role of the apostles and prophets will have a place in the building up of the body of Christ in every successive generation. Apostles and prophets are generational ministries along with the other fivefold ministry gifts. Prophets are ministry gifts to the church.

Christ gave the prophets to the church as a gift. The main function of a prophet is to equip the saints to do the work of service. The prophet equips the church with eyes to see and ears to hear. The grace that prophets carry can literally cause people to be able to hear the voice of the Spirit. Prophets have the authority to correct and direct because they are part of the government of God. Prophets represent the following in the New Testament role in the office to the church:

And He Himself gave some to be apostles, some prophets, some evangelists, and some pastors and teachers, for the equipping of the saints for the work of the ministry, for the edifying of the body of Christ, till we all come in the unity of the faith and of the knowledge of the Son of God, to a perfect man, to the measure of the stature of the fullness of Christ (Ephesians 4:11-13).

The prophet is the foundation ministry of the New Testament church in the following that helps the church become a habitation of God on earth:

Now, therefore, you are no longer strangers and foreigners, but fellow citizens with the saints and members of the household of God, having been built on the foundation of the apostles and prophets, Jesus Christ Himself being the chief cornerstone, in whom the whole building, being fitted together, grows into a holy temple in the Lord, in whom you also are being built together for a dwelling place of God in the Spirit (Ephesians 2:19-22).

Prophets are supernatural ministers of revelations, secrets, and mysteries of God in the following. Prophets and apostles have phenomenal grace to reveal, unlock, and unpack revelation. They function in the revelatory realm:

For this reason I, Paul, the prisoner of Christ Jesus for the sake of you Gentiles—Surely you have heard about the administration of God's grace that was given to me for you, that is, the mystery made known to me by revelation, as I have already written briefly. In reading this, then, you will be able to understand my insight into the mystery of Christ, which was not made known to people in other generations as it has now been revealed by the Spirit to God's holy apostles and prophets (Ephesians 3:1-5 NIV).

Prophets are revelators of the mind, will, heart, and intent of God. They reveal the very secrets and counsels of God. Prophets are secret counselors of God and minister from the unseen realm: *"Surely, the Lord God does nothing, unless He reveals His secret to His servants the prophets"* (Amos 3:7).

Prophets have the grace to impart a dimension of the prophetic that is upon them into other Christian believers such as the gift of prophecy and other spiritual gifts through prophecy and the laying on of the hands and by the prophetic leadership or biblically correct eldership of the church in the following: *"Do not neglect the gift that is in you, which was given to you by prophecy with the laying on of the hands of the eldership* [presbytery]" (1 Timothy 4:14).

The prophetic office has the ability to impart spiritual and prophetic gifts through the laying of hands according to the following: *"Therefore, I remind you to stir up the gift of God which is in you through the laying on of my hands"* (2 Timothy 1:6).

The ministry office of the apostle and prophet long to impart and implant spiritual gifts into their spiritual sons and daughters in the same way that Paul longed to impart spiritual gift to his son in the gospel, Timothy, in order to establish and strengthen him: *"I long to see you, that I may impart to you some spiritual gift to make you strong"* (Romans 1:11 NIV).

CHAPTER 13

THE OFFICE OF THE PROPHETESS

The Seventh Dimension of the Prophetic Realm

Now this man had four virgin daughters who prophesied.
—ACTS 21:9

The realm and office of the prophetess is the highest prophetic dimension for women in prophetic ministry. The term "prophetess" is simply a female prophet. There has been much debate and controversy over the role of women in prophetic ministry today. The primary question is, can a woman function in the role and office of a prophet? The answer is yes, *absolutely!* A woman can function in the role of a prophet today just as a man can function in the role of a prophet. The role and function of the prophetess is not a lesser role and function compared to a male prophet.

There is still controversy in some denominations, circles, streams, and movements about women in church leadership roles such as elders, pastors, bishops, and even apostles. It is important to follow what the Scriptures teach and reveal regarding this topic when considering the entirety of the Bible. There are a number of Scriptures that support the ministry of women in the history of the Bible and in the New Testament church as well. God placed certain women in key, prominent leadership roles such as a judge (Judges 4:4), shepherdess (Genesis 29:9), and deaconess (Romans 16:1) and for these purposes, the office of the prophetess.

The vast majority of scriptural prophesies were delivered by men, but that doesn't mean women didn't prophesy. In fact, the Lord's covenant people have been saved many times by a spiritually in-tune daughter of God. And though many women, including Rebekah, Hannah, Elisabeth, and Mary all prophesied, there are only a few who were actually designated as prophetesses in the Bible.

In the New Testament ministry of the prophetic, we see in the following two Scriptures women being used to prophesy. The spirit prophecy, gift of prophecy, and the office of prophecy is not just for men, but also for women who prophesy:

> And it shall come to pass in the last days, says God, that I will pour out of My Spirit on all flesh; your **sons and daughters shall prophesy....** And on My **menservants** and on My **maidservants** I will pour out of My Spirit in those days; and **they shall prophesy** (Acts 2:17-18).

> On the next day we who were Paul's companions departed and came to Caesarea, and entered the house of Philip the evangelist, who was one of the seven, and stayed with him. Now this man had four virgin **daughters who prophesied** (Acts 21:8-9).

Women can prophesy!

Many Bible scholars and theologians have ignorantly or erroneously misinterpreted the role and ministry function of women in the New Testament in order to silence the voice of women. They use these two verses by Paul in 1 Corinthians 14:34-35 to support their erroneous beliefs:

> Let your women keep silent in the churches, for they are not permitted to speak; but they are to be submissive, as the law also says. And if they want to learn something, let them ask their own husbands at home; for it is shameful for women to speak in church.

These two verses have created much confusion and indictment against the voice of the prophetess. It is my strong opinion that this way of thinking is of the enemy through cultural issues between gender roles inside and outside the church and through male chauvinism that Paul's intent has been misinterpreted. Unfortunately, if these verses are read without context and historical background the theory is validated. However, this is not quite the meaning Paul was sending to the Corinthians.

Paul was establishing apostolic order in the church of Corinth with respect to the operation and function of the spiritual gifts, the function of the prophecy and tongues, the order of prophets speaking in public settings, and of course the function of women speaking in the local church with respect to prophesying. This was not a universal and strict mandate for all churches in the New Testament, Paul was providing apostolic oversight and governance over the operation of gifts. It was important for him to set order and guidelines in this particular local body of believers.

The church at Corinth was a very charismatic and spiritually gifted church—and there was no orderly and decent flow of the Spirit. Certain women were out of order in disruptively asking questions publicly in the already chaotic service with all of the tongue talkers, prophetic utterances, and mixed cultural expression of spiritual activity. There needed to be some regulations to their free-for-all, anything-goes services. The prophets, tongues-speakers, and women needed to submit to the apostolic commandments given by the apostle Paul. He stated in 1 Corinthians 14:37-40 (NIV):

> *If anyone thinks they are a prophet or otherwise gifted by the Spirit, let them acknowledge that what I am writing to you is the Lord's command. But if anyone ignores this, they will themselves be ignored. Therefore, my brothers and sisters, be eager to prophesy, and do not forbid speaking in tongues. But **everything should be done in a fitting and orderly way.***

There are those today who have taken this commandment for the Corinthian women in that culture of that day and made it an absolute prohibition and even an indictment on any activity of prophesying or ministry of a woman in the church. God used women in the Old Testament, and the New Testament is no different; in fact, women tend to have an enhanced role. Paul was not saying women cannot speak or be used in the realm of praying and prophesying in the churches of the saints.

We can see from the following example that women in the New Testament church did in fact pray and prophesy: *"But every woman who prays or prophesies with her head uncovered dishonors her head, for that is one and the same as if her head were shaved"* (1 Corinthians 11:5). A married woman who uncovered her head in public would have brought shame on her husband and it dishonored him. The action may have connoted sexual availability or may have been an indication and sign of being unmarried. Culturally, a woman in that time who did not wear a head covering indicated to men that she was unmarried and available. It is similar in many cultures today if wives do not wear a wedding ring, people assume she is unmarried and available. In other words, in cultures where women's head coverings are not a sign of being married, wives do not need to cover their heads in worship, but they could obey this command by wearing some other physical symbol of being married, such as the wedding ring.

The key point is wives are to honor their husbands even when praying and prophesying in the local church. And if they have a question, they should ask their husbands when they get home instead of disrupting the service or shouting out questions, which is a sign of lack of submission to headship, leadership, and those in authority. It is important to understand the culture and who Paul was talking to in the context of the Scripture. This Scripture is taken out of context when it is used as the basis for the Scripture. This Scripture is taken out of context when it is used as the basis for the absolute prohibition and restriction of women today. Paul was given as an apostle to that body of believers to guide them apostolically; yet today we preserve the Spirit of the letter to Corinthians for churches in this hour.

Gender Difference—Same Prophetic Office

In the Old Testament, women were also divinely inspired of the Lord to prophesy in their generation. They were called prophetesses. The term "prophet" is unisex and can also describe a woman in the prophetic office. However, a male prophet cannot and must not be referred to as a prophetess. This term and title are clearly designated for a woman in the office of prophecy.

Different Gender—Same Prophetic Function

I have heard some women prefer to be called prophet instead of prophetess because culturally they feel that being called a prophetess is a lesser degree, role, and function of their office compared to a male prophet. They think that being called a prophet culturally makes them equal to a male prophet and gives them more spiritual authority. That is sadly not the case; but in fact, I believe if a woman who tries to function outside of who she is as a woman to compete with a man is clearly operating in a lesser authority and grace.

Some say there is no gender in the spiritual, but there is. The Spirit of God functions specifically in male and female respectfully, and there should not be any confusion in that regard. The function of the prophet is the same in both male and female. The woman prophet has the same authority as the male prophet.

The Holy Spirit does not function more or less in one gender than He would in the other gender. He shows no favoritism, therefore women should embrace fully the office of the prophetess because there is a certain grace and anointing that women possess that men will never comprehend; women see with a different set of lenses and vice versa. In fact, in most cases, female prophets are more sensitive and apt to worship openly and more expressively than male prophets. It does not mean the male prophet is not sensitive to the Spirit, men are just genetically wired different—but ultimately the Spirit can use both genders for God's glory. There are gender differences but the same Spirit operating powerfully in both the prophet and the prophetess.

THE REALM AND VOICE OF THE PROPHETESS

The following are some Old and New Testament examples of women prophets and the impact that women's prophetic voices bring to the prophetic ministry.

Miriam

Miriam the prophetess, the sister of Moses and Aaron, was assigned to watch Moses when he lay as a baby in the bulrushes. She was Moses's older sibling whose prophetic gifting and expression was in the realm of music and dance. She sang the song of the Lord and used the art of prophetic dance: ***"Miriam the prophetess,*** *the sister of Aaron, took the timbrel in her hand; and all the women when out after her with timbrels and with dances"* (Exodus 15:20).

The Lord spoke directly to Miriam and Aaron when they took pride in their prophetic gifts—and He cursed Miriam with leprosy. They usurped their authority in thinking that they were equal in rank as prophets with Moses. It was against God's constituted authority stated in Numbers 12:1-16. Miriam is later named as one of the three who helped and played a prominent role in delivering the children of Israel out of Egypt: *"For I brought you up from the land of Egypt, I redeemed you from the house of bondage; and I sent before you Moses, Aaron, and Miriam"* (Micah 6:4).

Deborah

Deborah, a prophetess, wife, and the fourth judge in Israel was a prophetic judge who was directed by the Lord to know when to go to battle, helping to liberate the kingdom from the subjugation of a foreign king. Israel came to her to settle judicial and civil disputes. It is the role of the prophet to settle disputes and to judge righteously.

> ***Deborah, a prophetess,*** *the wife of Lapidoth, was judging Israel at that time. And she would sit under the palm tree of Deborah between Ramah and Bethel in the mountains of Ephraim. And the children of Israel came up to her for judgment* (Judges 4:4-5).

Deborah's emergence and role as a mother in Israel came as a result of the lack of life in the village. She arose prophetically as a judge to overrule and spiritually overturn the lack of life. Prophets as spiritual judges can overturn in the spirit things that will bring life and new birth in the womb of the spirit: *"Village life ceased, it ceased in Israel, until I, Deborah, arose, arose a mother in Israel"* (Judges 5:7).

Huldah

Huldah was a wife and a prophetess whom God used to prophesy and teach the Word of the Lord in Jerusalem; she lived in the time of righteous King Josiah. Huldah the prophetess was also the keeper of the king's wardrobe and prophesied that the wicked people of Judah would feel the wrath of God, but that Josiah the king would be blessed because of his humility before the Lord.

King Josiah discovered the Book of the Law and realized that the wrath of God was upon his people because his forefathers did not obey the word of the Lord. Therefore, he sent men to the prophetess Huldah to inquire of the Lord about the impending judgment upon Israel:

> *"Go, inquire of the Lord for me, and for those who are left in Israel and Judah, concerning the words of the book that is found; for great is the wrath of the Lord that is poured out on us, because our fathers have not kept the word of the Lord, to do according to all that is written in this book." So Hilkiah and those the king had appointed went to* **Huldah the prophetess,** *the wife of Shallum the son of Tokhath, the son of Hasrah, keeper of the wardrobe. (She dwelt in Jerusalem in the Second Quarter.) And they spoke to her to that effect. Then she answered them, "Thus says the Lord God of Israel, 'Tell the man who sent you to Me'"* (2 Chronicles 34:21-23).

> *So Hilkiah the priest, Ahikam, Achbor, Shaphan, and Asaiah went to* **Huldah the prophetess,** *the wife of Shallum the son of Tikvah, the son of Harhas, keeper of the wardrobe. (She dwelt in Jerusalem in the Second Quarter. And they spoke with her* (2 Kings 22:14).

Isaiah's Wife

Isaiah the prophet considered his wife. There is little information about Isaiah's wife other than Isaiah calls her "the prophetess" and bore him children who were named by the Lord. Therefore, husband and wife can both be prophets. Today some married prophets minister together or separately, *"Then I went to the prophetess, and she conceived and bore a son. Then the Lord said to me, 'Call his name Maher-Shalal-Hash-Baz'"* (Isaiah 8:3).

Anna

Anna was an 84-year-old widow who was prophetess and intercessor. She fasted and prayed for the coming of the Messiah. She was a prophetic intercessor who through relentless praying and fasting, without departing the temple, saw the manifestation of the Lord. She is a picture of the intercessory prophet. Prophets are to pray without ceasing, and intercession is an aspect of the ministry office of the prophet. The realm of intercession is key to things being birthed and manifested. Anna was present when Jesus was brought to the temple as a baby.

There is mantle of intercession by prophets who serve God in prophetic prayer and fasting who will not relent until they see manifestations of God. There are mothers in Zion who commit their lives to prayer as prayer warriors and intercessors. Mothers in Zion will prophetically conceive and will become birthers in the realm of the Spirit and carry it until the manifestation. The following example is an example regarding the intercessory mantle of the prophetess Anna who was about to bear witness to the manifestation of the Messiah:

> *Now there was one, **Anna, a prophetess**, the daughter of Phanuel, of the tribe of Asher. She was of a great age, and had lived with a husband seven years from her virginity; and this woman was a widow of about eighty-four years, who did not depart from the temple, but served God with fastings and prayers night and day. And coming in that instant she gave thanks to the Lord, and spoke of Him to all those who looked for redemption in Jerusalem* (Luke 2:36-38).

PROPHETIC TYPES OF WOMEN

The following are a few more key women in the Bible who were used as prophetic types or women who were prophetic in nature.

Jael's Prophetic Mantle

Jael, the wife of Heber, took her mantle (rug) to cover and hide Sisera, the commander of the army who had recently escaped for his life, the casualty of war, and hid in her tent. The prophetic mantle was used as a strategy, a plan to cover and protect Sisera from death by assassins. But Deborah the prophetess prophesied to Barak declaring that the Lord had delivered Sisera into his hands (Judges 4:14). The Lord routed Sisera and all his chariots and all his army, where he fled on foot. He found himself at the tent of Jael.

See what the prophetic mantle of Jael was able to accomplish under the prophetic word of Deborah the prophetess in Judges 4:17-22:

> *However, Sisera had fled away on foot to the tent of Jael, the wife of Heber the Kenite; for there was peace between Jabin king of Hazor and the house of Heber the Kenite. And Jael went out to meet Sisera, and said to him, "Turn aside, my lord, turn aside to me; do not fear." And when he had turned aside with her into the tent, she covered him with a blanket [mantle]. Then he said to her, "Please give me a little water to drink, for I am thirsty." So she opened a jug of milk, gave him a drink, and covered him. And he said to her, "Stand at the door of the tent, and if any man comes and inquires of you, and says, 'Is there any man here?' you shall say, 'No.' "Then Jael, Heber's wife, took a tent peg and took a hammer in her hand, and went softly to him and drove the peg into his temple, and it went down into the ground; for he was fast asleep and weary. So he died. And then, as Barak pursued Sisera, Jael came out to meet him, and said to him, "Come, I will show you the man whom you seek." And when he went into her tent, there lay Sisera, dead with the peg in his temple.*

I love the prophetic word that John Eckhardt wrote in his book, *The Prophet's Manual*, regarding the Jael anointing saying:

> This is a prophetic word God gave me for women using the example of Jael driving a nail through the head of Sisera. Then Jael the wife of Heber took a peg and a hammer in her hand and went quietly to him, for he was fast asleep and tired. She drove the tent peg into his temple, and it went down into the ground, so he did (Judges 4:21).
>
> Hit the nail on the head means "to get to the precise point; to do or say something exactly right; to be accurate; to hit the mark; to detect and expose (a lie, scandal, etc.)." Prophetic women, get ready to "hit the nail on the head." Your prophetic utterances will "hit the mark."

The following is a list of other women in the Bible who ministered in the prophetic and who had the gift of prophecy:

- Daughters of Zelophehad who were given a prophetic inheritance from fathers. Apostolic fathers will bless and release spiritual inheritance not only to their sons but also their daughters (Numbers 27:1-7)
- Women in the upper room (Acts 1:14)
- Son and daughters (men and women) shall prophesy (Joel 2:28-29; Acts 2:17-18)
- Philip's four daughters prophesied (Acts 21:9)
- Women praying and prophesying in the Corinthian church (1 Corinthians 11:5)

FALSE PROPHETESSES

In the Old and New Testaments, there were false and pseudo prophets who operated outside of the realm of the genuine prophetic. The following examples are women in the Bible who were false prophets:

Noadiah

Noadiah was a false prophetess during the season and time of restoration from the enslavement in Babylon. She joined with others in trying to prevent Nehemiah from rebuilding the walls of Jerusalem. False prophets will try to tear down prophetically what God is trying to build or rebuild. The ministry of the prophet is a building ministry. Genuine prophetic ministry will edify, encourage, and build you up or encourage restoration.

False prophets are agents of discouragement and fear. Nehemiah perceived that God had not sent the false prophet Shemaiah, who was hired to intimidate him into stopping the work of building the wall. There was clearly a conspiracy and inside job against Nehemiah to instigate an evil report about him. Noadiah, the false prophetess, was part of the plot against the work of restoring and building the wall.

In the following biblical example of Nehemiah's discernment of Noadiah, he said of another "prophet" who sought to discourage him that he perceived that God had not sent him.

> *Afterward I came to the house of Shemaiah the son of Delaiah, the son of Mehetabel, who was a secret informer; and he said, "Let us meet together in the house of God, within the temple, and let us close the doors of the temple, for they are coming to kill you; indeed, at night they will come to kill you." And I said, "Should such a man as I flee? And who is there such as I who would go into the temple to save his life? I will not go in!" **Then I perceived that God had not sent him at all**, but that he pronounced this prophecy against me because Tobiah and Sanballat had hired him. For this reason he was hired, that I should be afraid and act that way and sin, so that they might have cause for an evil report, that they might reproach me. My God, remember Tobiah and Sanballat, according to these their works, and the prophetess Noadiah and the rest of the prophets who would have made me afraid (Nehemiah 6:10-14).*

Jezebel

Jezebel was a false prophetess in the Thyatiran branch of the church mentioned in the Book of Revelation: *"Nevertheless I have a few things against you, because you allow that woman Jezebel, who calls herself a prophetess, to teach and seduce My servants to commit sexual immorality and eat things sacrificed to idols"* (Revelation 2:20).

Jezebel is described as a pseudonym for a woman who influenced the church prophetically in Thyatira in the same manner that Jezebel the queen did in the Old Testament. She seduced Jews into idolatry, immorality, and support of false prophets and priests at her table (see 1 Kings 21:25-26).

Jesus deals with the corrupt church for allowing false prophecy, seductive teaching and activities to influence the church. False prophets will corrupt the church with their teaching and spiritual influence. Churches must ward against false prophets and teachings of devils and evil men and women. (See 2 Peter 2.)

Slave Girl

The slave girl mentioned in Acts 16:16 whom Paul and Silas encountered was vexed and possessed with a spirit of divination who had made her masters much profit by fortune telling. The word "divination" comes from the Latin word *divinare* meaning "to foresee" or "to be inspired by a god." To practice divination is to uncover hidden knowledge by supernatural means. It is in the pseudo realm of the supernatural to operate as a prophet or revealer of knowledge. It is associated with occult and demonic practices and involves fortune telling or soothsaying. In ancient times, people used divination to gain knowledge of the future or as a way to make money or profit.

These types of practice are by those who claim to possess supernatural abilities and insight through reading palms, tarot cards, tea leaves, star charts, and more. Practice of divination in any form is a sin and those, even Christians, who seek such open up the demonic realm, sickness, spirits of torments, and spiritual bondages into their lives. Christians should avoid all practice and participation related to divination including fortune telling, astrology, tarot cards, witchcraft, Ouija board games, omens, voodoo, necromancy, and spell casting, just to list a few.

OLD TESTAMENT EXAMPLES AGAINST DIVINATION

We are to avoid the wicked and abominable practices and customs outlined in Deuteronomy 18:9-14:

> *When you come into the land which the Lord your God is giving you, you shall not learn to follow the abominations of those nations. There shall not be found among you anyone who makes his son or his daughter pass through the fire, or one who practices witchcraft, or a soothsayer, or one who interprets omens, or a sorcerer, or one who conjures spells, or a medium, or a spiritist, or one who calls up the dead. For **all who do these things are an abomination to the Lord**, and because of these abominations the Lord your God drives them out from before you. You shall be blameless before the Lord your God. For these nations which you will dispossess listened to soothsayers and diviners; but as for you, the Lord your God has not appointed such for you.*

Samuel the prophet describes King Saul's rebellion as similar to the sin of divination and witchcraft in 1 Samuel 15:23: *"For rebellion is as the sin of witchcraft [divination], and stubbornness is as iniquity and idolatry. Because you have rejected the word of the Lord, He also has rejected you from being king."*

Practicing divination is listed as one of the reasons for Israel's exile in the following example in 2 Kings 17:17-18 (NIV):

> *They sacrificed their sons and daughters in the fire. **They practiced divination** and sought omens and sold themselves to do evil in the eyes of the Lord, arousing his anger. **So the Lord was very angry** with Israel and removed them from his presence. Only the tribe of Judah was left.*

Jeremiah spoke of the false prophets of his day regarding practicing worthless divination, prophesying lying visions and deceptions in Jeremiah 14:14:

> *And the Lord said to me, "The prophets prophesy lies in My name. I have not sent them, commanded them, nor spoken to them; they prophesy to you a false vision,* **divination, a worthless thing, and the deceit of their heart.***"*

New Testament Example of the Spirit of Divination

Paul and Silas encountered the possessed slave girl as they were on their way to prayer. There are those who are operating in the church with the spirit of divination who are false prophetic voices. They are functioning as fortune tellers and using ministry as another means of monetary gain; and sadly, the church has become a for-profit organization through the pseudo prophetic. An increase of "charismatic witchcraft" and "charismatic fortune telling" has leaked into the stream and nature of genuine forth telling and foretelling. Prophetic ministry has become a *for-profit* organization that causes churches to settle as *non-prophet* ministries instead of becoming for-prophet churches and ministries.

> *Now it happened, as we went to prayer, that a certain slave girl possessed with a spirit of divination met us, who brought her masters much profit by fortune-telling* (Acts 16:16).

CHAPTER 14

THE PROPHECY OF SCRIPTURE

The Eighth Dimension of the Prophetic Realm

We also have the prophetic message as something completely reliable, and you will do well to pay attention to it, as to a light shining in a dark place, until the day dawns and the morning star rises in your hearts. Above all, you must understand that no prophecy of Scripture came about by the prophet's own interpretation of things. For prophecy never had its origin in the human will, but prophets, though human, spoke from God as they were carried along by the Holy Spirit.

—2 PETER 1:19-21 NIV

The eighth dimension of the realms of the prophetic is the prophecy of Scripture, which is the highest form of prophecy in the prophetic. Anyone who desires to move into any realm of the prophetic that we previously discussed must understand that this is the most important aspect of all of the prophetic. This is the foundation of all prophetic operation—the written, infallible word of God. It is the very sacred written and documented word of prophecy of God Himself. God Himself inspired the hands of His prophets to pen His words, instructions, prophecy, and intentions. His words were compiled into sixty-six books comprising what is known globally as the Holy Bible or Holy Writ.

This realm of the prophet is the most important of all the dimensions of the prophetic realm. Understanding this dimension will increase the prophetic capacity in all the other realms of the prophetic. This is where the prophetic is born; and if we do not understand the prophecy of Scripture and the Word of God, it will minimize our ability to prophesy with accuracy and with authority. We cannot prophesy beyond the level, degree, and realm of our understanding and interpretation of the Word of God.

Prophets must be extraordinarily studious and able to rightly interpret, divide, and teach biblical truths as told in 2 Timothy 2:15 (KJV): *"Study to shew thyself approved unto God, a workman that needeth not to be ashamed, rightly dividing the word of truth."*

THE REALM OF INFALLIBILITY

In Kevin J. Conner's book *The Church in the New Testament,* he shares some important truths about the "prophecy of Scripture" that we will discuss in this chapter:

> In II Peter 1:19-21 the expression "prophecy of Scripture" is used to refer to the prophetical books of the Old Testament. Because the Scriptures are the inspired Word of God, the prophecy therein must be regarded as inspired and infallible revelation (II Timothy 3:15, 16). This then is the highest degree of prophecy and requires the most careful and systematic interpretation.

Kevin J. Conner is essentially saying and confirming that the prophecy of Scripture is the highest degree of prophecy in the prophetic realm and must be regarded as the absolute word of prophecy as it is the highest authority of God's word. The other dimensions and realms of the prophetic that we have previously discussed in this book are fallible, which means they are subject to human error—but the prophecy of Scripture is infallible. The word "infallible" means incapable of making mistakes or being wrong.

It also means never failing and always effective, according to the Merriam Webster's Dictionary. The infallible word of God written by the prophets in the Old Testament and New Testament by the apostles is unerring, faultless, flawless, impeccable, perfect, precise, accurate, and meticulous.

The realms of the prophetic that we have covered in this book are only true to the degree to which they agree with prophecy of the Bible. All prophetic activity, function, and operation, and importantly any prophecy today, must be in agreement with the Scriptures, both Old and New Testaments. This is the place where we weigh and judge genuine prophecy and prophetic activity in the church. The written Word of God is the most accurate form and nature of prophecy. In fact, the written prophecy and words in the Bible are the most resourceful and most reliable prophet. Prophets today can error and miss it when ministering in the realm of prophecy, but the Scriptures are 100 percent accurate, dependable, certain, trustworthy, unerring, guaranteed, effective, and foolproof.

The Bible is the only infallible prophecy in the Word. Everything that is written in it is pure and complete. In the Book of Revelation, John the apostle wrote the revelation of Jesus Christ and words of His prophecy. The Bible was written in the spirit of prophecy, according to Revelation 19:10 (NIV), *"At this I fell at his feet to worship him. But he said to me, 'Don't do that! I am a fellow servant with you and with your brothers and sisters who hold to the testimony of Jesus. Worship God! For it is the Spirit of prophecy who bears testimony to Jesus.'"* Therefore, all of the Scriptures whether read, taught, or preached carry the spirit of the prophets who have written it for their age and ages to come.

THE *LOGOS* AND *RHEMA* OF GOD

There are two primary words in the Greek that describe the Old and New Testament Scriptures: 1) *logos* and 2) *rhema*. *Logos* and *rhema* are two realms in the prophecy of Scripture that are very important to understand in regard to the other levels of the prophecy. The following passage confirms that all Scripture is given by the inspiration of God:

All Scripture is God-breathed and is useful for teaching, rebuking, correcting and training in righteousness, so that the servant of God may be thoroughly equipped for every good work (2 Timothy 3:16-17 NIV).

God's Word is useful for:

- Teaching (doctrine)
- Reproof or rebuking
- Correction
- Instruction, training in righteousness
- Perfection (completion) and fitting in, having special aptitude for given uses
- Thoroughly furnishing, training, and equipping for all good works

WHAT IS *LOGOS?*

The word *logos* is the Greek term translated as word, speech, principle, or thought. In Greek philosophy, it also referred to as universal, divine reason or the mind of God. *Logos* is simply the entire *written word of God* in the Bible. The word *logos* refers principally to the entire inspired Word of God written by the prophets and apostles—the Bible. The written word of God is the first realm of prophecy. It is God-inspired and breathed upon by the Spirit and provides doctrine, reproof, correction, and instruction in righteousness for humans, according to 2 Timothy 3:16.

The prophecy of Scripture speaks of the revelatory and declaratory elements of the Word of God. It is the highest revelation of God known to humankind. All prophetic utterance, prophecy, and prophetic operation must be judged by the prophecy of Scripture. We judge prophecy to see if it is in line with the Scripture—the source of the prophetic.

Logos refers to the constant, written Word of God, recorded today in the Bible. It is given to us as a guide to teach us practically about the ways of God, salvation, the overall will, plan, and purposes of God for humanity. God raised up priests in the Old Testament through Moses the prophet to teach the Law, the Torah. The priests were appointed to teach the ways of the Lord to God's peculiar and special people Israel (Leviticus 10:11; Deuteronomy 31:9-13; Malachi 2:7). *Logos* is where we come to know God objectively; but knowing Him by experience personally, intimately, and subjectively is through the second realm of the prophecy of Scripture, which is the *rhema* of God. We will discuss the rhema word of God later in this chapter.

The word *logos* is the Greek word meaning "logic." In the dictionary the word "logic" means a science that deals with the rules and tests of sound thinking and proof by reasoning. It speaks of relatively divine reasoning or divine logic. In other words, it is the mind of God written as a way to connect readers to knowing the ways and the reasonings of God. It is also the divine wisdom manifest in the creation, government, and redemption of the world and often identified with the second person of the Trinity defined in the Merriam Webster Dictionary. *Logos* means reason in ancient Greek philosophy and is the controlling principle in the universe. The Greeks understood the logos of God as the speech, word, or reason of God. In other words, the *logos* is the legend of God.

The first use of the term logos is in reference to Jesus Christ as the eternal Word or *Logos:*

> *In the beginning was the Word* [Logos], *and the Word* [Logos] *was with God, and the Word* [Logos] *was God. He was in the beginning with God. All things were made through Him, and without Him nothing was made that was made. In Him was life, and the life was the light of men* (John 1:1-4).

The Holy Scriptures reveal that the Old Testament prophecy of Scripture, both written in the Law and the Prophet, was speaking about the living *Logos*—Jesus Christ. The Old Testament reveals Jesus Christ in two ways. First, there were hundreds of prophecies about Him. Second, Jesus is shown through types and shadows.

The following list of New Testament Scriptures bear witness to the truth that the Old Testament was written prophecy about Jesus. This is why Jesus could state:

> *You study the Scriptures diligently because you think that in them you have eternal life.* **These are the very Scriptures that testify about me** (John 5:39 NIV).

> *If you believed Moses, you would believe, for* **he wrote about me** (John 5:46 NIV).

> *This is what I told you while I was still with you: Everything must be fulfilled that is* **written about me** *in the Law of Moses, the Prophets and the Psalms* (Luke 24:44 NIV).

> *Here I am—* **it is written about me** *in the scroll—I have come to do your will, my God* (Hebrews 10:7 NIV).

The New Testament records:

> *And beginning at Moses and all the Prophets,* [Jesus] *expounded to them in* **all the Scriptures the things concerning Himself** (Luke 24:27).

> *Philip found Nathanael and said to him, We have found Him of* **whom Moses in the law, and also the prophets, wrote— Jesus** *of Nazareth, the son of Joseph* (John 1:45).

BIBLICAL EXAMPLES OF *LOGOS*

The following Scripture passages are examples of the logos of God:

> *In the beginning was the Word* [Logos], *and the Word* [Logos] *was with God, and the Word* [Logos] *was God* (John 1:1).

> *They believed the Scripture, and the word* [logos] *which Jesus had said* (John 2:22).

If He called them gods, to whom the word [logos] *of God came and the Scripture cannot be broken* (John 10:35).

...The seed is the word [logos] *of God* (Luke 8:11).

WHAT IS *RHEMA?*

He who believes in Me, as the Scriptures has said, out of his heart will flow rivers of living water (John 7:38).

The second realm of the prophecy of Scripture is the Greek word *rhema,* which refers to the spoken word. *Rhema* literally means an utterance—individually, collectively, or specifically. The word *rhema* simply means the spoken word of God. It is a word that has been uttered by a living voice. It is the speech or discourse of what one has said, spoken, or uttered.

In addition, *rhema* can be best defined as a series of words joined together by a voice into a sentence—a declaration of one's mind made in words. *Rhema* is an inspired utterance, verse, or portion of Scripture that the Holy Spirit brings to our attention with application to a current situation or need for direction. We say someone is "speaking their mind" or speaking what is on their mind or heart.

The *rhema* of God is the utterance spoken of His mind, which is prophetic and an inspired utterance. This is the realm of speaking what is on the mind of God. *The prophecy of Scripture is simply the written (logos) and spoken (rhema) words of God.* God's written and spoken communication of His mind is imparted to us through the prophecy of Scripture. This is the true meaning and definition of prophecy, which is the communication of the mind of God to humans, whether written or spoken—the inspired writings and utterances of God.

Christians have different views regarding rhema and how it should be understood. Some charismatics view rhema as the voice of the Holy Spirit speaking to them at the present moment. They believe they should be guided by the Holy Spirit through inner feelings, impressions, and experiences. Some believe that the direct words of God to the individual can also be imparted through the words of others, such as a preacher in a worship service or a friend who counsels them. Through these avenues, the Christian experiences God's direct leading.

We need both the logos and the rhema of God as the whole counsel of God. This means that we as believers and those who intend to operate in any dimension and realm of the prophetic must have without question a biblical and concrete understanding of the written and spoken word of God in agreement with all Scriptures. Every word of God is inspired and God breathed. It is the Holy Spirit who illuminates particular Scriptures for application in a daily walk with the Lord.

Rhema is prophecy. The rhema words of Jesus are significant on this point in Matthew 4:4 (NIV): *"Jesus answered, 'It is written, "Man shall not live on bread alone, but on every word* [rhema] *that comes from the mouth of God."'"*

Rhema is the Spirit of Prophecy. Jesus also stated the same in John 6:63 (NIV): *"...The words* [rhema] *I have spoken to you, they are full of the Spirit and life."*

Dr. Jeremy Lopez best explains the word *rhema* as an inspired utterance or prophecy in relation to *logos,* the written word of God, in his book *School of the Prophets—A Training Manual for Activating the Prophetic Spirit Within.* He states:

> Prophecy or Rhema, the spoken word from the Lord that comes through the mouths of people cannot be on an equal term with the Bible, the Logos word of God. It is there to confirm from and line up with the Word of God. The prophecy of scripture is the only kind of prophecy that can claim this level of inspiration. All other prophecy should be inspired by God but will not be direct revelation. We must hold the Logos, written word of God—the Bible, as the highest and purest form of communication from God that exists.

The *rhema* word of God is commonly known as a "right now" word—it speaks to us in the now and should always be in agreement and in total alignment with the written Word of God. The rhema of God must be in agreement with the *logos* of God. They work as scriptural witnesses. Any prophecy spoken that does not agree and line up with the teaching of the written Word of God should be disregarded. If any prophetic activity and functions by prophesiers, those with the gift of prophecy and those who walk in the office of the prophet, do not line up with the ministry of Jesus Christ in word and deed, those activities and functions need to be reconsidered. The rhema word of God must be in conjunction with the Bible, the logos Word.

PROPHECY OF SCRIPTURE VERSUS PROPHECY OF MAN

Rhema works with the *logos* word of God when the Holy Spirit illuminates particular passages of Scripture for application purposes. You may be praying about a particular situation regarding family, finances, career move, education, decisions, owning a business, marriage, etc. The Spirit of God will quicken a rhema with the answers or solution. This is how this works in the realm of the prophetic where many today seek a prophetic word of prophecy from a human vessel of God regarding some of these issues and concerns. People today prefer personal prophecy from a person—who may be manipulated, miss it, give an off-prophecy, or error totally—over the prophecy of Scripture. The prophecy of Scripture is the most trusted form of prophecy, much more than people on any day.

What does it mean that the Bible is God-breathed? In 2 Timothy 3:16 (NIV), Paul states, *"All Scripture is God-breathed and is useful for teaching, rebuking, correcting and training in righteousness."* This is the only time the Greek word *theopneustos* is used, which means God-breathed, inspired by God, due to the inspiration of God. Other passages support the basic premise of Scripture being inspired by God. The very Spirit and life of God is upon the letters of Scripture. The power of the breath of God in divine inspiration pervades Scripture.

In the Merriam Webster Dictionary, the word "inspiration" means the act or power of moving the intellect or emotions—inhalation. It comes from the word "inspire" or "the breath of life," which means to influence, move or guide by divine or supernatural inspiration. God through the agency of prophecy communicated to man supernaturally to write and speak His mind, will and purposes.

Dr. Jeremy Lopez defines "inspiration" in his book, *School of the Prophets*, as "the supernatural influence of the Spirit of God on the human mind by which the apostles and prophets and sacred writers were qualified to set forth divine truth without any mixture or error according to the Webster's Dictionary definition."

The follow passages of Scripture are examples of the breath of God imparting life:

- God breathed into Adam in Genesis 2:7: *"And the Lord God formed man of the dust of the ground, and breathed into his nostrils the breath of life; and man became a living being."*

- Jesus Christ breathed on His disciples in John 20:22: *"And when He had said this, He breathed on them, and said to them, 'Receive the Holy Spirit.'"*

- In 2 Peter 1:21 (NIV) we are told that the origin of prophecy is not will of man or by the origin of man but simply humans being inspired and moved by God to speak: *"Prophecy never had its origin in the human will, but prophets, though human, spoke from God as they were carried along by the Holy Spirit."*

BIBLICAL EXAMPLES OF *RHEMA*

The following Scripture passages give examples of the rhema of God:

- When Jesus told Peter to cast the fishing nets on the other side of the boat, Peter answered, *"Master, we have toiled all*

night and caught nothing; nevertheless at Your word [rhema]
I will let down the net" (Luke 5:5).

▪ When the angel told Mary that she would have a child,
*"Mary said, 'Behold the maidservant of the Lord! Let it be to
me according to your word* [rhema]" (Luke 1:38).

▪ Simeon recalled the promise that he would see Christ
before he died: *"Lord, now You are letting Your servant
depart in peace, according to Your word* [rhema]'" (Luke
2:29).

▪ God gave John the message he was to preach as a fore-
runner to Christ: *"The word* [rhema] *of God came to John"*
(Luke 3:2).

How to Receive a *Rhema* Word

In the regular course of our daily reading of God's Word *(Logos)*, we need
to ask God to speak to us through His Word and give us insight into it.
The Holy Spirit can cause certain passages to stand out with significant
meaning or application for our lives. These are the *rhemas* of Scripture and
should become part of our daily thoughts and actions.

CHAPTER 15

JESUS THE PROPHET

*So the multitudes said, "This is Jesus, the
prophet from Nazareth of Galilee."*
—MATTHEW 21:11

*The woman said to Him [Jesus], "Sir, I
perceive that You are a prophet."*
—JOHN 4:19

This chapter will reveal the prophet ministry of Jesus Christ as the flawless model of the office of the prophets. You will learn to understand Jesus's concepts of the prophetic and how to move and operate in the heart of the Prophet—Jesus Christ. The goal and emphasis of this chapter is to examine key prophetic functions of Jesus Christ in the lens of the Gospels. The greatest Prophet of all time and history is Jesus Christ who walked in the office of King, Priest, and Prophet. The New Testament example of true prophetic ministry must be viewed through the eyes of our Lord Jesus.

The highest prophetic office is the office of the Christ. As we have studied the different dimensions and realms of the prophetic, I believe this realm of studying the prophetic ministry of Jesus through the writings of the Holy Scriptures gives us a blueprint and master template to follow as New Testament prophets. Jesus declared that He did not come to abolish the Law and the Prophets but to fulfill it; therefore, we today as prophets, prophetic people, and prophetic generations have a comprehensive, historical documentation of the Master Prophet Jesus recorded by His very own disciples.

The following are just a few key examples in Scriptures of the prophetic functions of the office of the Christ we will examine in this chapter. There are, of course, more, however this chapter is not intended to be exhaustive. I highlight a few prophetic functions that reveal the type of prophetic ministry that Jesus has already set foundationally for all of the prophets He has given as gifts to His Church.

Jesus Christ has given us an extension and measure of His ministry gift of prophet, according to Ephesians 4:7-11 (NIV):

> But to each one of us grace has been given as Christ apportioned it. This is why it says: "When he ascended on high, he took many captives and gave gifts to his people."
>
> (What does "he ascended" mean except that he also descended to the lower, earthly regions? He who descended is the very one who ascended higher than all the heavens, in order to fill the whole universe.) So **Christ himself gave** the apostles, **the prophets,** the evangelists, the pastors and teachers.

Prophets today are an extension of Jesus's own prophetic ministry; therefore, we are to model and strive to be like Jesus, the Prophet. He set the tone for what genuine prophetic ministry is to look like in the New Testament.

IMITATE THE PROPHETIC MODEL

> Then He [Jesus] said to them, "Follow Me, and I will make you fishers of men." They immediately left their nets and followed Him (Matthew 4:19-20).

The ministry of the prophet is an extension of Jesus's own prophetic grace that He Himself gave as a gift to us. Those who operate and function in the New Testament ministry of the prophet have a measure of the same grace and anointing of His same prophetic Spirit in them by the Holy

Spirit. We walk in the same administrative and prophetic function. However, I believe that this chapter will better help us, to view in light of the Scripture, to better identify with a few of those functions. With respect to the prophetic office, ministry, and gift of prophecy, we can strive to follow Christ in the same manner that Paul the apostle imitated Him: *"Imitate me, just as I also imitate Christ"* (1 Corinthians 11:1).

The word "follower" in 1 Corinthians 11:1 is the Greek word *mimetes*, which simply means an imitator, to imitate someone. According to the dictionary, the word "imitator" comes from the root word "imitate" that means to follow as a model, to resemble or to produce a copy of something. Jesus is our model for the prophetic ministry after whom we can model our ministry. He is the perfect example and image of what genuine prophetic ministry is to look like. We are to emulate Him and to follow the examples that He left for all generations. The Holy Spirit in us is to reproduce the Jesus Christ kind of prophetic ministry in saints in every generation.

Prophets are followers—imitators—of Christ. *"Then Jesus said to His disciples, 'If anyone desires to come after Me, let him deny himself, and take up his cross and follow Me'"* (Matthew 16:24).

Peter, Andrew, James, and John, who were fishermen, left everything after being called to follow Christ. Prophets are disciples and students of Christ in the prophetic:

> *As Jesus was walking beside the Sea of Galilee, he saw two brothers, Simon called Peter and his brother Andrew. They were casting a net into the lake, for they were fishermen. "Come, follow me," Jesus said, "and I will send you out to fish for people." At once they left their nets and followed him. Going on from there, he saw two other brothers, James son of Zebedee and his brother John. They were in a boat with their father Zebedee, preparing their nets. Jesus called them, and immediately they left the boat and their father and followed him* (Matthew 4:18-22 NIV).

Prophets walk in the same manner as Jesus walked: "He who says he abides in Him ought himself also to walk just as He [Jesus] walked" (1 John 2:6).

In Strong's Concordance, the word "walk" in 1 John 2:6 is the word *peripateo*, which literally means to regulate one's life conduct and to live just like or to follow as a companion or votary. In other words, as His companions, we are to walk and live just as Jesus lived.

Prophets of Love

Whoever does not love does not know God, because God is love (1 John 4:8 NIV).

The New Testament ministry of the prophet is a ministry of love. There is a stereotype in the church today that in order to be a prophet you have to be rough, tough, stern, and firm—lacking or showing any signs of emotions. We have an Old Testament view and paradigm of prophetic ministry that is doom and gloom, where ancient prophets were mean, calling fire down from Heaven, slaying false prophets, prophesying judgment and the wrath of God upon wicked kings and nations. However, Jesus revised, redefined, and reshaped the prophetic role and function in fulfilling the Law and the Prophets. Therefore, the New Testament ministry of the prophets is not doom and gloom but groom and bloom.

Christ fulfilled the law's prophetic utterance regarding Himself (Luke 24:44). He also fulfilled the demands of the Mosaic Law that called for perfect obedience under threat of a curse according to Galatians 3:10,13. Therefore, He emphasized in the New Testament the spirit of the Law and the Prophet, which is a spiritual law that all believers and ministry gifts obey, is love. Love is the law of the prophetic that governs our ministry. Love is the greatest commandment in the New Testament, onto which all the Law and the Prophets hang. Love activates the gift of prophecy and the prophetic realm because without love our ministry is nothing.

Look at what Paul says about the greatest gift of love as it relates to the gift of prophecy and faith 1 Corinthians 13:2: *"And though I have the gift of prophecy, and understand all mysteries and all knowledge, and though I have all faith, so that I could remove mountains, but have not love, I am nothing."*

Prophets are commanded to love according to Matthew 22:37-40: *"Jesus said to him, 'You shall love the Lord your God with all your heart, with all your soul, and with all your mind.' This is the first and great commandment. And the second is like it: 'You shall love your neighbor as yourself.' On these two commandments hang all the Law and the Prophets."*

The prophet code of honor is love. The prophet functions and operates with love as the heartbeat of the ministry to serve all mankind for Christ. Love is the badge of honor of the New Testament prophets.

There are two laws of love under the New Testament of Jesus Christ that we follow:

1. Love the Lord—with all your heart, with all your soul, and with all your mind.

2. Love your neighbor—as you love yourself: *"Love does no wrong to a neighbor. Therefore love is the fulfillment of the law"* (Romans 13:10 NET).

SONSHIP PROPHETS

For as many as are led by the Spirit of God, these are sons of God (Romans 8:14).

And because you are sons, God has sent the Spirit of His Son into our hearts, crying out, "Abba! Father!" (Galatians 4:6).

Jesus introduced the radically new ministry of sonship. This is a new paradigm and relationship to the prophetic office. The ministry of sonship is the New Testament ministry of the prophet. Just as the ancient prophets had a company of prophets who were their spiritual and prophetic sons and protégés, likewise we are the sons of the Prophet who is Jesus Christ. We have been given the spirit of adoption as New Testament prophets and prophetic people (Galatians 4:6). We are prophets who are also sons and daughters of God (Romans 8:14). This is a radically different paradigm from that of the Old Testament prophetic office. New Testament prophets have a more Father-son relationship as prophets. The Old Testament prophets functioned as servants more than sons.

SERVANT-SON PROPHETS

Old Testament Servants: *"Surely the Lord God does nothing, unless He reveals His secret to His servants the prophets"* (Amos 3:7).

The following are examples of the new position of the prophet in the New Testament where prophets are no longer servants of God, they function as sons of God. The role of the prophetic in relationship with God changes the office of the prophet radically to mirror the same relationship that Jesus had with the Father. Jesus introduced the New Testament prophets as sons and daughters of God who are born-again believers.

New Testament Sons: *"But as many as received Him, to them He gave the right to become children of God, to those who believe in His name: who were born, not of blood, nor of the will of the flesh, nor of the will of man, but of God"* (John 1:12-13).

Prophets are also friends of God as Jesus reveal the Father to them: *"No longer do I call you servants, for a servant does not know what his master is doing; but I have called you friends, for all things that I heard from My Father I have made known to you"* (John 15:15).

Prophets as sons reveal through the Spirit, the Christ and the Father. Jesus gives revelation of the Father to His New Testament prophets. The greatest revelation of a prophet is his or her revelation of Christ. This revelation is revealed out of an intimate relationship with Christ. Jesus will reveal the Father and make Him known to whomever prophet He wills: *"All things have been delivered to Me by My Father, and no one knows the Son except the Father. Nor does anyone know the Father except the Son, and the one to whom the Son wills to reveal Him"* (Matthew 11:27).

PROPHETIC RELATIONSHIP WITH THE FATHER

The following are ten attributes of Jesus's relationship with the Father for the New Testament prophetic ministry from John 5:17-37:

1. Prophets are reflections of the Father as sons. Prophets work as the Father is working in the same manner as Jesus (John 5:17).

2. Prophets are totally dependent on the Father and can do nothing on their own accord. They do not speak on their own accord because they are spokespersons who only speak on the behalf of God as prophets. Prophets see things that God in Christ reveals to them. He reveals what he or she sees in the Spirit. New Testament prophets do not conjure up visions or anything on their own, they only share what God shows them. God will reveal and show us greater works, and people will marvel (John 5:19-20).

3. Prophets in the New Testament ministry office have faith in the heavenly Father's love for them. They function out of that unconditional love of the Father. Prophets are secure in their office and do not put their faith in people's opinion of them and the work that they were sent to do; they care only of the Father's opinion. There is security in the love of God and His trust in him to complete the assignment that he was sent to do (John 5:20).

4. Prophets will honor Christ Jesus through bringing glory to God. The New Testament office of the prophet is a ministry of honor. They see every ministry opportunity to honor Jesus. When they obey the Spirit, God is gloried in the Son through His prophetic ministry in us (John 5:23).

5. Prophets have revelation of what the Father is doing. Jesus is working in His prophets by the Spirit to do the greater works (see John 14:12).

6. Prophets will work together with the Father to speak and release life. The New Testament prophets are about their Father's business (see Luke 2:41-52) (John 5:21,24-29).

7. Prophets understand that the Father has given them great prophetic responsibility and burden of ministry.

8. Prophets are sent ones and the works of their ministry are spiritual credentials that God has authorized. There will be dimensions of the supernatural upon their ministry in the form of divine revelation, physical healing, and deliverance (John 5:36).

9. Prophets in the New Testament ministry of Christ will live for the will of the Father and not their own (John 5:30).

10. Prophets are ministers of the gospel of Jesus Christ and will cause others to believe in the Son of God whom the Father sent to give everlasting life (John 5:24).

PROPHETIC INTERCESSION

I do not pray for these alone, but also for those who will believe in Me through their word; that they all may be one, as You, Father, are in Me, and I in You; that they also may be one in Us, that the world may believe that You sent Me. And the glory which You gave Me I have given them, that they may be one just as We are one: I in them, and You in Me; that they may be made perfect in one, and that the world may know that You have sent Me, and have loved them as You have loved Me (John 17:20-23).

Intercession is a key function of the prophetic ministry and what Jesus lived by. He gave His students the blueprint, the template of prayer and intercession when they asked Him to teach them how to pray (Luke 11:1). Jesus taught His disciples how to pray (Luke 11:2-4)—it was the earmark of His ministry. His disciples had no doubt noticed Jesus's prayerfulness, which provoked them to want to model Him, knowing prayer produced incredible realms and would thrust them into supernatural power as was evident in His ministry. Prophets must have a ministry of prayer and intercession.

PROPHETIC INTERCESSORY MANTLE OF CHRIST

Prophets in the ministry of Christ will pray and intercede with the Spirit the will of God and not according to their own will, purposes, or intentions according to Romans 8:26-27. Jesus continually made intercession for the saints. The following are a few examples of Jesus's intercessory ministry as the Prophet that we should follow:

- Prophets will withdraw from people, places, and things to pray. *"So He* [Jesus] *Himself often withdrew into the wilderness and prayed"* (Luke 5:16).

- Prophets will pray and intercede all night continually to God. *"Now it came to pass in those days that He* [Jesus] *went out to the mountain to pray, and continued all night in prayer to God"* (Luke 6:12).

- Prophets pray until Heaven opens. *"When all the people were baptized, it came to pass that Jesus also was baptized; and while He prayed, the heaven was opened"* (Luke 3:21).

PROPHETIC ANOINTING

Elijah the prophet who was human like us had a powerful ministry of intercession that empowered him to prophesy open and closed heavens.

> *The Spirit of the Lord is upon Me, because He has anointed Me to preach the gospel to the poor; He has sent Me to heal the brokenhearted, to proclaim liberty to the captives and recovery of sight to the blind, to set at liberty those who are oppressed; to proclaim the acceptable year of the Lord* (Luke 4:18-19).

According to Luke 4:18-19, the prophetic anointing upon the prophets of Christ of the New Testament are anointed by the Spirit generally, which gives them an extension gift of His mantle to do the following:

- Preach the gospel
- Send ones
- Healing
- Deliverance
- Revelation
- Proclaim the year and favor of the Christ Jesus

The following are a few examples of the anointing of Christ in His prophets:

- Prophets are anointed by God with the Holy Spirit and with supernatural, miracle-working power. *"How God anointed Jesus of Nazareth with the Holy Spirit and with power, who went about doing good and healing all who were oppressed by the devil, for God was with Him"* (Acts 10:38).

- Prophets are filled with the Holy Spirit and are led by the Spirit. *"Then Jesus, being filled with the Holy Spirit, returned from the Jordan and was led by the Spirit into the wilderness"* (Luke 4:1).

- Prophets walk in the power of the Spirit that will cause fame and notoriety to his prophetic ministry. *"Then Jesus returned in the power of the Spirit to Galilee, and news of Him went out through all the surrounding region"* (Luke 4:14).

REVELATORY PROPHETS

No longer do I call you servants, for a servant does not know what his master is doing; but I have called you friends, for all things that I heard from My Father I have made known to you (John 15:15).

Prophets function regularly and heavily in the revelatory gifts and anointing that sets their ministry apart from the other fivefold ministry gifts of apostle, evangelist, pastor, and teacher. They carry a supernatural ability to see things in someone's past, present, and future. This is one of the key functions demonstrated and modeled in the prophetic ministry of Jesus. Prophets operating in the revelatory gifts function with extraordinary prophetic ability that causes others to recognize the genuine essence and office of the prophet.

We see the powerful manifestation of the Spirit function in Jesus's prophets with incredible detail and accuracy. Scripture references are cited next to each manifestation of Jesus's revelatory ministry to aid in your study of this topic. Jesus-type prophets today walk in the revelatory ministry of Christ. The three revelatory gifts of the Holy Spirit that prophets operate in primarily, but are not limited to, are the following according to 1 Corinthians 12:8-10:

1. Word of Knowledge (John 4:19; John 1:45-50)

2. Word of Wisdom (Luke 19:29-34)

3. Discerning of Spirits (1 Corinthians 12:10; John 2:23-25; Hebrews 4:12; Matthew 9:4; Mark 2:8)

MIRACLE, HEALING, AND DELIVERANCE PROPHETS

"What things?" Jesus asked. "The things that happened to ***Jesus****, the man from Nazareth," they said. "He was a* ***prophet who did powerful miracles****, and he was a mighty teacher in the eyes of God and all the people"* (Luke 24:19 New Living Translation).

The prophets in the New Testament ministry of Jesus the Prophet will function in the realm of the supernatural. They will do signs, wonders, and miraculous healing as prophets. The following are a few examples of Jesus's supernatural Kingdom ministry that demonstrate the power of God.

- Prophets are sent from God with the ability to do the supernatural. People will testify and validate the prophet's ministry. *"If this Man were not from God, He could do nothing"* (John 9:33).

- Prophets will minister with Jesus Christ in the Spirit as He works with them with accompanying signs. *"So then, after the Lord had spoken to them, He was received up into heaven, and sat down at the right hand of God. And they went out and preached everywhere, the Lord working with them and confirming the word through the accompanying signs. Amen"* (Mark 16:19-20).

- Jesus Christ's New Testament prophets' commissioning is stated in Matthew 10:6-8: *"But go rather to the lost sheep of the house of Israel. And as you go, preach, saying, 'The kingdom of heaven is at hand. Heal the sick, cleanse the lepers, raise the dead, cast out demon. Freely you have received, freely give.'"*

Prophets will walk in a realm and dimension of the supernatural where they will do notable—documented and undocumented—and unusual miracles as signs they are prophets of Christ (Acts 4:16 NIV). Prophets will do special miracles through God in their prophetic ministry. We will even see special miracles demonstrated literally by the mouth of the prophet. There will be creative miracles performed as prophets prophesy (Ezekiel 37; Acts 19:11-12). We will see apostolic prophets emerge and function in miracle ministries. Prophets will be mighty in deed and in word before God and all the people they are sent to minister.

Jesus was recognized as a mighty Prophet by the multitude in Luke 24:19 (Berean Literal Bible): *"And He said to them, 'What things?' And they said to Him, 'The things concerning Jesus of Nazareth, a man who was a prophet, mighty in deed and word before God and all the people.'"*

TEACHING AND PREACHING PROPHETS

Jesus's prophetic ministry was a ministry of teaching and preaching. When He taught or preached, He captivated the multitude. The office of Christ in the prophetic carries a supernatural mantle to see manifestations of the power of God. This demonstration of power will not just come when the prophets prophesy, it will visibly and notably be seen as they teach and preach the Word of God. Powerful, prophetic preaching and teaching will be the mark of the New Testament prophetic office.

A prophet is an expounder and interpreter of the divine truths of Scripture. Therefore, this implies that an expounder who is a prophet is an inspired teacher. The word "expound" means to explain by setting forth in careful and often elaborate detail or to interpret with accurate detail. A prophet has the prophetic ability as an inspired expounder of the Word of God to clarify, make clear, construe, demonstrate, elucidate, explain thoroughly, explicate, illuminate, illustrate, and simply spell out what God is saying to us. I say all that to simply say that a prophetically inspired expounder, a prophet, has the ability to teach and preach.

The Realm of Prophetic Teaching

Prophets teach as having authority. *"And so it was, when Jesus had ended these sayings, that the people were astonished at His teaching, for He taught them as one having authority, and not as the scribes"* (Matthew 7:28-29).

Prophets teach with wisdom and mighty works of miracles. *"When He had come to His own country, He taught them in their synagogue, so that they were astonished and said, 'Where did this Man get this wisdom and these mighty works?'"* (Matthew 13:54). *"The officers answered, 'No man ever spoke like this Man!'"* (John 7:46).

Here are a few other Scripture references of Jesus's astonishing teaching ministry that His prophets will function in—Matthew 4:23; Mark 1:27; Luke 4:32; John 8:28 and John 14:21-24.

The Realm of Prophetic Preaching

Prophets prepare the way of the Lord through their preaching and messages. They are a prophetic voice in their generation who will turn people's hearts toward the Father as we see in the following example of John the Baptizer in Matthew 3:1-3:

> *In those days John the Baptist came preaching in the wilderness of Judea, and saying, "Repent, for the kingdom of heaven is at hand!" For this is he who was spoken of by the prophet Isaiah, saying: "The voice of one crying in the wilderness: 'Prepare the way of the Lord; Make His paths straight.'"*

Prophets preach the gospel of the Kingdom of God and Heaven. "The law and the prophets were until John. Since that time the kingdom of God has been preached, and everyone is pressing into it" (Luke 16:16).

Prophets preach the message of repentance and reformation. *"From that time Jesus began to preach and to say, "Repent, for the kingdom of heaven is at hand"* (Matthew 4:17). *"Now after John was put in prison, Jesus came to Galilee, preaching the gospel of the kingdom of God"* (Mark 1:14).

Prophets like Jesus understand the purpose and power of preaching in different places. *"But He said to them, "Let us go into the next towns, that I may preach there also, because for this purpose I have come forth"* (Mark 1:38).

SENT-ONES PROPHETS

The following are two additional passages of Scripture to show you that Jesus mandated to preach everywhere in every city, town, village, etc. as one sent by God (Luke 4:43; 8:1).

> *So Jesus said to them again, "Peace to you! As the Father has sent Me, I also send you"* (John 20:21).

Jesus was sent by the Father; therefore, He also sends us as His prophets. Prophets will endure great persecution, opposition, and attacks from the religious and those who do not understand God's mandate upon their lives and the prophetic ministry as His sent ones. New Testament prophets are not just called, they are commissioned as sent by Jesus Christ with the Word of the Lord and the agendas of Heaven.

Therefore I am sending you prophets and sages and teachers. Some of them you will kill and crucify; others you will flog in your synagogues and pursue from town to town (Matthew 23:34 NIV).

DISCIPLESHIP—MAKING DISCIPLES

Go therefore and make disciples of all the nations, baptizing them in the name of the Father and of the Son and of the Holy Spirit, teaching them to observe all things that I have commanded you; and lo, I am with you always, even to the end of the age. Amen (Matthew 28:19-20).

Prophets' minds are opened by the Spirit and they unlock the secret and mysterious understanding of the Scriptures for others. *"And He [Jesus] opened their understanding, that they might comprehend the Scriptures"* (Luke 24:45).

Prophets receive an impartation of the Spirit of Christ upon them. *"And when He had said this, He breathed on them, and said to them, "Receive the Holy Spirit"* (John 20:22). *"Behold, I send the Promise of My Father upon you; but tarry in the city of Jerusalem until you are endued with power from on high"* (Luke 24:49).

Here a few more Scriptures for you to understand your prophetic appointment as one who walks in the prophetic office of Jesus Christ— John 15:16 and Acts 1:8.

Prophets teach the distinction of true and false ministries especially false prophets. *"Beware of false prophets, who come to you in sheep's clothing, but inwardly they are ravenous wolves. You will know them by their fruits. Do men gather grapes from thornbushes or figs from thistles?"* (Matthew 7:15-16).

PROPHETS OF FAITH

> *He replied, "Because you have so little faith. Truly I tell you, if you have faith as small as a mustard seed, you can say to this mountain, 'Move from here to there,' and it will move. Nothing will be impossible for you"* (Matthew 17:20 NIV).

> *Jesus replied, "What is impossible with man is possible with God"* (Luke 18:27 NIV).

REALM OF HUMILITY

The following are just a few examples of Jesus's ministry of humility as a prophet:

- Jesus gave up His divine privileges (Philippians 2:7-9 New Living Translation)
- Humility comes before honor (Proverbs 18:12)
- Prophets walk in humility, not pride (Matthew 23:12; 1 Peter 5:6; Luke 14:11)
- Jesus rode on a donkey (Mark 11:1-11; Zechariah 9:9)
- Jesus, after healing, told the man to tell no one (Luke 5:14-16)

BEATITUDES OF THE PROPHETS

Jesus taught the following Beatitudes to His disciples; these should be standards for New Testament prophetic ministers. Matthew 5:3-10 (NIV):

1. *Blessed are the poor in spirit, for theirs is the kingdom of heaven.*
2. *Blessed are those who mourn, for they will be comforted.*
3. *Blessed are the meek, for they will inherit the earth.*
4. *Blessed are those who hunger and thirst for righteousness, for they will be filled.*

5. *Blessed are the merciful, for they will be shown mercy.*

6. *Blessed are the pure in heart, for they will see God.*

7. *Blessed are the peacemakers, for they will be called children of God.*

8. *Blessed are those who are persecuted because of righteousness, for theirs is the kingdom of heaven.*

CHAPTER 16

FALSE AND PSEUDO PROPHETS

*Beware of false prophets, who come to you in
sheep's clothing, but inwardly they are ravenous
wolves. You will know them by their fruits.*
—MATTHEW 7:15-16

As we have discussed extensively in previous chapters regarding the authenticity of the prophets and prophecy, I share now about the counterfeit ministry of false prophets and pseudo activities.

Just as there are true and valid prophetic ministries, prophets, and prophecies, there are also the opposite. It is my duty in this literary work on the realms of the prophetic to make a clear distinction in identifying fictitious ministries and prophetic activities. It is very easy to be deceived if there is a lack of understanding of what to look for when exposed to a false prophet.

In an audio recording teaching I purchased from Bill Johnson Ministries on the subject of *Creating a Kingdom Culture,* Bill Johnson, senior pastor of Bethel Church in Redding, California, made a powerful statement about the recognition of the counterfeit, "You don't recognize counterfeit dollar bills because you study counterfeit dollar bills, you recognize counterfeit because you studied the real thing." Likewise, the more acquainted we become with studying true prophets, it becomes easier to recognize and identify the false. To Bill Johnson's point, it is similar to our familiarity with continually handling and knowing authentic paper money, dollars. You know how it feels and what it looks like. Therefore, when you have a fake or counterfeit dollar, sometimes without even looking you know immediately that it is not the real thing.

WHAT IS A FALSE PROPHET?

The earmarks and nature of false prophets and pseudo activities need to be identified. In the Old Testament, the phrase "false prophet" is not found—though there are a number of Scriptures that identify them. The word "false" in the Merriam Webster's Dictionary means not genuine, artificially made or assumed, intentionally untrue; adjusted or made so as to deceive, tending to mislead, and deceptive. The realm of false prophets and prophecy is synonymous with being artificial, bogus, fake, imitation, phony, mechanical, a sham, synthetic, unnatural, crooked, deceitful, fraudulent, spurious, inaccurate, erroneous, and inexact.

In religion, a false prophet is one who falsely claims the gift of prophecy or divine inspiration, or who uses that gift for evil ends, greed, manipulation, and sorcery. False prophets are people who teach destructive and false doctrine in order to lead people away from the true gospel message and teaching of God found in the Bible.

Jesus warned about false prophets in Matthew 24:24 stating that in the last days many false prophets would arise and deceive: *"For false christs and false prophets will rise and show great signs and wonders to deceive, if possible, even the elect."*

Most religions and cultures in the world, including Judaism, Christianity, Islam, ancient Greece and others have had prophets. Out of all the world religions that have prophets, only the prophets of Jesus Christ's Church are the true messengers of God. The origin of the prophetic is in Christ (Revelation 19:10). Any prophet or prophecy that leads you away from Christ Jesus is a false prophet and prophecy.

An important function of a true prophet is found in a statement from God to the ancient Israelites through Moses, *"I will raise up for them a*

Prophet like you from among their brethren, and will put My words in His mouth, and He shall speak to them all that I command Him" (Deuteronomy 18:18). God was foretelling that, like Moses, Jesus Christ would come as a true Prophet and God would speak through Him. The Bible explains that, in addition to true prophets, there would also be false ones. Anyone who falsely claims to speak God's words or who teaches errors in His name is not a true prophet.

Why are there false prophets and prophecy? We know that satan is the father of lies and has deceived the whole world (John 8:44; Revelation 12:9). His goal has been to twist and falsify the truth of God and to discourage humanity from following the path of Christ who is the Way, the Truth, and eternal Life (John 14:6). To assist him in this effort, the devil manipulates and influences people to become counterfeit prophets. Also, some people speak from their own imagination. God says, *"Woe to the foolish prophets, who follow their own spirit and have seen nothing!"* (Ezekiel 13:3). Throughout the centuries, numerous false prophets have emerged because of their own desires and satan's influence.

Preceding the apostle Paul's death, he predicted that some brethren would be easily led astray by false teachers:

> *For the time will come when they will not endure sound doctrine, but according to their own desires, because they have itching ears, they will heap up for themselves teachers; and they will turn their ears away from the truth, and be turned aside to fables* (2 Timothy 4:3-4).

God warned through Moses of presumptuous prophets. *"But the prophet who presumes to speak a word in My name, which I have not commanded him to speak, or who speaks in the name of other gods, that prophet shall die"* (Deuteronomy 18:20).

Peter explained that false prophets had come in the past and that false teachers would continue to come with harmful and destructive messages. *"But there were also false prophets among the people, even as there will be false teachers among you, who will secretly bring in destructive heresies, even denying the Lord who bought them, and bring on themselves swift destruction"* (2 Peter 2:1).

The following are some signs of false and pseudo prophetic operations:

- A warning for the generation just before Christ's return
- False anointing upon the prophets and teachers
- Destructive heresies and doctrines of men and devils (1 Timothy 4:1-3)
- Lying (deceiving) signs, wonders, and miracles
- Counterfeit spirits masquerading as genuine prophets
- Emergence of false prophetic anointing and prophetic voices

During His earthly ministry, Christ described conditions in the last days just before His return to earth in glory to set up His Kingdom. He said false prophets would have power to show great counterfeit miracles that would almost deceive even the faithful. *"For false christs and false prophets will rise and show great signs and wonders to deceive, if possible, even the elect. See, I have told you beforehand"* (Matthew 24:24-25).

THE DANGER OF FALSE PROPHETS

In both the Old and New Testaments we are repeatedly warned about false prophets. They are in the church. They may even do miracles. The issue here is not the power to prophesy, it is the prophet's character and teaching. We are to beware of false prophets disguised as sheep who are ravenous wolves and greedy prophets.

False prophets will do deceitful and lying signs and wonders.

For false christs and false prophets will rise and show great signs and wonders to deceive, if possible, even the elect (Matthew 24:24).

Many will say to Me in that day, "Lord, Lord, have we not prophesied in Your name, cast out demons in Your name, and done many wonders in Your name?" And then I will declare to them, "I never knew you; depart from Me, you who practice lawlessness!" (Matthew 7:22-23)

Do not listen to prophets who speak against the Bible.

To the law and to the testimony! If they do not speak according to this word, it is because there is no light in them (Isaiah 8:20).

Yet we cannot ignore all prophecies out of fear of false prophets—we should test them.

Do not despise prophecies. Test all things; hold fast what is good (1 Thessalonians 5:20-21).

False prophets will emerge with twisted teaching to draw or persuade people to them.

Even from your own number men will arise and distort the truth in order to draw away disciples after them (Acts 20:30 NIV).

False prophets will follow their own spirit:

*Thus says the Lord God: "Woe to the **foolish prophets, who follow their own spirit and have seen nothing!** O Israel, your prophets are like foxes in the deserts. You have not gone up into the gaps to build a wall for the house of Israel to stand in battle on the day of the Lord. **They have envisioned futility and false divination,** saying, 'Thus says the Lord!' But the Lord has not sent them; yet they hope that the word may be confirmed. Have you not seen a futile vision, and have you not spoken false divination? You say, 'The Lord says,' but I have not spoken"* (Ezekiel 13:3-7).

The following are examples of the foolishness of false prophets and pseudo practices according to Ezekiel 13:3-7:

- Foolish, lying, silly, goofy prophets
- Delusive vision (seers)
- Divination (false prophetic spirit), clairvoyance, witches, warlocks, mediums, psychics, and palm and tarot card readers, ESP, etc.
- Soulish, carnal, and fleshly prophets
- False prophets receive inspiration from demons

Dr. Paula A. Price, in her book, *The Prophet's Handbook: A Guide to Prophecy and Its Operation*, provides us with the root definition of false prophecy:

- Erroneous revelation or prediction
- Untrue revelation or prediction
- Wrong revelation or prediction
- Mistaken revelation or prediction
- Deceitful revelation or prediction

False prophets' teachings and prophecies are not biblical.

*If **anyone thinks they are a prophet** or otherwise gifted by the Spirit, let them acknowledge that what I am writing to you is the Lord's command (1 Corinthians 14:37 NIV).*

*But **there were false prophets** also among the people, even as there shall be false teachers among you, who privily shall bring in damnable heresies, even denying the Lord that bought them, and bring upon themselves swift destruction (2 Peter 2:1).*

False prophets do not operate in the Spirit of God.

They operate in spirit of the antichrist (1 John 4:3), error and divination.

Beloved, do not believe every spirit, but test the spirits, whether they are of God; because many false prophets have gone out into the world (1 John 4:1).

False prophets prophesy by others gods and other religions.

The priests did not say, "Where is the Lord?" and those who handle the law did not know Me; the rulers also transgressed against Me; the prophets prophesied by Baal, and walked after things that do not profit (Jeremiah 2:8).

False prophets will prophesy lies in the name of Jesus Christ.

The Lord said to me, "The prophets prophesy lies in My name. I have not sent them, commanded them, nor spoken to them; they prophesy to you a false vision, divination, a worthless thing, and the deceit of their heart" (Jeremiah 14:14).

False prophets will emerge to deceive many. They are deceptive in nature.

Then many false prophets will rise up and deceive many (Matthew 24:11).

Like anyone in the ministry, a true prophet's life must be an example of holiness and decency.

There is no other standard. On the other hand, beware of those who are deceitful:

- False prophets and prophetesses will operate in a Jezebel spirit
- Witchcraft is a pseudo-prophetic spirit
- False teaching, seducing doctrines of demons and humans
- Fornication, idolatry, and extra biblical traditions, rituals, practices, and sexual immorality is not the nature of a holy and righteous prophet

Nevertheless I have a few things against you, because you allow that woman Jezebel, who calls herself a prophetess, to teach and seduce My servants to commit sexual immorality and eat things sacrificed to idols (Revelation 2:20 NIV).

A false prophet will excuse the flesh, particularly prophesying approval of sexual immorality. False prophets often direct people into their sinful lusts or give spiritual licensure to satisfy the lusts of their eye, flesh, and pride of life. Mostly these types of prophets are dealing with areas of sexual sin, compromise, and immorality. False prophets and prophetesses are "self-appointed" and will compromise integrity, honor, and holiness to get ahead and to sell themselves out to promote their own fanfare, financial status, and lavish lifestyles (1 Kings 18:19)

False prophets promote themselves. *"Jezebel, who calls herself a prophetess"* (Revelation 2:20).

False prophets operate under the law rather than grace. They criticize, attack, and condemn others of sin, rather than weep and plead for repentance. Jonah was rebuked by the Lord for his lack of compassion on Nineveh (Jonah 1-3).

- False prophets are not accountable to leadership; they are vagabonds, rebellious, and unteachable. They are driven to control meetings, not respecting leadership or letting themselves be tested.

- True prophets know how to operate under proper leadership and are not afraid to be examined, corrected, and judged by their prophetic leaders. *"Let two or three prophets speak, and let the others judge. …And the spirits of the prophets are subject to the prophets"* (1 Corinthians 14:29,32). False prophets are unaccountable to leadership.

False Prophetic and Prophecy

The Bible warns of false prophets many times, especially in these "last days" or "end times." False prophets masquerade as genuine prophets. *"Beware of false prophets, who come to you in sheep's clothing, but inwardly they are ravenous wolves"* (Matthew 7:15). Genuine prophets are known by their fruit, not necessarily by their gifts. *"You will know them by their fruits"* (Matthew 7:16).

A false prophet is not someone who gives a bad or inaccurate word—it is someone who prophesies from a wrong spirit or an evil heart. A false prophet is able to prophesy accurately from a demonic spirit. Apostle Paul encountered such a person in Acts 16:16-18, the story about the possessed slave girl who was a fortune teller by the spirit of divination. Some false prophets operate in the spirit of divination, which may appear as if they are functioning in the spirit and gift of prophecy. The fortune teller gave accurate information, but from the wrong source.

Demons can operate accurately in the gift of the word of knowledge because they can see and hear. Demons cannot prophesy the future; if they could, the devil would never have put into the hearts of the people to crucify Jesus (1 Corinthians 2:8).

There are times when a person becomes a false prophet over time. He or she started out right, but allowed compromise, sin, dabbling in witchcraft, occult or other religions, greed, and love of money into their lives and has fallen away from God. Yet, they can still operate in the prophetic gift: *"For the gifts and the calling of God are irrevocable"* (Romans 11:29).

Characteristics of False Prophets and Prophecy

The characteristics of false prophets and prophecy are that they:

- Operate in pride, arrogance, and with a haughty spirit
- Operate from a spirit of divination
- Knowingly deceive people

- Knowingly use signs and wonders to deceive people (Mark 13:22)

- Use flattery, seduction, and manipulation (Jezebel spirit)

- Have a wounded heart

- Lose accountability to the Scripture and place themselves above the Word of God

- Have a heart that is closed to new revelation and are unwilling to allow people to test their prophecy

- Seek to promote themselves and their own personal agendas

- Prophesy for personal gain, either wealth or influence. They prophesy what people want to hear for personal gain

- Draw people to themselves instead of Jesus Christ

- Are known by their fruit—they do not walk in the Fruit of the Spirit, which is love (see Matthew 7:15-20)

PART III

UNLOCKING THE REALMS OF THE PROPHETIC

CHAPTER 17

PROPHETIC COMMUNICATIONS, CHANNELS, AND CONDUITS

Then He said, "Hear now My words: If there is a prophet among you, I, the Lord, make Myself known to him in a vision; I speak to him in a dream."
—NUMBERS 12:6

My sheep hear My voice, and I know them, and they follow Me [Jesus].
—JOHN 10:27

God is always speaking. He has created us as sons and daughters to live from a place of intimate relationship and communication with Him. Individually, each believer is prophetic, and together we are a prophetic generation. Yet many people do not recognize when God is speaking to them. God speaks in many different and unusual ways. Some of the ways He speaks are quite dramatic and earthshaking. Other times His voice is very soft and subtle.

The purpose of this chapter is to show you some of the many different ways that God communicates and inspires openness to hearing His voice. This chapter is not intended to be exhaustive in the many ways God speaks or various types of prophetic encounter, which I will save for another book, but to simply highlight a few key areas in which God speaks to us. The primary emphasis of this chapter is activating your five prophetic senses in the realms of the prophetic where God can use you as a prophetic voice—supernatural communicators, channels, and conduits.

REALM OF VISIONS AND DREAMS

He said, "Listen to my words: When there is a prophet among you, I the Lord, reveal myself to them in visions, I speak to them in dreams" (Numbers 12:6 NIV).

One of the most common ways the Lord communicates with us is through visions and dreams. God reveals Himself to prophets in visions and speaks to them in dreams. This is one of the primitive means of God speaking and unlocking His secrets to His spokespersons. The word "vision" in the Old Testament Hebrew in Strong's Concordance is *marah,* which means a mode of revelation, a mirror. A vision was a mode of revelation that God used to speak to ageless prophets. It also means a mirror, a method God employed to cause the prophet see the image of something or reflection. A vision is God's reflection that He desires to communicate through His prophets. The root meaning of vision is the word *mareh,* which is a view, act of seeing, and appearance, phenomenon, spectacle, a supernatural vision.

VISION AND DREAMS

In the first year of Belshazzar king of Babylon, Daniel had a dream, and visions passed through his mind as he was lying in bed. He wrote down the substance of his dream (Daniel 7:1 NIV).

The term "dream" in the Hebrew is *chalown* which is a dream with a prophetic meaning. Dreams are simply night visions or sleeping visions where God reveals His instructions in dreams (Job 33:16). Dreams are one of ways God can speak to us. When He speaks, it is important to journal and write down the dream, telling the main facts with the ability supernaturally to interpret the meanings of visions and dreams as Daniel did (Daniel 1:17).

REALM OF TRANCES

When I returned to Jerusalem and was praying in the temple, I fell into a trance (Acts 22:17 NIV).

Trances take us from our natural mind as we are overcome by the Spirit of God. They are a dream-like state while we are awake. Trances are vehicles that the Lord uses to take us into an encounter, such as a when doctor puts you "under" before surgery or an operation. The Greek word for "trance" is *ekstasis* in Strong's Concordance, which means a displacement of the mind, to remove out of its place or state, i.e., bewilderment, or ecstasy. Trances can last for any length of time, from a few seconds to several hours.

The following are a few biblical examples that could describe various forms of an ecstatic prophetic state, a trance-like state:

- Awestruck, amazed, trembling, bewildered (Mark 16:8 NKJV, NIV)
- The hand of the Lord (Ezekiel 1:3)
- A deep sleep from the Lord (Genesis 2:21; Job 33:15; Daniel 8:18)
- Falls down, eyes wide open (Numbers 24:4,16)

REALM OF ANGELS

And when Herod was about to bring him out, that night Peter was sleeping, bound with two chains between two soldiers; and the guards before the door were keeping the prison. Now behold, an angel of the Lord stood by him, and a light shone in the prison; and he struck Peter on the side and raised him up, saying, "Arise quickly!" And his chains fell off his hands (Acts 12:6-7).

The angelic realm is another common way God uses messengers to communicate His purpose to us. Throughout the New Testament are examples of how angels visited and manifested themselves to people. We know that an angel of the Lord visited Joseph in a dream concerning the plot of Pharaoh to find and kill baby Jesus (Matthew 2:13-23). Sometimes strangers are angels from another world. Angels coexist within the affairs of humankind.

> *Do not forget to entertain strangers, for by so doing some have unwittingly entertained angels* (Hebrews 13:2).

The following is a short reference list of the diverse ways God communicates to us supernaturally:

- Spiritual perceptivity (John 8:38)
- Open heaven (Acts 7:55-56; Ezekiel 1:1-4; Matthew 3:16-17)
- Audible voice (Matthew 3:17; Acts 9:3-5)
- Caught up in the Spirit (2 Corinthians 12:2-3)
- Mind perceptivity or perception of minds (Luke 6:7-8; 9:47; 11:17)
- Translation and transportation in the spirit (Acts 8:39-40)
- Pictorial vision (Numbers 12:6)
- Appearances or seeing apparitions (Luke 1:11, Genesis 32:24-31; Joshua 5:13-15; Luke 1:26-38; Acts 10:1-6)
- Out-of-body encounters (Ezekiel 8:3 and 2 Corinthians 12:2-4)
- Third heaven experience or visitation (2 Corinthians 12:2; Psalm 11:4; Nehemiah 9:6)
- Second heaven: the outer space, sun, moon, stars, planets (Genesis 1:16-17)

- First heaven: atmospheric level with the sky, dome or expanse above the earth (Matthew 16:1-3)

- Still small voice (1 Kings 19:11-12)

- Prophetic song of the Lord or inspired songs (Colossians 3:16)

ACTIVATING YOUR FIVE PROPHETIC SENSES

But solid food belongs to those who are [mature] *of full age, that is, those who by reason of* [practice] *use have their senses exercised to discern both good and evil* (Hebrews 5:14).

It is important to understand that just as we have five natural senses—sight, hear, touch, taste, and smell—that help us to comprehend the world around us in the natural realm, likewise in the realm of the spirit we also have senses. We need to activate our five spiritual senses, especially in supernatural ministry, to help us minister and understand the world in the spirit. We have been born again from above (John 3:3-8) from Heaven, and therefore we have spiritual senses that we must put into practice. So in the natural first, also in the spirit where we can be in touch with a dimension beyond the natural (1 Corinthians 15:46).

We are so used to functioning and operating in the natural that we are ignorant of the spiritual world that coexists with us on earth. The five spiritual or prophetic senses will open, give you access to flow and function in the prophetic realm. We have spiritual gifts but the seer realm of the prophetic also corresponds with our spiritual senses. This is a powerful combination when ministering in the prophetic. Prophets in the office are Hebrew 5:14 prophets who by reason of practice, habit, and usage have trained and exercised their senses to discern both good and evil, natural and spiritual, prophetic and pseudo powers of God and the power of hell.

The following are Scripture examples of the ancient prophets functioning in the five prophetic senses.

1. Prophetic Sense of Sight

And Elisha prayed, and said, "Lord, I pray, open his eyes that he may see." Then the Lord opened the eyes of the young man, and he saw. And behold, the mountain was full of horses and chariots of fire all around Elisha (2 Kings 6:17).

Jesus saw in the spirit what the Father was doing. The key to Jesus's spiritual eyes remaining open was being obedient and continuing to do what He saw the Father doing. Spiritual sight is connected to spiritual obedience:

Then Jesus answered and said to them, "Most assuredly, I say to you, the Son can do nothing of Himself, but what He sees the Father do; for whatever He does, the Son also does in like manner" (John 5:19).

Paul reveals a key to unlocking spiritual vision and sight, which is faith. By faith we understand and comprehend the unseen, supernatural realm. Faith activates the ability to see in the invisible spiritual or God realm. Faith is the key to opening the unseen realm according to these Scripture passages:

For we walk by faith, not by sight (2 Corinthians 5:7).

Now faith is the substance [realization] *of things hoped for, the evidence* [confidence] *of things not seen"* (Hebrews 11:1).

Elisha the prophet prayed for his servant's eyes to be opened that he could see in the unseen realm. The veil and scale of the invisible realm of the supernatural was pulled off so that his servant could see an army of chariots of fire that was reinforcing the mantle of the prophet. Elisha was not unnerved by the army of men surrounding him because his spiritual eyes were open as a prophet to see in the realm of the prophetic and supernatural (2 Kings 6:17).

Prophetic Key: The prophetic sense of sight is one of the most powerful senses in the realm of the prophetic. Ask a prophet to pray over you and impart the ability to see in the realm of the spirit. Prophets can impart supernatural vision. Typically, when you get around prophets or prophetic people or if you are discipled, mentored, coached, or fathered by a prophet, you will begin to see like the prophet. Learn to practice the presence of God; many times Jesus would go away to be alone with His Father to pray and spend time with God. The more you are in the presence of God and praying in the Spirit, the more your spiritual eyes will see in the realms of the prophetic. You can pray and ask the Lord to open your eyes in the spiritual world, but the key is that your motive and agenda have to be pure—that your request is unto the glory of Jesus Christ, not to be proud or super spiritual. This helps the prophet in the realm of seeing supernaturally in visions, dreams, and open-eye visions and trances.

2. Prophetic Sense of Hearing

Adam heard the voice, the sound of the Lord walking. He knew the presence of God by the vibration of a sound moving in the cool (spirit) of the day. Adam was in tune with the frequency of God's voice and sound. He knew God's walk and movement. He knew it was the voice of God because of the distinction in His walk. Adam reveals a key—that we must spend time in the presence of God to learn and know His voice, sound, and walk, His movements among us.

> *And they heard the sound* [voice] *of the Lord God walking in the garden in the cool* [wind, spirit, or breeze] *of the day, and Adam and his wife hid themselves from the presence of the Lord God among the trees of the garden* (Genesis 3:8).

Believers can hear the voice of Jesus Christ in the spirit or in our spirit. He speaks into the spiritual hearing. The key to spiritual hearing is to know by experience Jesus Christ. The more you know Him and learn about Him, the more you will hear His voice in order to follow Him as a sheep follows a shepherd. Those who know Him obey His leading and His voice. Followers of Christ will hear in the realm of the supernatural the voice of God

My sheep hear My voice, and I know them, and they follow Me. And I give them eternal life, and they shall never perish; neither shall anyone snatch them out of My hand (John 10:27-28).

Anyone with ears to hear should listen and understand (Matthew 11:15 New Living Translation).

Whoever has ears, let them hear what the Spirit says to the churches (Revelation 2:29).

Prophetic Key: The prophetic sense of hearing is the most critical of all the five prophetic senses for the prophetic realm. Praying continually in the Spirit will open your sensitivity to hear the voice of God (Jude 20). It is important as prophets and prophetic people to desire and long to hear the voice of God. Being prophetic is primarily hearing more than it is speaking. Prophets are inspired listeners or hearers first before they ever become inspired speakers.

3. Prophetic Sense of Touch

For we have not an high priest which cannot be touched with the feeling of our infirmities; but was in all points tempted like as we are, yet without sin (Hebrews 4:15 KJV).

Jesus felt the woman with the issue of blood *touch* the anointing of the Spirit for healing as He said, "Who touched Me?" Her touch was a supernatural release and pulling on His anointing in the Spirit.

And Jesus said, "Who touched Me?" When all denied it, Peter and those with him said, "Master, the multitudes throng and press You, and You say, 'Who touched Me?'" But Jesus said, "Somebody touched Me, for I perceived power going out from Me." Now when the woman saw that she was not hidden, she came trembling; and falling down before Him, she declared to Him in the presence of all the people the reason she had touched Him and how she was healed immediately (Luke 8:45-47).

Prophetic Key: We can use our prophetic sense of touch to feel someone's pain or infirmities or even what someone is going through in the spirit. Many times as you are ministering in the prophetic, you can feel them hurting, which helps to activate the gift of prophecy to build them up, console, and encourage them. There have been many times when I touch someone or lay hands on someone and I immediately feel the area that God desires to minister. Those functioning in the area of healing will have more spiritual capabilities activated in them to release physical, emotional, and mental healing. Spiritual touch allows us to feel the presence of God. There is a heightened sensitivity to the presence of God and the touch of God; you feel Him and may start weeping in His presence or feel His love toward you or someone else.

4. Prophetic Sense of Taste

Ezekiel the prophet ate the scroll that God had commanded him to eat and he described the taste of the Word of God as he digested it.

> *Then he said to me, "Son of man, eat this scroll I am giving you and fill your stomach with it." So I ate, and it tasted as sweet as honey in my mouth* (Ezekiel 3:3 NIV).

Ezekiel the prophet was able to taste the Word of God supernaturally, which means there is a spiritual sense of taste that can be activated. His sense of spiritual taste was activated when he ate the scroll. This is key to unlocking this realm in the prophetic. You can prophesy through your spiritual taste buds. I actually get words for people through this sense in the realm of the Spirit.

John the apostle, in the Book of Revelation, was given a scroll to eat by an angel, God's messenger. It is symbolic that in order to be an effective messenger of God, spokesperson, and mouthpiece of God, the prerequisite is consuming the Word of God. The Bible should be the diet of the prophets.

> *Then I took the little book out of the angel's hand and ate it, and it was as sweet as honey in my mouth. But when I had eaten it, my stomach became bitter* (Revelation 10:10).

Your spiritual taste is connected to your sight. Taste can activate your vision to see even the goodness of the Lord. Someone can blindfold you and allow you to taste a banana or an orange, etc. and you do not necessarily have to see the fruit to identify with detail which fruit you taste. Likewise, your prophetic taste gives you prophetic eyes to see if something is good, bitter, sweet, or sour.

> *Oh, taste and see that the Lord is good; blessed is the man who trusts in Him!* (Psalm 34:8)

Prophetic Key: Eating—by studying, mediating, and reading—the Word of God activates the prophetic sense of taste. We must develop more of an appetite as prophets and prophetic people to have an insatiable hunger for the Word of God. Prophets love to digest the Word of the Lord that activates the prophetic in their mouths to prophesy. A prophet must feed on the Word like Ezekiel, which will activate supernatural taste.

I have found myself in a number of instances as a seer prophet ministering to someone and could taste something sour in my mouth, which is a prophetic impression or inclination that something in that person's life has gone sour, or it could be coming to an end and be bittersweet. Spiritual taste is a prophetic tool that I use when ministering as a prophet. Seer prophets are able to see with all of their spiritual senses, and this one I use often to get the Word of the Lord for someone.

5. Prophetic Sense of Smell

We as believers are to God the pleasing aroma of Christ. *"For we are to God the fragrance of Christ among those who are being saved and among those who are perishing"* (2 Corinthians 2:15).

Jesus is described as our Rose of Sharon. Roses smell lovely and are symbolic of love and beauty. We can smell the love and presence of Jesus Christ.

> *I am the rose of Sharon, and the lily of the valleys* (Solomon 2:1).

And when He had called His twelve disciples to Him, He gave them power over unclean spirits, to cast them out, and to heal all kinds of sickness and all kinds of disease (Matthew 10:1).

Because they were saying, "He has a foul spirit" (Mark 3:30 Aramaic Bible in Plain English).

What is an unclean or foul spirit? Your prophetic sense of smell will allow you to smell demons, unclean, impure, and foul-smelling spirits. An unclean spirit is simply a New Testament synonym, a more descriptive Jewish term, for a demon. We can see that the terms "unclean spirit" and "demon" seem to be used interchangeably in Scripture. There is no clear difference in their definitions. Some translations refer to them as "impure spirits."

Throughout the New Testament, the word "unclean spirits" is *akathartos* in the Greek language in Strong's Concordance, and is mentioned more than twenty times. Throughout those passages we read that unclean spirits can possess people and cause them sickness and harm (Matthew 10:1; Mark 1:26; Acts 5:16, 8:7).

Prophetic Key: The prophetic sense of smell can be activated by spending time in the presence of God worshipping, soaking, and basking. When in strong worship and when ministering to the Lord, I can sense that He has walked into the room by the aroma, fragrance, and scent of His presence. It can smell sweet like roses, perfume, or some lovely fragrance. I can sense angelic activity by smelling in the spirit. I can also smell a demonic presence or even sicknesses or infirmities in someone's body due to this gift being activated in my life.

Foul and Unclean Spirits

I can recall one incident where this powerful sense of smell was activated when I had a relative who was hiding some sexual immoralities and needed deliverance. Whenever I would get near him, I would smell a foul or pungent odor coming from him. I knew it was not a natural odor because he would smell either like a skunk or a wet dog. I just could not shake the smell whenever I was around him. As I sought the Lord about what I was sensing regarding him, the Lord revealed the characteristics of the skunk and the wet dog to me as He highlighted the sexual nature of these animals. My relative had unclean and foul spirits. He was demonically possessed with an impure spirit. God was revealing an impure lifestyle of sexual immorality and perversion.

The Lord gave me a revelation that the smell of the dog represented a dog "in heat" (a mating call or odor) looking to mate. I later discovered that this relative was involved in prostitution and paying for sex. There is a saying that "If you lay down with dogs, you get up with fleas." Well, my relative spiritually had a flea of demons, no pun intended. The smell of the skunk was a confirmation to the revelation of the wet dog smell coming from my cousin. I learned that for skunks, the season of February through March in North America is mating season for the striped, hog-nosed, and hooded skunk. Mating season translates into the "skunk smell" according to my research online at the Skedaddlewildlife.com website on skunks.

It is said that the stink occurs when the male tries to court females who may not be in the mood. When this happens, the female skunks generate an aroma to repel their rejected suitors. My point is that the smell of skunk was a key to unlock revelation into what I was sensing from my cousin to help minister deliverance and salvation to him and break off the spirits of immorality in his life. My cousin was in his mating season and he was being rejected, which created the incredibly foul odor.

One of my strongest senses is my prophetic sense of smell that enables me to detect and discern evil spirits, coupled with the revelatory gifts of discerning of spirits. I have even detected various diseases and cancers in people's bodies and they were miraculously healed through deliverance of spirits. My brother gave me the nickname "K-9," a nickname for a police dog with keen sense of smell to locate illicit drugs and hidden or inconspicuous activities. We need prophetic K-9s to detect hidden spiritual activities.

CHAPTER 18

PROPHETIC FAMINE

"Behold, the days are coming," says the Lord God,
"That I will send a famine on the land, not a famine
of bread, nor a thirst for water, but of hearing the
words of the Lord. They shall wander from sea to
sea, and from north to east; they shall run to and fro,
seeking the word of the Lord, but shall not find it."
—AMOS 8:11-12

There is a season of God that many are not aware of that comes in certain times to manifest the intent of God. This season is what I call a "Prophetic Famine." According to Amos 8:11-12, God declared through Amos the prophet, that there would be days when the Lord would send upon the land a season of famine, which would be something uniquely different. This type of famine was not your typical famine of scarcity and shortage of food or lack of water in a dry season. I believe this type of famine was the lack of hearing prophetically—hearing the Word of the Lord. A prophetic famine is not being able to hear the voice of God. Spiritually, it is likened to not receiving any bread (fresh revelation) or water (fresh outpouring of the Spirit). This is a spiritual drought at its finest.

Many people are experiencing this type of famine in their personal lives as well as cities, regions, and nations. Historically, Israel had consistently rejected the words of the Lord that were sent by the prophets and turned away from God to follow other gods. Famine was symbolic, representing the withdrawal of God's word and the destruction of idols (Zephaniah 2:11).

RARE PROPHETIC SEASONS AND TIMES

In seasons of prophetic famine there will be little to no revelation. *"Now the boy Samuel ministered to the Lord before Eli. And the word of the Lord was rare in those days; there was no widespread revelation"* (1 Samuel 3:1).

The word of the Lord was rare in the time of the judges and it was a period of extremely limited prophetic activity and encounters. During that era, the people each did what was right in their own hearts because there was no king (Judges 21:25). They followed their own will and had no interest in the will of God through His prophets. The few visions that God did give during that time were not widely known or experienced.

There was a scarcity of divine revelation mediated through prophetic voices, visions, and dreams. The spiritual and prophetic climate was dark in the days of Samuel, similar to what we are experiencing in this hour as many churches, territories, cities, regions, and nations are lacking authentic prophetic activities. Much of this is a result of the hardness of human hearts, unbelief, and fear of the supernatural, disobedience, idolatry, spiritual blindness, erroneous doctrines in the church, gross perversion, and growing sin.

When there is no prophet (1 Kings 22:7) in the land, there will be no widespread revelation or prophetic encounters through dreams, visions, and the prophets according to Psalm 74:9: *"We do not see our signs; there is no longer any prophet; nor is there any among us who knows how long."*

God sends rare prophetic seasons of famine and drought to call rare prophetic voices to emerge in these moments to cause movements and revivals. God sends times and seasons of famine of hearing the word of the Lord to develop a greater hunger and thirst for more of the Word of God. It produces a greater desire in the hearts of His people to seek after Him. God allows global epidemics, warfare, sickness and diseases, murders, and social and economic declines to come to a boiling point to cause people to seek

Him for solutions and answers to the world's problems. Rare ministries are raised in seasons of famine. Samuel the prophet was called in a time when the prophetic voices had become irrelevant, obsolete, and ignored. Dark times in Israel called for drastic prophetic measures, where the vitality of Israel's existence hinged on the word of the Lord.

God is raising up rare prophetic ministries today who will carry prophetic relief and revival and keys in the midst of famine, who will bring the glory rain, breakthrough, healings, revival, restoration, deliverance, miracles, signs, and wonders. They will carry a peculiar anointing in their day as keys to opening the heavens and changing spiritual climates. We are about to see a resurgence of these types of prophetic anointings in this hour when the prophets and prophetic people are hearing rare revelations in seasons of famine and drought to release the breakthrough of Heaven that the earth needs.

Understanding Prophetic Famine

The prophet Amos spoke of times when there would be a *"famine on the land, not a famine of bread, nor a thirst for water, but of hearing the words of the Lord"* (Amos 8:11). There are three types of famines to consider according to Amos 8:11:

1. Famine—hunger for bread (food)

2. Thirst—drought (lack of water)

3. Hearing—prophetic word of the Lord (no prophetic word)

Famine deals with us spiritually in all three realms: 1) spiritual hunger; 2) spiritual thirst; and 3) spiritual hearing.

What is prophetic famine?

- The word "famine" in the Hebrew is *ra'ab* in Strong's Concordance, which means hunger in a land, nation, or individuals. Famine is to be hungry or voracious, to suffer the lack of food. Famine in its purest sense of the word, is extreme lack that persists for an extended season. The biblical understanding of famine is an extreme shortage of food and even water, resulting in hunger and thirst. Spiritually, famine means you are wrestling with a landscape of extreme lack in your life in various areas. Famine affects the spiritual landscape similar to natural famine.

- The word "drought" means a long spell of dry weather. Biblically, the word "drought" means dryness, desolation, heat, parch and waste.

- The word "hearing" is *shama* in Hebrew in Strong's Concordance, which means to listen or hear with attention or interest to obey. Hearing in the biblical sense is to listen in order to obey. In other words, hearing means those who genuinely hear obey what they hear.

This chapter examines just a few prophetic types and ancient prophets who had the ability to break the season of prophetic shortage, scarcity, drought, and barrenness in times of famine. These examples serve as keys in allowing us to learn how to break the spirit of prophetic famine. Amos the prophet was dealing with Israel's refusal to hear the word of the Lord from His prophets or what was written in the Law of the prophets. Therefore, God sent famine that would cause an inability to hear from Him directly through prophets, the Urim and Thummin and through visions, dreams, and prophetic encounters, in the case of Saul (1 Samuel 28:3-6; 16-18). The prophetic has more to do with hearing the voice of God than speaking forth the word of God. Being genuinely prophetic has everything to do with hearing from God.

PROPHETIC KEYS OF SUPERNATURAL REVIVAL

This section of the chapter is written to reveal prophetic keys used by the following five ancient prophets and prophetic types to break the power of spiritual and prophetic famine, drought, and depravity to usher in the Holy Spirit outpouring. We will examine the following key people and note what they did in times, seasons, and years of famine. There are powerful keys that we can use in our personal lives to unlock and release the power of revival that will bring us supernatural breakthroughs, healings, miracles, signs, and wonders through the realm of the prophetic.

1. Abraham—Moved by Faith

Now there was a famine in the land, and Abram went down to Egypt to dwell there, for the famine was severe in the land (Genesis 12:10).

There was a famine in the land, besides the first famine that was in the days of Abraham... (Genesis 26:1).

Abraham's Prophetic Key: Open new things and wells.

The following are key points that Abraham activated during his time of famine:

- Abraham obeyed the voice of God (Genesis 26:3-5). During prophetic famine it is important to obey the voice of God. While others are not hearing Him, prophetic people steward hearing the Word of the Lord.

- He moved to Egypt; famine initiates movement.

- The first recorded famine in the Bible reveals the key of faith to move out of a place where there is lack and move into a place of abundance (Egypt). Key movements are created with those who are hungry, thirsty, and hearing for more.

- He moved by faith and obeyed God. The Bible says, *"By faith Abraham obeyed when he was called to go out to the place which he would receive an inheritance. And he went out, not knowing where he was going. By faith he dwelt in the land of promise as in a foreign country, dwelling in tents with Isaac and Jacob, the heirs with him of the same promise"* (Hebrews 11:8-9).

- To reserve water, Abraham dug wells and opened up new wells because of the famine. (Genesis 26:18). He was not settled in famine, he moved to a new territory, and out of his obedience to do something in a time when the climate or forecast was not ripe for it, he came out of Egypt very wealthy (Genesis 13:1-2). Obey the voice of God in famine; there is a wealth of revelation you will receive from it.

2. Isaac—Re-digging the Wells

There was a famine in the land, besides the first famine that was in the days of Abraham. And Isaac went to Abimelech king of the Philistines, in Gerar (Genesis 26:1).

Isaac's Prophetic Key: Re-digging the wells and creating new space.

There was a famine in the land similar to that in the days of Abraham, Isaac's father. Isaac did not travel and dwell in Egypt like Abraham. The Lord appeared to him and instructed him to stay in Gerar and dwell in that land during the famine. Isaac, trusting the voice of God, stayed in Gerar in the land of the Philistines, which was a foreign place. "Gerar" means in Hebrew "a lodging place."

The following are key points that Isaac activated during his time of famine:

- Isaac followed the same pattern of his father—he obeyed the voice of God in famine (Genesis 26:1-6).
- Isaac sowed in the midst of famine and reaped a hundred times harvest in the same year (Genesis 26:12-14). He continued to prosper and the Philistines in the territory envied him. It is important to know that God caused him

to prosper and grow wealthy like his father, even during the famine.

Sow your way out of famine and watch God supernaturally prosper you right in the middle of a dry season. Your miracle is in the seed of obedience in God's word. Only God can cause seed to grow with limited or no water at all. He can cause it to rain on your crop, yet the crop of your neighbor can experience drought.

An example of this is when God made it rain on one city and withheld rain from another city. Amos 4:7 (NIV) says: *"I also withheld rain from you when the harvest was still three months away. I sent rain on one town, but withheld it from another. One field had rain; another had none and dried up."*

After his death, the Philistines plugged up all the wells with dirt that Abraham and his servants had dug. During ancient times in the desert, water was so precious that wells were essential. Plugging someone's well was ruinous and caused serious acts of aggression, often leading to war. Because of Isaac's wealth and growth, the Philistines sent him away from them because he had become mightier. Isaac moved from there and pitched his tent in the Valley of Gerar. In the middle of the valley season, yet it did not stop Isaac.

Isaac's additional prophetic keys: Isaac re-dug the ancient wells of his father and Isaac discovered a "well of running water" or "well of springing water" there in the Valley of Gerar (Genesis 26:19). The word "springing" in the Hebrew is *chay*, which means reviving, renewal, revival, living, alive, flowing, fresh, active, and life. He found a well of revival. The key to revival is that you have to continue to dig for it. Isaac's anointing was his ability to re-dig and find new wells of water. Everywhere Isaac and his servants dug, they found water.

Well of God's Space—Rehoboth

There were three wells that Isaac dug in the Valley of Gerar. Two of the three caused contention with a Philistine who tried to claim ownership until God made room for him at the well of Rehoboth in Genesis 26:20-22:

- *Esek*—the well of running water (revival). *"The herdsmen of Gerar quarreled with Isaac's herdsmen, saying, 'The water is ours.' So he [Isaac] called the name of the well Esek because the people quarreled with him"* (Genesis 26:19-20).

- *Sitnah*—the second well of water that Isaac dug was also fought over. *"They quarreled over that one also. So he [Isaac] called its name Sitnah [which literally means enmity]"* (Genesis 26:21).

- *Rehoboth*—the well that Isaac dug that the Philistines did not quarrel and contend over it. *"So he [Isaac] called its name Rehoboth [meaning spaciousness], because he said, 'For now the Lord has made room for us, and we shall be fruitful in the land'"* (Genesis 26:22). God gave Isaac and his servants their own space. God will make room for you too and will cause you to prosper and be fruitful.

3. Joseph—Opened all the Storehouses

And the seven years of famine began to come, as Joseph had said. The famine was in all lands, but in all the land of Egypt there was bread. So when all the land of Egypt was famished, the people cried to Pharaoh for bread. Then Pharaoh said to all the Egyptians, "Go to Joseph; whatever he says to you, do." The famine was over all the face of the earth, and Joseph opened all the storehouses and sold to the Egyptians. And the famine became severe in the land of Egypt. So all countries came to Joseph in Egypt to buy grain, because the famine was severe in all lands (Genesis 41:54-57).

Joseph's Prophetic Key: Open the storehouses during famine.

I will not take much time on the story of Joseph, as I have already written extensively in this book about him in "The Dreamers Are Coming" chapter, where you learned of this powerful prophet. However, for the purpose of this section, I want to highlight a few keys that Joseph used in the season of famine that were critical to God's divinely orchestrating his emergence and rise to power as second-in-command in all of Egypt to Pharaoh himself—and how Joseph opened stores in the middle of a seven-year famine (Genesis 41:37-57).

He opened stores of grain and bread in a season when there was a shortage of bread. Have you noticed a pattern with the previous key people mentioned with respect to how they prospered and grew wealthy when following the voice and inspiration of God? Joseph is no different. The key point is that famine will move you into wealth. Joseph, being thirty years old (Genesis 41:46), was in prison and summoned by Pharaoh by the recommendation of the butler who remembered him interpreting his dream. Pharaoh had a puzzling dream that needed to be interpreted; none of the magicians could explain it (Genesis 41:1-24). Joseph interprets Pharaoh's dream in Genesis 41:14-32.

There are four critical and pivotal moments that set up Joseph as a prophet to have the ear of Pharaoh the king:

1. Pharaoh summoned Joseph because of his prophetic gift of interpretation of dreams as a master of dreams (Genesis 40-41).

2. Pharaoh discloses his dream (Genesis 41:17-24).

3. Joseph interprets the dream as a prophetic famine, seven years of plenty and after that seven years of famine of food and bread (Genesis 41:25-32).

4. Joseph provides strategic advice to Pharaoh on what to do during the seven years of famine.

Strategic Prophetic Reserve

The following is the strategy that Joseph gave Pharaoh that we can use when experiencing prophetic famine of hearing the voice of God or experiencing the lack of His presence. God will give you a famine strategy for prophetic reservation before difficult times and seasons:

Now therefore, let Pharaoh select a discerning and wise man, and set him over the land of Egypt. Let Pharaoh do this, and let him appoint officers over the land, to collect one-fifth of the produce of the land of Egypt in the seven plentiful years. And let them gather all the food of those good years that are coming, and store up grain under the authority of Pharaoh, and let them keep food in the cities. Then that food shall be as a reserve [supply] *for the land for the seven years of famine which shall be in the land of Egypt, that the land may not perish* [cut off or die] *during the famine* (Genesis 41:33-36).

Two keys that are important to note:

1. Joseph saved his posterity (future generations and remnant) from dying in famine. Both Egypt and Israel survived through the strategic key of advice and interpretation of the famine dream to preserve and meet the supply and demand of grain and food before the famine.

2. The seven-year famine provided an opportunity for Joseph to be a business owner of stores that sold bread to meet the demand for food.

Famine made Joseph wealthy in famine; he had the keys to open up all the storehouses:

The famine was over all the face of the earth, and Joseph opened all the storehouses and sold to the Egyptians. And the famine became severe in the land of Egypt. So all countries came to Joseph in Egypt to buy grain, because the famine was severe in all lands (Genesis 41:56-57).

4. David the King—Broke Spiritual Cycles

Now there was a famine in the days of David for three years, year after year; and David inquired of the Lord. And the Lord answered, "It is because of Saul and his bloodthirsty house, because he killed the Gibeonites" (2 Samuel 21:1).

David's Prophetic Key: Breaking spiritual cycles and renewing covenants.

There was an unusual three-year famine in the land during the days of David. David clearly discerned that the famine was abnormal, so he inquired of the Lord. God gave him revelation about how the nature of the famine was spiritual and prophetic. David exercised spiritual keys in the realm of the spirit and exercised his ruling and kingly authority to prohibit and lock up the cycle of famine that Saul opened up through a breach for it to legally affect the kingdom.

The following are three key points that David activated during his time of famine:

1. David inquired of the Lord in the midst of famine and God gave him revelation of what was behind the three-year famine cycle that Saul's bloodthirst created for killing the Gibeonites. Inquire and seek revelation from God about any illegal soul ties, covenants, allegiance, and contracts in the realm of the spirit that need to be broken (2 Samuel 21:1).

2. David repented on behalf of Saul breaking a 400-year covenant and renewed it by sacrificing the life and blood of the seven sons of Saul. He avenged the Gibeonites for the sake of Israel (2 Samuel 21:2-9).

3. God accepted what David did and broke the famine off the land and heeded the prayer of the people again. David's key of repentance on behalf of Saul, who had already died, broke the spirit and cycle of famine and opened heaven for rain, revival, and answered prayer to be restored to the land. David gathered the bones of Saul, Jonathan, and the seven sons, that he sacrificed by death for the Gibeonites, and gave them all a proper burial.

The prophetic famine was broken by the keys of David:

They buried the bones of Saul and Jonathan his son in the country of Benjamin in Zelah, in the tomb of Kish his father. So they performed all that the king commanded. And after that God heeded the prayer for the land (2 Samuel 21:14).

Isaiah the prophet understood the burden of responsibility of a key holder of the keys of David—having the power to open and close doors. It is our prophetic responsibility to inquire of the Lord to get revelatory knowledge and wisdom and divine intelligence on how to exercise our authority in prayer and intercession to break spiritual cycles and to bind and loose on earth God's will and pray for the land like King Solomon received from his father David. The secret key to breaking famine is discovered in 1 Kings 8:35-40 NIV:

*When the heavens are shut up and there is no rain because your people have sinned against you, and when they **pray** toward this place and **give praise** to your name and **turn from their sin** because you have afflicted them, then **hear** from heaven **and forgive** the sin of your servants, your people Israel. **Teach them the right way to live**, and send rain on the land you gave your people for an inheritance. When famine or plague comes to the land, or blight or mildew, locusts or grasshoppers, or when an enemy besieges them in any of their cities, whatever disaster or disease may come, and when a **prayer or plea is made** by anyone among your people Israel—being aware of the afflictions of their own hearts, and spreading out their hands toward this temple—then **hear from heaven**, your dwelling place. **Forgive and act**; deal with everyone according to all they do, since you know their hearts (for you alone know every human heart), so that they will **fear you all the time** they live in the land you gave our ancestors.*

We are repairers of the breach or broken (Isaiah 58:12). David repaired the broken agreement by Saul that Israel had with the Gibeonites, established over 400 years prior, with Joshua (Joshua 9).

> *The key of the house of David I will lay on his shoulder; so he shall open, and no one shall shut; and he shall shut, and no one shall open* (Isaiah 22:22).

5. Elijah—Open and Shut the Heavens

> *And Elijah the Tishbite, of the inhabitants of Gilead, said to Ahab, "As the Lord God of Israel lives, before whom I stand, there shall not be dew nor rain these years, except at my word"* (1 Kings 17:1).

Elijah's Prophetic Key: Power of prayer and intercession.

Elijah's ancient key is of prayer and intercession to birthing supernatural revival. He had the key to supernaturally shut up the heavens through his prayer of intercession. He prayed that God would close the heaven over Ahab and Jezebel economically. Prophets have economy in their mouths where they can open the heavens through prayer and release supernatural relief. The prophetic key was intercession. His prayers created a recession in Israel that produced a spiritual famine in the kingdom ruled by Ahab and Jezebel. He declared boldly that there would be no rain or dew for three and a half years accept at his word, command. Rain was in the mouth of the prophet. Revival was the word of the Lord in the mouth of Elijah.

God entrusted Elijah with that spiritual climate. It is interesting that prophecy was developed in a season of fervent prayer and intercession until God gave him the command to go and prophesy (James 5:17-18). The effectual prayer of a righteous person avails much. But he had the power of God to open and close the heavens with a word, then it tells us that His mouth was a key to whether an entire nation would eat or starve.

Jesus recognized the power of Elijah and his ministry impact during famine when he was sent, not to satisfy the needs of many Israelite widows, but to a Gentile widow in Zarephath in need:

> But I tell you truly, many widows were in Israel in the days of Elijah, when the heaven was shut up three years and six months, and there was a great famine throughout all the land; but to none of them was Elijah sent except to Zarephath, in the region of Sidon, to a woman who was a widow (Luke 4:25-26).

Elijah's Prophetic Process to Spiritual Revival

Here is how you as a believer can create or break spiritual drought and famine illustrated by Elijah the prophet:

1. Availing Prayer and Intercession. *"Confess your trespasses to one another, and pray for one another, that you may be healed. The effective, fervent prayer of a righteous man avails much. Elijah was a man with a nature like ours, and he prayed earnestly that it would not rain; and it did not rain on the land for three years and six months. And he prayed again, and the heaven gave rain, and the earth produced its fruit"* (James 5:16-18).

2. Prophesy. *"And Elijah the Tishbite, of the inhabitants of Gilead, said to Ahab, 'As the Lord God of Israel lives, before whom I stand, there shall not be dew nor rain these years, except at my word'"* (1 Kings 17:1).

OBADIAH INTERCESSORS

During times of spiritual and prophetic famine of revelation, the supernatural, the word of the Lord, hearing the voice of God, financial strain and deficit, stock market plummets, spiritual starvation, dry churches and ministries, lack of the move of the Spirit and much more, God will raise up intercessors who will preserve the prophets in those seasons and times of prophetic famine. While others were not receiving bread and water during famine, God had hidden prophets who did not bow their heads to eat from the tables of Jezebel and Ahab who supported and fed false prophets. She massacred the prophets of the Lord and supported her 450 false prophets (1 Kings 18:22). Jezebel fed and financially supported false prophetic operations in Israel that caused the shutdown in the heavens by the genuine prophets in intercession (1 Kings 18:19). Jezebel fed her false prophets, but God used Obadiah to preserve His.

PROPHET PRESERVATION

Obadiah had fed one hundred prophets of God during the famine:

> *So Elijah went to present himself to Ahab; and there was a severe famine in Samaria. And Ahab had called Obadiah, who was in charge of his house. (Now Obadiah feared the Lord greatly. For so it was, while Jezebel massacred the prophets of the Lord, that Obadiah had taken one hundred prophets and hidden them, fifty to a cave, and had fed them with bread and water.) And Ahab had said to Obadiah, "Go into the land to all the springs of water and to all the brooks; perhaps we may find grass to keep the horses and mules alive, so that we will not have to kill any livestock" (1 Kings 18:2-5).*

PROPHETIC BIRTHING OF REVIVAL

The following Scripture passage reveals the intercessory birthing position of prophets and the declaration of the end of the drought by Elijah:

> *Then Elijah said to Ahab, "Go up, eat and drink; for there is the sound of abundance of rain." So Ahab went up to eat and drink. And Elijah went up to the top of Carmel; then he bowed down on the ground, and put his face between his knees, and said to his servant, "Go up now, look toward the sea." So he went up and looked, and said, "There is nothing." And seven times he said, "Go again." Then it came to pass the seventh time, that he said, "There is a cloud, as small as*

a man's hand, rising out of the sea!" So he said, "Go up, say to Ahab, 'Prepare your chariot, and go down before the rain stops you.'" Now it happened in the meantime that the sky became black with clouds and wind, and there was a heavy rain. So Ahab rode away and went to Jezreel. Then the hand of the Lord came upon Elijah; and he girded up his loins and ran ahead of Ahab to the entrance of Jezreel (1 Kings 18:41-46).

Elijah was in somewhat of a fetal position equivalent to a baby in the womb waiting for the time of birthing. Elijah was in intercessory prayer that God would send the rain. He was, through intercession, bringing it forth in the spirit. Before he ever prophesied "revival rain" is coming, he incubated rain in prayer. Prayer is the cradle of revival. All great revivals started in prayer before manifesting.

REVIVAL RAIN

An ancient prophetic key that we can learn from the prophet Elijah is how he was able to open and close the heavens. Rain represents spiritual blessings. Closed heavens are a form of spiritual and prophetic drought. The key to seeing revival and breakthrough in your life, family, church, city, region, territory, bloodline, nation, and generation is in your mouth. We as believers must pray fervently without ceasing (1 Thessalonians 5:17) until God puts rain in our mouths to declare a change in the prophetic forecast—that the drought is over and you see rain coming. The release was in Elijah's mouth and his servant had to go up to see the manifestation of the release several times until it became a cloud the size of a man's hand. The hand represents power and release. The power of release was in the continual intercession of the prophet. There is a powerful release in your mouth and in your intercession. This is key to breaking the prophetic famine.

THE DROUGHT IS OVER!

And it came to pass after many days that the word of the Lord came to Elijah, in the third year, saying, "Go, present yourself to Ahab, and I will send rain on the earth" (1 Kings 18:1).

Men and women of God will carry the rain in their mouths like Elijah the prophet declaring the drought is over. We are about to experience revival rain upon us and we will be soaked and drenched in the glory of God. Elijah-type ministries are coming to declare that the drought in people's lives is over after they have been praying fervently in a birthing posture to hear supernaturally the sound of abundant rain (see 1 Kings 18:41). Before there was a supernatural relief of rain, Elijah told Ahab to "Go up, eat, and drink." God is sending prophetic relief through the words and voices of the prophetic to bring supernatural rain.

CHAPTER 19

RE-DIGGING ANCIENT WELLS AND LANDMARKS

Then Isaac departed from there and pitched his tent in the Valley of Gerar, and dwelt there And Isaac dug again the wells of water which they had dug in the days of Abraham his father, for the Philistines had stopped them up after the death of Abraham. ...Also Isaac's servants dug in the valley, and found a well of running water there.
—GENESIS 26:17-19

*Remove not the ancient landmark,
which thy fathers have set.*
—PROVERBS 22:28 KJV

FAMINE OF HEARING THE WORD OF GOD

Isaac, the son of Abraham, in Genesis chapter 26, began to experience famine in the land that was similar to the first recorded famine in the Bible in the days of his father. This famine was very grievous and severe in the land. There are approximately fifteen documented famines in the Scriptures. Amos the prophet gives us what type of famine I believe we are experiencing today and in seasons to come:

> *"Behold the days are coming," says the Lord God, "that I will send a famine on the land, not a famine of bread, nor a thirst for water, but of hearing the words of the Lord. They shall*

wander from sea to sea, and from north to east; they shall run to and fro, seeking the word of the Lord, but shall not find it" (Amos 8:11-12).

As you read in Chapter 18, Amos the prophet prophesied that God was sending a famine on the land, not for food or water but a famine of hearing (prophetically) the words of the Lord. I believe God is initiating this type of famine in various seasons to shift and change the prophetic landscape of voices in every season, time, age, era, and generation. Famine creates new movements. This is what God strategically uses to raise up and upgrade His next wave of apostolic and prophetic voices.

THIRSTY FOR REVIVAL

In the Bible, there were four important happenings and encounters that took place at a well that I believe we are about to see take place in locations where believers, leaders, ministries, and churches are commencing to re-dig ancient wells and dig new ones. There are four types of people who are thirsty for revival coming to the wells:

1. Sheep
2. Sons
3. Soldiers
4. Samaritans

THE SHEEP ARE COMING!

*So Jacob went on his journey and came to the land of the people of the East. And he looked, and saw a well in the field; and behold, there were **three flocks of sheep lying by it; for out of that well they watered the flocks**. A large stone was on the well's mouth. Now all the flocks would be gathered there; and they would roll the stone from the well's mouth, water the* *sheep, and put the stone back in its place on the well's mouth* (Genesis 29:1-3).

*So he said to them, "Is he well?" And they said, "He is well. And look, his daughter Rachel is coming with the sheep." Then he said, "Look, it is still high day; it is not time for the cattle to be gathered together. Water the sheep, and go and feed them." But they said, "We cannot until all the flocks are gathered together, and they have rolled the stone from the well's mouth; then **we water the sheep*** (Genesis 29:6-8).

The first happening at a well is when Jacob meets Rachel and helps water her sheep from a well near Haran (see Genesis 29:1-8). At this well in Haran, Jacob saw three flocks of sheep lying by it; for out of that well they water the flocks. Rachel, a shepherdess, was bringing her sheep to the same well for water:

Now while he [Jacob] was still speaking with them, Rachel came with her father's sheep, for she was a shepherdess. And it came to pass, when Jacob saw Rachel the daughter of Laban his mother's brother, and the sheep of Laban his mother's brother, that Jacob went near and rolled the stone from the well's mouth, and watered the flock of Laban his mother's brother (Genesis 29:9-10).

In the middle of famine, the wilderness, the valley, or a drought, God is about send sheep to drink from the wells of churches, ministries, and leaders who are willing to re-dig and dig for revival in their city, region, nation, or sphere of influence. God is raising up supernatural ministers who will dig relentlessly and tirelessly through praying, seeking, and rediscovering supernatural wells for sheep to drink from Heaven. Get ready to water more sheep in this season. The sheep are coming!

THE SONS ARE COMING!

> *Then Isaac departed from there and pitched his tent in the Valley of Gerar, and dwelt there. And Isaac dug again the wells of water which they had dug in the days of Abraham his father, for the Philistines had stopped them up after the death of Abraham. He called them by the names which his father had called them. Also Isaac's servants dug in the valley, and found a well of running [springing] water there (Genesis 26:17-19).*

The second happening at a well was when Isaac's servants dug a new well in the valley of Gerar and discovered a well of fresh running, or springing water there (Genesis 26:17-19 KJV). There was something very significant about this particular well that Isaac found. This was a "well of springing water," as termed in the King James Version of the Bible. "Springing" in Hebrew means living, flowing fresh, revival, or renewal. Isaac found a well of fresh water.

Spiritually, Isaac dug again and reopened a well in the valley of Gerar, a *Well of Revival!* God is placing an anointing of Isaac upon those in this next wave of leaders and prophetic voices to open new and reopen ancient wells of revival in desolate, wasted, and dry places. Isaac was a digger of wells who had an anointing of his father upon him to reopen what the Philistines had stopped up with dirt to hide what his father Abraham had done in his days.

Unfortunately, Isaac's re-digging and opening old and new wells caused him to clash with the Philistines over the ownership of the wells that his father had dug (Genesis 26:20-21). Today's diggers may encounter tremendous opposition and contention from the enemy at places where they are reopening ancient and ancestral wells and digging new wells of revival.

Demonic resistance and opposition are sent at revival wells to stop them from producing. Isaac found fresh flowing water in the valley of Gerar. Water represents the Holy Spirit and its manifestations. People will be sent to oppose and stop the next movement of the apostolic and prophetic voices from flowing, releasing, and experiencing fresh moves of the Spirit. Isaac moved on from the wells of contention, opposition, and strife and began to dig again another well that the Philistines did not fight them over.

Well of God's Space

The next well Isaac dug he named Rehoboth, meaning well of God's space:

> *And he moved from there and dug another well, and they did not quarrel over it. So he called its name Rehoboth [spaciousness], because he said, "For now the Lord has made room for us, and we shall be fruitful in the land* (Genesis 26:22).

This well was prophetic in that God gave him space to be fruitful and to further prosper in the middle of the valley. Rehoboth also means spaciousness. The word "space" in the dictionary means some small measurable distance, area, or volume. God had given Isaac an area in which to be fruitful. It was measured out as a God space. Within that line, jurisdiction, and measure of influence, God was giving him the grace for the space to grow exponentially. Isaac had an extraordinary grace to open up wells and to find hidden wells that were hidden on earth. God would cause him to flourish in the land.

The Lord appear to Isaac and reaffirmed His promise to multiply his descendants for the sake of Abraham, his father. He was a son, the beneficiary of the promise. He built an altar at the place where God appeared to him and worshipped God there. He also dug a well there at the place of God's appearance.

Isaac built an altar and a well at the place of God's presence:

> *Then he went up from there to Beersheba. And the Lord appeared to him the same night and said, "I am the God of your father Abraham; do not fear, for I am with you. I will bless you and multiply your descendants for My servant Abraham's sake." So he built an altar there and called on the name of the Lord, and he pitched his tent there; and there Isaac's servants dug a well* (Genesis 26:23-25).

Well of Oath and Agreement

There was such anointing on Isaac that even his servants carried the spirit of Isaac to be able to find water in different places in Genesis 26:32-33:

> It came to pass the same day that Isaac's servants came and told him about the well which they had dug, and said to him, "We have found water." So he called it Shebah [Oath]. Therefore the name of the city is Beersheba [Well of the Oath] to this day.

Isaac, a son, followed the ancient patterns, wells, markers, and landmarks set by his father and rediscovered them and intentionally began reopening them so his flock and family would be able to live and survive in seasons of famine in the valley. God supernaturally gave Isaac revelation to seek and find the wells of water the Philistines tried to hide or cover up with dirt; the markers of revival wells.

I believe this type of revelation is given through sonship and will unlock the mysteries of revival in seasons of famine when sons will dig new wells in uncommon places. There will be new discoveries, releases, and moves of the Spirit in unusual places by apostolic and prophetic sons and daughters of God. The next movement will be reinitiated by sons coming thirsty to rediscover what their spiritual fathers have left behind for them as landmarks, to drink from wells of ancient glory. The sons are coming!

THE SOLDIERS ARE COMING!

> And David said with longing, "Oh, that someone would give me a drink of the water from the well of Bethlehem, which is by the gate!" So the three mighty men [soldiers] broke through the camp of the Philistines, drew water from the well of Bethlehem that was by the gate, and took it and brought it to David. Nevertheless he would not drink it, but poured it out to the Lord. And he said, "Far be it from me, O Lord, that I should do this! Is this not the blood of the men [soldiers] who went in jeopardy of their lives?" Therefore he would not drink

> *it. These things were done by the three mighty men* [soldiers]
> (2 Samuel 23:15-17).

The third happening at a well is when three out of thirty of David's soldiers risked their lives to bring him water from a well near Bethlehem. David was at the cave of Adullam, the place where he trained, equipped, and raised up mighty men of war in obscurity. He literally took unqualified men and turned them into the bravest and most outstanding soldiers that the kingdom had known. These elite soldiers were known as "David's Mighty Men." During this time, David was within the stronghold and garrison of the Philistines in the valley of Rephaim, and he was thirsty. He requested that someone give him a drink from the well of Bethlehem, which is by the gate.

Three of David's mighty soldiers broke through the camp of the Philistines and risked their lives to draw water from this particular well. God is sending these types of mighty men to the well of apostolic and prophetic churches to help upgrade churches in seasons and times of spiritual warfare. They will carry water from Bethlehem, the house of bread. God is sending soldiers in the army of God who will come to the well, drawing from a place where there is spiritual food, substance, and bread. Deliverance is the children's bread.

These men were able to break through the stronghold of the Philistines, the enemies of God and His people, Israel. These mighty soldiers carried an anointing of breakthrough in a season of warfare to penetrate the enemies' defenses, resistance, and strongholds. God is sending these types of soldiers to wells—churches—that are positioned at gates in cities, regions, territories, and nations. They will be soldiers who are "gatekeepers" manning the wells of ministries and churches to protect the water to make sure there are no contaminants or stoppage in the flow.

In addition, these types of mighty men are coming to the well to draw from it to bring supernatural breakthroughs against principalities, powers, and spiritual wickedness in high places and rulers of the darkness of this world in this age. God is sending warriors who are "bloodthirsty" to see wells of continual flowing of deliverance, victories, and breakthrough in spiritual warfare. The soldiers are coming!

THE SAMARITANS ARE COMING!

But He [Jesus] needed to go through Samaria. So He came to a city of Samaria which is called Sychar, near the plot of ground that Jacob gave to his son Joseph. Now Jacob's well was there. Jesus therefore, being wearied from His journey, sat thus by the well. It was about the sixth hour. A woman of Samaria came to draw water. Jesus said to her, "Give Me a drink" (John 4:4-7).

The fourth and last happening at a well is in the New Testament when Jesus Christ needed to go through Samaria and came to Sychar where He encountered a Samaritan woman (see John 4:4-15). Jesus was exhausted from His travels; He stopped and sat at a well known as Jacob's well. It was about noon and a Samaritan woman came to draw water. Jesus was thirsty from His journey and asked her for a drink of water. She questioned Jesus about asking her, a Samaritan woman, for a drink because Jews had no dealings with Samaritans.

Jesus answered her with a very powerful statement, which I believe whet her spiritual thirst, saying, *"If you knew the gift of God, and Who it is who says to you, 'Give Me a drink,' you would have asked Him, and He would have given you living water"* (John 4:10). Moreover, Jesus, in His discourse with the woman at the well, told her that *"Whoever drinks of this water* [from Jacob's well] *will thirst again, but whoever drinks of the water that I will give him will never thirst. But the water that I will give him will become in him a fountain of water springing up into everlasting life"* (John 4:13-14).

THE HOLY SPIRIT IS THE LIVING WATER

The living water that Jesus was referring to is the Holy Spirit who is the Source of spiritual life. He reveals who the living water is in John 7:37-39:

*On the last day, that great day of the feast, Jesus stood and cried out, saying, "If anyone thirsts, let him come to Me and drink. He who believes in Me, as the Scripture has said, out of his heart will flow rivers of **living water.**" But this **He spoke concerning the Spirit**, whom those believing in Him would receive; for the Holy Spirit was not yet given, because Jesus was not yet glorified.*

We see that in both Scripture accounts that Jesus was referencing the Holy Spirit as the *"living water"* that the Samaritan would receive if she believed in Him and would drink from the water that He would give her. The Holy Spirit would become in her a fountain or well of water flowing eternally. We become wells of the Spirit that will draw Samaritans to us in order to bring spiritual transformation to outsiders, sinners, unchurched, and the types of people who the religious do not want to deal with. We are becoming wells of God where people will encounter Jesus Christ in our meetings, churches, and ministries. Churches are to become wells of God for all types of people to come and experience the manifestation of Christ— to drink from Him. The Samaritans are coming!

About the Author

Dr. Naim Collins is an emerging leader and catalyst with an apostolic heart and prophetic voice. He carries a peculiar anointing in the prophetic, healings, and the supernatural. He has been featured on various multimedia outlets such as Sid Roth's television program, *It's Supernatural!* and The Word Network. He is the visionary leader of Naim Collins Ministries and Fan the Flames Global Ministries based in Wilmington, Delaware, USA.

MINISTRY CONTACT INFORMATION

Naim Collins Ministries
c/o Dr. Naim Collins
P.O. Box 25225
Wilmington, DE 19899

naimcollinsworldwide@yahoo.com
bookingtwinprophets@gmail.com
info@naimcollinsministries.com
www.naimcollinsministries.com

SOCIAL MEDIA CONTACT INFORMATION

Facebook: www.facebook.com/naimcollinsministries
Twitter: @NaimCollins
Instagram: naim_collins
YouTube: naim collins or prophet naim collins

DONATION INFORMATION

www.naimcollinsministries.com/donate
www.paypal.me/naimcollins
Cash App: $drnaim